BRITISH CONSERVATISM AND TRADE UNIONISM, 1945–1964

Modern Economic and Social History Series

General Editor: Derek H. Aldcroft

Titles in this series include:

Taste, Trade and Technology
The Development of the International Meat Industry since 1840
Richard Perren

Alfred Herbert Ltd and the British Machine Tool Industry, 1887-1983
Roger Lloyd-Jones and M.J. Lewis

Rethinking Nineteenth-Century Liberalism
Richard Cobden Bicentenary Essays
Edited by Anthony Howe and Simon Morgan

Governance, Growth and Global Leadership
The Role of the State in Technological Progress, 1750–2000
Espen Moe

Triumph of the South
A Regional Economic History of Early Twentieth Century Britain
Peter Scott

Aspects of Independent Romania's Economic History with Particular Reference
to Transition for EU Accession
David Turnock

Estates, Enterprise and Investment at the Dawn of the Industrial Revolution
Estate Management and Accounting in the North-East of England, c.1700-1780
David Oldroyd

Across the Borders
Financing the World's Railways in the Nineteenth and Twentieth Centuries
Edited by Ralf Roth and Günter Dinhobl

Economics in Russia
Studies in Intellectual History
Edited by Vincent Barnett and Joachim Zweynert

Mining Tycoons in the Age of Empire, 1870–1945
Entrepreneurship, High Finance, Politics and Territorial Expansion
Edited by Raymond E. Dumett

British Conservatism and Trade Unionism, 1945–1964

PETER DOREY
Cardiff University, UK

ASHGATE

Published by
Ashgate Publishing Limited
Wey Court East
Union Road
Farnham
Surrey GU9 7PT
England

Ashgate Publishing Company
Suite 420
101 Cherry Street
Burlington
VT 05401-4405
USA

www.ashgate.com

British Library Cataloguing in Publication Data
Dorey, Peter, 1959–
    British conservatism and trade unionism, 1945–1964 1. Conservative Party (Great Britain) – History – 20th century 2. Labor unions – Great Britain – History – 20th century 3. Labor unions – Government policy – Great Britain – History – 20th century 4. Great Britain – Politics and government – 1945–1964
    I. Title
    331.8'8'0941'09045

Library of Congress Cataloging-in-Publication Data
Dorey, Peter, 1959–
    British conservatism and trade unionism, 1945–1964 / Peter Dorey.
        p. cm. – (Modern economic and social history)
    Includes bibliographical references and index.
    ISBN 978-0-7546-6659-2 (alk. paper)
    1. Conservatism–Great Britain–History–20th century. 2. Conservative Party (Great Britain)–History–20th century. 3. Labor unions–Great Britain–Political activity–History–20th century. 4. Labor policy–Great Britain–History–20th century. 5. Great Britain–Politics and government–1945–1964. I. Title.

    JC573.2.G7D67 2009
    322'.2094109045–dc22

                                                                                2008043880

ISBN 978 0 7546 6659 2

Mixed Sources
Product group from well-managed forests and other controlled sources
www.fsc.org Cert no. SA-COC-1565
© 1996 Forest Stewardship Council

Printed and bound in Great Britain by
MPG Books Ltd, Bodmin, Cornwall.

Contents

List of Tables

Modern Economic and Social History Series General Editor's Preface

Economic and social history has been a flourishing subject of scholarly study during recent decades. Not only has the volume of literature increased enormously but the range of interest in time, space and subject matter has broadened considerably so that today there are many sub-branches of the subject which have developed considerable status in their own right.

One of the aims of this series is to encourage the publication of scholarly monographs on any aspect of modern economic and social history. The geographical coverage is world-wide and contributions on the non-British themes will be especially welcome. While emphasis will be placed on works embodying original research, it is also intended that the series should provide the opportunity to publish studies of a more general thematic nature which offer a reappraisal or critical analysis of major issues of debate.

Derek H. Aldcroft
University of Leicester

Acknowledgements

As will become evident to the reader, this book is primarily based on research involving primary sources and archival materials, particularly those concerned with Cabinet meetings, the detailed deliberations of sundry Cabinet committees, Ministerial correspondence, the advisory work of senor civil servants and discussions involving different organisations and personnel in the Conservative Party itself; not only its MPs, but key sections of the extra-parliamentary Party who sought to shape Conservative policies towards the trade unions from 1945 to 1964.

I would, therefore, like publicly to express my genuine gratitude to the staff of the National Archives (formerly the Public Records Office) in Kew, London, and the Conservative Party Archivists at the Bodleian Library, Oxford University – especially Jill Spellman, Emily Tarrant and Jeremy Mcilwaine – for their invaluable assistance in tirelessly retrieving documents and papers for me. My sincere thanks to all of them.

Pete Dorey
Bath, Somerset

Introduction

The relationship between British Conservatism and trade unionism has often been a fraught one, characterised by mutual suspicion and sporadic open hostility. While reciprocal antipathy between the Conservatives and the trade unions was most pronounced during the 1980s and 1990s, when the Governments of Margaret Thatcher and John Major systematically reduced the power and role of trade unions, the history of British Conservatism contains various examples of antipathy towards, or anxiety about, the trade unions, most notably the 1799–1800 Combination Acts, the 1927 Trade Disputes Act, and the perennial demands for legislation emanating from individual Conservative MPs and constituency activists. This image of animosity has frequently been compounded through numerous speeches by senior Conservatives denouncing specific aspects of British trade unionism, most notably their 'irresponsibility' in pursuing strike action, their 'greed' in seeking allegedly excessive wage increases, their resistance to the introduction of new technologies and working practices, their transgression into the political sphere (via widespread union links with the Labour Party, and the associated 'political levy') and their denial of individual liberty through their former operation, in many cases, of the closed shop, entailing compulsory trade union membership for all employees in an industry or company.

In many respects, this antipathy has not been particularly surprising, given the different philosophies and principles which British Conservatism and trade unionism have enshrined or subscribed to. The Conservative Party has traditionally espoused such values and tenets as individualism, the importance and inevitability of inequality, private property, authority (including managerial authority in the workplace – what Margaret Thatcher termed 'management's right to manage'), competition and the virtue of profit. By contrast, trade unionism has tended to laud or symbolise the principles of collectivism, egalitarianism (albeit loosely or vaguely defined), a greater degree of public ownership or governmental regulation of the economy, an enhanced voice for employees in the workplace and protection against over-mighty employers, co-operation and solidarity, and suspicion towards profits, on the grounds that large profits derive, ultimately, from exploitation of workers who do not share in those profits. Ultimately, British Conservatism has been concerned to maintain Capitalism, while many trade unions have been formally committed to Socialism. Admittedly, many of these trade union tenets are often rhetorical rather than real – for example, the principle of collectivism and workers' solidarity has often been compromised by the pursuit of sectional or short-term interests by employees and trade unions in different sectors of the economy, while the espousal of egalitarianism and equality has routinely been undermined by the determination of skilled workers to maintain or restore pay differentials *vis-à-vis* their less-skilled or lower-paid 'comrades'. As such, for many trade unions, 'socialism' is a vague aspiration to be attained at some unspecified time in the distant future, but in lieu of which, each union will strive to secure the best possible terms and conditions for its members, with little regard for the impact on other workers and unions, or even the wider economy. Of course, this is something which Conservative critics of trade unionism have often been quick to condemn, although it could be argued that the unions are merely acting in accordance with the logic of the Capitalist system which Conservatives themselves revere.

In spite of these ideological or normative differences, though, the period from 1945 to 1964 was characterised by considerable conciliation and co-operation between the Conservative Party and the trade unions, certainly to a degree never previously seen, nor witnessed since (and extremely unlikely to be in the future, either). A number of younger, more progressive Conservatives had already been advocating a more constructive approach to, and role for, the trade unions during the late 1920s and through the 1930s, and some of these individuals rose to occupy senior positions in the Conservative Party during the following decades, thereby enabling them to put some of their principles into practice. Of course, their case for a closer and more constructive partnership with the trade unions was greatly strengthened by the successful involvement, at the highest political levels, of organised labour during the Second World War.

Having heavily lost the 1945 general election to the Labour Party, these progressive Conservatives devoted considerable time and energy crafting a new and positive approach to industrial relations and trade unionism, and in so doing, sought to play down the former animosity and conflicts between British Conservatism and trade unionism. The emphasis was now on the vital importance of the trade unions in national life, and their indispensability to future economic success. As such, the latter half of the 1940s convinced many Conservatives that, both economically and electorally, their Party would have to adopt a much more conciliatory approach to organised labour, one which would henceforth treat the trade unions as allies, rather than adversaries.

Thus it was that from 1951 to 1964, the vast majority of senior Conservatives, and especially those serving as Ministers of Labour, steadfastly refused to introduce legislation to regulate the behaviour or internal affairs of the trade unions, even though the Party continued to disapprove of such features as the closed shop and aspects of the political levy. A critique was enunciated which insisted that many industrial relations problems were not amenable to legislative solutions, but could only be tackled by promoting greater trust and partnership between management and workers, and between Conservative Ministers and the trade unions. To those Conservatives who continued to demand trade union legislation, Ministers invariably retorted that Acts of Parliament were not appropriate to the problems involved, and would not be practicable or enforceable anyway. Indeed, legislation would almost certainly antagonise the trade unions, and alienate the moderates therein (whom the Conservative leadership was painstakingly trying to win the trust of in order to marginalise the Left). Ultimately, therefore, mutual dialogue was to replace Ministerial diktats, and collaboration was to supersede confrontation.

This is not to say that relations between the Conservative Party and the trade unions were always amicable or harmonious during this period, but they were certainly more constructive than they had ever been previously, and in spite of their own occasional frustrations with the unions, most Ministers adhered to this constructive approach right through to 1964, by which time, pressure in the Party for a Royal Commission on Trade Unionism and/or legislation had become too strong to be disregarded. Prior to this date, though, there had been 13 years of unprecedented cordiality and dialogue between senior Conservatives and many trade union leaders. What follows is a study of the interplay between the ideas, key individuals, and circumstances which facilitated this unique period of relative calm in the often tempestuous history of British Conservatism and trade unionism.

Finally, a brief word ought to be offered about the manner in which trade unions, trade unionism and trade unionists are referred to in this study. In many of the Conservative Party's own internal publications and archives, references to trade unions or trade unionism are hyphenated; i.e., trade-unions, etc. This study will therefore adhere to this usage of hyphens when quoting directly from a Conservative Party archive or document which itself hyphenates, but will not use the hyphen outside of verbatim quotes.

Chapter 1

Conservatism and Trade Unionism
prior to 1945

The period of British history briefly covered in this chapter encompassed the whole range of Conservative attitudes towards the trade unions, ranging from repression born of fear, toleration or grudging acceptance, more positive attempts at incorporation, and indifference or non-commitment. Often, there seemed to be a disjuncture between aspects of trade unionism and key principles of Conservatism, most notably the principle of collectivism symbolised by the trade unions, in contrast to the emphasis on individualism intrinsic to much of Conservatism. Similarly, whereas trade unions often urged governmental intervention in the economy to provide jobs and employment rights for industrial workers, and legal protection for the activities of the trade unions – albeit strongly resisting governmental intervention in the unions' own internal affairs and activities – Conservatives worshipped at the shrine of 'the market', and, in principle, believed that jobs and wages, along with prices and conditions of employment, were best determined by the immutable laws of supply and demand. Indeed, for many Conservatives, one of the few forms of state intervention which was justified was when curbs apparently needed to be placed on the trade unions themselves, due to their alleged interference with the smooth operation of market forces, the threat to individual liberty, or impeding of managerial authority in the workplace.

Another issue which often caused tension between the British Conservatism and trade unionism concerns the professed political objectives and loyalties of the unions, namely their tendency to espouse generally left-wing principles, and/or (from 1906) affiliation to the Labour Party, while often denouncing, particularly through speeches and resolutions at their respective conferences, the iniquities of capitalism and the greed or selfishness of big business and those earning enormous salaries from the sweat and toil of industrial workers. In this context, Conservatives have often drawn a distinction between the industrial and political roles of trade unions, with the former – concerning work-place issues – deemed entirely legitimate, while their political dimension was routinely condemned, particularly after the formation of the Labour Party at the start of the twentieth century, and the subsequent affiliation to it of many trade unions. Yet just over a century earlier, there had been deep anxiety among Tories, as the Conservatives were generally known prior to the early 1830s, that the nascent trade unions might contain within them the seeds of revolution, so alarming did the notion seem of workers combining together to demand better wages and conditions of employment. This heralded the most notable example of Tory hostility towards the trade unions, and the most draconian anti-union legislation ever enacted in Britain. After this episode, however, the Conservatives gradually, albeit sometimes hesitantly, came to terms with trade unionism, although controversies and conflicts continued to occur periodically.

The Combination Acts

It was a Tory Government, led by William Pitt the Younger, which introduced the 1799–1800 Combination Acts. Hitherto, there had been no less than 40 different laws forbidding collective action by workers, on the grounds that this constituted either 'conspiracy' or 'restraint of trade', and hence a plethora of individual cases pursued by employers in different industries, trades and regions and at different times. What the Combination Acts did was to place all collective industrial action by workers within the ambit of an all-encompassing single law, with alleged breaches to be speedily determined by one magistrate, who might also be an employer in the defendants' trade or industry, so hardly likely to be impartial, and could require just one witness to provide evidence. As one labour historian has noted, with specific regard to the 1799 Combination Act, 'its crucial feature lay in its provision for summary trial', for 'the Act offered a speedy recourse to the law for employers faced by any combination of workmen to improve conditions or raise wages' (Stevenson, 1982: 16). Workers adjudged guilty under the Act were liable either to three months' imprisonment or two months' hard labour. The subsequent 1800 Combination Act made some slight changes to the previous year's legislation, the most notable amendment being that two magistrates should preside over cases pursued under the Act, and that these should not include an employer from the trade or industry in which the defendants were employed.

The impetus for the Combination Acts was two-fold. Firstly, the curbing of collective action by the emerging industrial working class reflected the ideological strength of economic liberalism at this juncture, with its emphasis on individualism and 'the market', both of which were hindered, or at least threatened, by trade unions. However, the enactment of such legislation highlighted one of the apparent paradoxes which often accompanies *laissez-faire* economics, namely the need for state intervention to tackle those institutions or practices which are deemed to constitute an impediment to the natural operation of the free market, and the laws of supply and demand; as the Thatcher Governments in Britain during the 1980s clearly showed, the principle of non-intervention by the state can only be pursued if the state actually does intervene, in order to impose its authority on obstructive or recalcitrant organisations, with trade unions often being a prime target.

Secondly, the passing of the Combination Acts reflected fear among Britain's political leaders of the potential dangers arising from the 1789 French Revolution, for there was anxiety that such insurrection, and its proclamation of equality and fraternity, might spread north across the English Channel. In this context, trade unions were viewed with the gravest suspicion, lest they contain within them the seeds of a British Revolution. This fear was compounded by a wave of industrial unrest which swept through Britain during the 1790s, thereby fuelling hostility towards nascent trade unions. According to the Duke of Portland, the then Home Secretary, 'even if nothing injurious to the safety of the government was actually being contemplated, associations so formed contained within themselves the means of being converted, at any time, into a most dangerous instrument' (quoted in Pelling, 1976: 25).

However, some historians have subsequently claimed that the apparent repressiveness, and therefore the impact, of the Combination Acts on trade unions has been somewhat exaggerated, with Dorothy George (1936: 172), for example, insisting that the legislation 'introduced no new principle and created no new offence', a view endorsed by D.F. Macdonald's claim that the Acts 'did not really represent any sudden, reactionary shift in state policy', but merely represented an extension of existing policy, and primarily modified the procedures for instigating legal action against combinations engaged in activities which were already unlawful (Macdonald, 1976: 18). Furthermore, many employers refrained from instigating legal proceedings for fear of exacerbating poor industrial relations and distrust between masters and workmen, a caution also shared by some Tory Ministers, for having introduced the Combination Acts, they did not then actively promote their enforcement, but insisted that this was a matter for employers. It seems that in spite of enacting this legislation, there was concern among senior Tories that vigorous enforcement of the Combination Acts, particularly if they were seen to be personally involved in promoting prosecutions, might well serve to encourage the very radicalism, industrial militancy and working class solidarity which they hoped to forestall.

In addition to this consideration, three other factors also tempered active Tory hostility towards the trade unions during the first two decades of the nineteenth century, thereby moderating the potentially devastating impact of the Combination Acts on collective action by industrial workers. Firstly, more contemplative Tories recognised that the professed liberal impartiality of the state would be seriously compromised if it was seen to be vigorously curbing trade unions without similarly suppressing employers' associations. Or as the Attorney-General, Spencer Perceval, observed in 1804:

> ... the impartiality of government would be awkwardly situated if, after undertaking a prosecution at the instance of the Masters, against the conspiracy of the journeymen, they were to be applied to on the part of the journeymen, to prosecute the same Masters, for a conspiracy against their men.
> (quoted in Pelling, 1976: 27)

Secondly, but not unrelated to this point, some Tories were anxious that if the State involved itself too closely or actively in industrial relations, then it might inadvertently become the target of lobbying by trade unions seeking improvements on behalf of their members or even the working class in general. Clearly, for those

Tory politicians concerned to defend the status quo, based on economic *laissez-faire* and individualism, it would be potentially dangerous if the state was then viewed by subordinate classes as a channel for social change and reform through collective action.

Thirdly, there was a concern about the enforceability and practicability of legislation, for although the Tories had introduced the Combination Acts, more prescient Ministers recognised that active implementation might prove problematic. This was a particularly important consideration during a period when Britain was at war with France, which meant that troops could not readily be called upon to quell social disorder or civil unrest, and in an era predating the formation of a national police force. Having passed the Combination Acts, some Tories were subsequently apprehensive about pressing for the vigorous implementation of this legislation, lest it prove unenforceable in practice.

Ironically, some of the factors which had prompted the passing of the Combination Acts were, 25 years later, instrumental in ensuring their repeal. In particular, the principles of economic *laissez-faire* and individual liberty were subsequently cited to promote the right of workers freely and voluntarily to combine for the purpose of seeking improvements in their terms and conditions of employment; a liberalism which prohibited such voluntary associations of employees was really no liberalism at all. Moreover, it was acknowledged that instead of resulting in a diminution of such associations, the Combination Acts had merely served to drive many of them underground, where their continued operation in a twilight world of clandestine secrecy was likely to render them even more pernicious, because any injustices or illegal acts perpetrated by them were obscured from the view of the authorities. Far better, it was eventually acknowledged, to allow combinations of workers to operate above board and above ground, by rendering their associations lawful.

Thus were the Combination Acts repealed in 1824, by Lord Liverpool's Tory administration, although some minor restrictions were reintroduced in 1825, following an outbreak of sometimes violent industrial unrest in the immediate aftermath of repeal. As Robert Peel, then Home Secretary and a subsequent Tory/ Conservative leader, argued in the parliamentary debates presaging repeal of the Combination Acts, men who possessed no property other than their manual skill and physical strength should be permitted to associate together, if they so wished, for the purpose of determining the price at which they were willing to sell their labour. Meanwhile, William Huskisson (President of the Board of Trade) lamented that the Combination Acts had contributed to a deterioration in relations between employers and employed, and fuelled mutual mistrust.

Disraelian Paternalism

Following the repeal of the Combination Acts, most of the remainder of the nineteenth century was characterised by a growing, if sometimes apprehensive,

Conservative acceptance of trade unionism, and while there remained, in some quarters, concern about the revolutionary potential of trade unionism, particularly when Karl Marx was at his most prolific during the 1840s and 1850s, some senior Conservatives firmly believed that the best antidote to potential insurrection was political incorporation, to neutralise the perceived susceptibility of trade unions to radical ideas and revolutionary doctrines by granting concessions within the existing socio-economic system. This perspective, which subsequently became firmly subscribed to by many 'progressive' or 'One Nation' Conservatives through the remainder of the nineteenth century and throughout most of the twentieth century, held that attempts at suppressing trade unionism for fear that they might prove to be agents of radical social change, was likely to prove a self-fulfilling prophecy; militant action against the trade unions would almost inevitably invite an equally militant response. If the Conservatives were perceived, by industrial workers, to be anti-working class or anti-trade union, then this was likely to lend credence to the claims of radicals and revolutionaries about what they deemed to be the exploitative and undemocratic nature of capitalism, and its subjugation of the workers who actually produced most of the wealth through their physical toil.

Indeed, the Conservative Party's concern to prevent the spread of socialist or syndicalist doctrines from continental Europe, and ensure that the industrial working class or trade unions were not seduced by such utopian promises, meant that two broad principles or strategies needed to be enacted simultaneously: social reform to ameliorate the worst excesses and inequalities of unfettered *laissez-faire* capitalism, and more explicit acceptance of the trade unions, in order to encourage responsible, constitutional trade unionism, both of which would convince the expanding industrial working class that material improvements could be attained through existing industrial and political channels.

The nineteenth-century Conservative leader who came to personify this approach was Benjamin Disraeli, a novelist who held various prominent political posts before serving as Prime Minister for nine months in 1868, and then from 1874 to 1880. Disraeli's condemnation of the excessive inequalities engendered by unregulated Capitalism, and the ensuing squalor in which much of the working class was compelled to live, was trenchantly expressed, in 1844, when he declared that:

> I had long been aware that there was something rotten in the core of our social system. I had seen that while immense fortunes were accumulating, while wealth was increasing to a superabundance, and while Great Britain was cited throughout Europe as the most prosperous nation in the world, the working classes, the creators of wealth, were steeped in the most abject poverty, and gradually sinking into the deepest degradation
> (Quoted in Monypenny and Buckle, 1929: 629)

Consequently, Disraeli's Government enacted a range of social reforms to improve the social conditions in which the working class lived, most notably the 1874 Factory Act, the 1875 Artisans' Dwellings Act, the 1875 Public Health Act and the

1876 Education Act. These measures were subsequently eulogised as 'the most notable instalment of social reform undertaken by any single government of the century' (Smith, 1967: 2).

Meanwhile, with regard to trade unionism, Disraeli had previously been largely responsible for the introduction of the 1859 Molestation of Workmen Act, while he was Chancellor in Lord Derby's Conservative Government. This legislation, which legalised peaceful picketing, reflected Disraeli's success in persuading his more sceptical Cabinet colleagues that a more constructive approach towards the trade unions was likely, in turn, to encourage more moderate and responsible behaviour. Several years later, when Disraeli himself was Prime Minister, he established a Royal Commission to consider improving the laws relating to 'master and servant'. The ensuing report prompted the introduction of the 1875 Employers and Workmen Act, which made employers and employees formally equal before the law, while also making breach of contract a civil, rather than a criminal, offence. In introducing this reform, the Home Secretary, Richard Austen Cross, asserted that, if public order was not jeopardised, then workers should enjoy the greatest possible freedom of action to promote or improve their material interests (House of Commons Debates [hereafter HC Debates], 3rd series, Vol. 651, col. 678). Also placed on the statute book in the same year was the Conspiracy and Protection of Property Act, which decreed that actions committed by workers in pursuance of a legitimate trade dispute would no longer be liable to prosecution for conspiracy if those same acts, when carried out by an individual, were not deemed unlawful.

Disraeli subsequently informed Queen Victoria that these two Acts represented the most important labour laws passed during her reign, and declared that: 'We have settled the long and vexatious contest between Capital and Labour' (quoted in Monypenny and Buckle, 1929: 711), while another of Disraeli's biographers adjudged this legislation to constitute 'much the most successful of the Conservative social reforms', and echoed the view that these Acts 'satisfactorily settled the position of labour for a generation' (Blake, 1969: 555). Indeed, these laws have been described as 'easily the most important of the government's social reforms. It gave the working class everything for which they had striven at the 1874 general election' (Smith, 1967: 217). Yet, as in 1859, Disraeli had to overcome considerable scepticism in presiding over the enactment of such permissive legislation, for a substantial body of Conservative opinion remained anxious about, or even antipathetic towards, the trade unions, and thus uncomfortable with Disraeli's liberal approach (Coleman, 1988: 147).

Renewed Conservative concern over trade unionism

Perhaps not surprisingly, this anxiety and antipathy towards trade unions was compounded by the pattern of trade union membership during the last third of the nineteenth century, for although there was an overall increase from 1870 to 1900, there were fluctuations within this period, these coinciding with occasional economic downturns. Both trends in union membership were viewed unfavourably by Conservative critics of trade unionism; in periods of rising membership, anxiety increased about the dangers of collectivism and working-class militancy, whilst in times of economic retrenchment, when trade union membership declined somewhat, their Conservative critics readily blamed the unions for having precipitated a downturn in the economy, either by pricing their members out of work through their wage demands, or by deterring investment and undermining business confidence. According to one Conservative MP, the trade unions were exercising a 'moral terrorism', and 'creating a new jurisdiction ... with oppressive effect', and as such, Parliament might need to take legislative action to curb this malign power (HC Debates, 3rd series, Vol. 125, cols 684–5). That such sentiments were widely shared among Conservatives suggests that Disraeli was either being naively presumptuous or deliberately provocative in declaring that the labour question had finally been 'settled'.

Moreover, although Disraeli had reasoned that extending the franchise to sections of the working class would reduce the likelihood of proletarian insurrection, as democratisation led to political assimilation and inculcation of the principles of parliamentarianism, his faith was not shared by those Conservatives who feared that the growing number of industrial workers and trade unions posed an increasing threat to capital. One of the most prominent Conservative proponents of this pessimistic prognosis was the (third) Marquess of Salisbury, who served as Party leader and Prime Minister at the end of the nineteenth century, yet who had, in the 1860s, warned that the extension of the franchise to a numerical majority in society might, rather than eradicating social evils, actually replace them with new, possibly worse, ones, including 'the strong, steady, deadly grip of the trade unions'. If such a scenario did occur, he asserted, 'we should welcome the military despotism that should relieve us' (Salisbury, 1860). Closer examination of Lord Salisbury's written ruminations suggest that it was not so much the enfranchisement of the working class which vexed him – he acknowledged that many *individual* industrial workers were thoroughly decent and patriotic (Taylor, 1975: 19) – but the potential that the working class, either industrially or politically, might act *en masse* (Salisbury, 1860, 1866). Instead of acting as *individual* workers or voters, they might act as a working *class*; that was the perceived danger, and the underlying source of Salisbury's trepidation about democratisation and trade unionism.

From elsewhere in the Conservative Party came the warning that if other classes in British society were given cause to fear the working class, then this was likely to destroy the confidence of capital, with dire consequences for the livelihoods of industrial workers. After all, capital could usually be put to other uses, or even moved somewhere more profitable, whereas labour was generally more fixed and relatively immobile. The prosperity of the working class thus depended, ultimately, on the confidence and profitability of capital, yet trade unions increasingly posed a threat to these vital characteristics (National Union of Conservative and Constitutional Associations, 1873: 3). This critique enjoyed considerable currency in the Conservative Party during the economic downturns which occurred in the last quarter of the century, on which occasions considerable blame was targeted at the trade unions.

Gradually coming to terms with trade unionism

Nonetheless, during the remainder of the nineteenth century, there was no direct attempt by the Conservatives to reverse the legal rights and privileges which the trade unions had been granted by Disraeli's Government, in spite of the anxieties which existed in sections of the Party. To have pursued any such repeal would have risked provoking precisely the kind of collective, class-based action which Conservatives such as Salisbury feared. At the very least, any measure which might have been construed as a Conservative attack on organised labour, and thus an attempt at turning back the clock in any way, would almost certainly have had serious electoral repercussions, for the Party was now competing – against the Liberals – for the votes of those industrial workers who had been enfranchised in 1867 and 1884. The Conservative Party's stance was thus, fully in accordance with its appellation, to maintain the status quo; to refrain from repealing the permissive trade union laws already enacted, but to refuse to pursue any further reforms which would further strengthen the trade unions by bestowing upon them additional legal privileges.

It is worth noting, though, that the issue of compulsory arbitration was occasionally raised by a few Conservative MPs, deriving from a concern that serious industrial disputes could have a detrimental impact on the economy and society, in which case the state ought to ensure that the national interest was protected (see, for example, John Gorst, HC Debates, 4th series, Vol. 31, col. 395). However, others were concerned that compulsory arbitration would entail the state becoming embroiled in major industrial disputes, which would both weaken the overall commitment to *laissez-faire* (which remained the dominant economic ideology or discourse during the late nineteenth century, in spite of Disraeli's social reforms), and possibly undermine the state's professed impartiality and neutrality between various societal interests and organisations. This perspective was endorsed by a Royal Commission on Labour, established in the last decade of the nineteenth century, which – in spite of an economic downturn and various outbreaks of industrial unrest – presented a rather optimistic view of industrial relations, whereby those representing capital and labour were expected to develop a closer and more trustful relationship in due course, once initial misapprehensions had been overcome. The Royal Commission's exhortation that compulsory arbitration should be avoided was heeded by the Conservative Government, now led by the (third) Marquess of Salisbury, which instead opted, via the 1896 Conciliation (Trade Disputes) Act, to establish a system of voluntary arbitration, available under the auspices of the Board of Trade – the Ministry of Labour not being created until 1916 – but only when both sides in an industrial dispute requested it.

The Conservative Government's willingness to avoid compulsion reflected a more general recognition that the Party's electoral and political interests would not be best served by antagonising or alienating the trade unions, even if senior figures like Salisbury were apprehensive about the rise of organised labour and the potential for collective action. Indeed, some Conservatives were now convinced that the Party needed to adopt a rather more positive and conciliatory stance towards organised labour, with Lord Randolph Churchill arguing that if the 'labour interest' felt confident that it could achieve its legitimate industrial objectives through existing political institutions and processes, then it would be happily reconciled to Britain's constitutional system and parliamentary democracy. However, he warned, if organised labour became convinced that it could not obtain its objectives through the existing political framework, and that the 'Constitutional' [Conservative] Party regularly showed itself to be much more sympathetic to the rights of capital and owners of private property, then 'the labour interest' might be persuaded that the existing constitutional system was intrinsically defective, and thereby seek to replace it altogether (quoted in Churchill, 1906: 458–60).

Had Lord Randolph Churchill's constructive approach been more widely shared among senior Conservatives during this period, then the Party leadership might have reacted rather differently to a landmark judicial decision at the very start of the twentieth century. The Taff Vale Railway Company in South Wales had sued the Amalgamated Society of Railway Engineers for loss of revenue, as a direct consequence of a strike, in 1900, by members of the union, whereupon the House of Lords, in 1901, adjudged that trade unions were indeed legally liable for action undertaken in their name, and could thus be sued for damages by those directly affected or targeted by such action. Many trade unions were naturally aghast at this judicial decision, and the clear implications for their ability to engage in strike action. However, the Conservative Government, now led by Arthur Balfour, declined to legislate to restore the trade unions' legal immunities, arguing that such was the power of organised labour and employers' organisations, that it was non-union workers and small businesses who were most in need of protection (HC Debates, 4th series, Vol. 122, cols 261–4). Indeed, at one of his weekly audiences, Balfour informed King Edward VII that the Taff Vale decision had been: 'In substance, right' (quoted in Egremont, 1980: 202).

Yet such was the controversy provoked by the Taff Vale decision that Balfour did authorise, in 1903, a Royal Commission on Trade Disputes and Trade Combinations, although its 1906 Report offered little succour to the trade unions. Indeed, it argued that the Taff Vale decision had been reasonable in its interpretation of the relevant law as it then stood, for no law had ever bestowed upon the trade unions total immunity from civil action, and as such, the case had raised no new issue of principle, nor had it actually altered the legal position or privileges of the trade unions (for an account of this episode, see Macdonald, 1976: 53–60). Nonetheless, the Report did presage new legislation to prevent a repeat of the Taff Vale scenario, by providing greater protection to the trade unions in pursuing industrial action, namely the 1906 Trade Disputes Act, although this was passed by a Liberal Government, Balfour's Government having lost the previous year's general election. Furthermore, while the Trade Disputes Bill was wending its way through Parliament, Balfour confessed his dislike of 'great powers given to any body of men without any power of making them answerable for the results of their action' (HC Debates, 4th series, Vol. 164, col. 911), a perspective which could readily be construed by the trade unions as further evidence of Conservative hostility towards them.

For most of the next two decades, the Conservative Party seemed to assume that a general parity of power had been established between employers and organised labour, and that this should henceforth facilitate orderly collective bargaining. Senior Conservatives therefore placed considerable emphasis on the virtues of industrial partnership, repeatedly urging capital and labour to work more closely together in a spirit of co-operation, whereupon mutual distrust and industrial conflict would steadily dissipate. Even Balfour now seemed to adopt a slightly more constructive or benign attitude, suggesting that some of the conflict in British industry derived from a lack of understanding among workers about the problems which employers faced, in which case, closer partnership would enable employers to educate their employees about some of the pressures which they faced in an increasingly competitive world (*The Times* 2 December 1908), a perspective also articulated by William Bridgeman, a junior Minister at the newly-created Ministry of Labour (*The Times* 4 October 1917. See also National Unionist Association, 1924). Of course, such advocacy of closer links and greater dialogue between employers and employees assumed particular resonance following the 1917 Bolshevik Revolution in Russia, for this exacerbated Conservative anxiety about the potential for revolutionary ideas to develop among the British working class. Industrial partnership was thus intended to be a means of enabling employers to win the trust of their employees, and thereby reduce the likelihood of class warfare or syndicalism. That Conservatives invariably denounced socialism as utopian and un-British did not eradicate their fear that sections of the working class and trade union movement might now look east for political inspiration, just as the Tories had feared, nearly 120 years earlier, that industrial workers and trade unions might be beguiled by political developments occurring to the south, in France; fear of the alien 'other' has always constituted an important component of British Conservatism and its promotion of nationalism.

In urging closer partnership and communication between the two sides of industry – capital and labour, or management and workers – Conservatives presaged the voluntarist paradigm which was to prevail throughout the 1950s and early 1960s, insisting that there was little that the state could do to ensure that employers and employees worked more harmoniously together. Industrial co-operation could only be generated from within industry itself, through the efforts and goodwill of employers and employees, or management and trade unions. This was not something which could be ensured through governmental legislation. Industrial partnership therefore had to develop voluntarily and organically, with the role of governments confined largely to exhortation and encouragement.

This stance was adopted or enunciated by virtually all Conservative leaders and Prime Ministers during the first third of the twentieth century, namely Arthur Balfour (*The Times* 20 January 1923), Stanley Baldwin (*The Times* 6 March 1925; HC Debates, 5th series, Vol. 34, col. 956), Andrew Bonar Law (*The Times* 22 May 1912) and Neville Chamberlain (*The Times* 16 October 1917).

The Political Levy

There was, however, one particular aspect of trade unionism which did offend most Conservatives during the first quarter of the twentieth century, namely the political levy, whereby many trade unions utilised a small proportion of their members' annual subscription fee to finance a separate political fund. In many cases, this effectively entailed trade unions making financial donations to the Labour Party, which had been formed by the trade unions and various socialists in 1906. It was this which rendered the political levy so controversial, because it meant that millions of trade union members who voted Conservative or Liberal were nonetheless – and often unwittingly – financing the Labour Party. In 1908, W. Osborne, who was both a local branch secretary of the Amalgamated Society of Railway Engineers (recently embroiled in the Taff Vale case) and a member of the Liberal Party, sought an injunction against the union to prevent it from spending money on political objectives, claiming that such expenditure was *ultra vires*. After some legal wrangling, the 'Osborne judgment', in 1909, upheld his claim, decreeing that the trade union had no authority to spend its members' fees on political (as opposed to industrial) matters or activity (Hedges and Winterbottom, 1930: 102–3; MacDonald, 1976: 63–6; Pelling, 1976: 130–32).

The Osborne judgment prompted the introduction of the 1913 Trade Union Act, which granted the unions the right to operate a political fund, financed by a small proportion of their members' annual subscription fee, but only on condition that any member who objected could 'contract out' of contributing to it. However, this immediately became a source of Conservative hostility, partly, of course, because the trade unions' political funds provided much of the Labour Party's own funding (and Labour was steadily replacing the Liberals as the main alternative to the Conservative Party), but also because 'contracting-out' placed the onus on individual trade union opponents of the political fund to extricate themselves from it. In many cases, it was alleged, trade union members failed to exercise their right to 'contract out' due to a combination of unawareness of the extent to which the political levy was being utilised to fund the Labour Party, apathy, or fear of intimidation; to formally request a 'contracting-out' form was effectively to declare to that one did not support the self-professed 'workers' party', which might make the employee unpopular with some their colleagues. If the trade unions were going to operate a political fund, and *de facto* use much of this money to bankroll the Labour Party, then individual trade unionists should, Conservatives insisted, be required to 'contract in' if they wanted to contribute to a political fund.

Of course, Conservatives also intimated that if the trade unions confined themselves to industrial and workplace matters, rather than becoming involved in party politics, these issues would not arise in the first place. This distinction between the legitimate industrial activities of trade unions, and their allegedly disreputable political objectives, was one which was crisply articulated by Andrew Bonar Law (Conservative leader from 1911 to 1921), when he declared that:

> from the time the trade unions became captured by a particular political party, and became a political organisation, I was opposed to them. But from the point of view of the purposes for which trade unions were created – the purpose of using combinations of men to obtain better terms for themselves, and a larger share of the profits in the business in which they work – I am entirely in favour of trade unions.
> (HC Debates, 5th series, Vol. 31, cols 1647–8)

Notwithstanding the flawed understanding of history enshrined in this statement – the trade unions were instrumental in forming the Labour Party to provide a parliamentary voice for their interests; they did not become 'captured' by the Party, although this claim has repeatedly been made by Conservatives and pro-Conservative newspapers ever since – the sentiments it expresses have been shared, and often reiterated verbally, by many senior Conservatives ever since.

Meanwhile, the Conservatives were inclined to pose the Labour Party an awkward question: was it a small or large minority of trade unionists who objected to paying the political levy? If it was only a small minority, then surely the Labour Party would have little to lose by allowing that minority to cease paying the political levy. If, however, it was a large minority, to the extent that their ceasing to pay the political levy would cause the Labour Party serious financial difficulties, then Labour was effectively engaging in a form of large-scale coercion and extortion. Thus it was that when the Conservatives were returned to Office after defeating the 1923–24 minority Labour Government, F.A. Macquisten, a Conservative backbencher, attempted to introduce a Political Levy Bill, which would replace 'contracting-out' (a form of 'political conscription', Macquisten claimed) with 'contracting-in', whereupon trade union members who wanted to pay the political levy would need to submit written authorisation to their union to this effect, rather than having to apply for exemption from payment. Consequently, the onus to take action would no longer be on those trade unionists who wanted to 'contract out'; trade union members would be assumed to *not* want to pay the political levy unless they expressly stated, in writing, that they wished to do so (HC Debates, 5th series, Vol. 181, col. 816, col. 822).

Yet in spite of the hostility which the political levy attracted among a great many Conservatives, Macquisten's Bill itself caused some anxiety in the parliamentary Party, with a deputation of Conservative MPs visiting Prime Minister Stanley Baldwin, to convey their concerns. Although they broadly shared the objections to the political levy in principle, they were not convinced that a Private Members'

Bill was the most appropriate means of tackling the problem, partly because it only sought to deal with one particular aspect of contemporary trade unionism, and partly because some working men might consider the Bill to be 'a blatant show of partiality' – after all, there was no corresponding proposal to limit donations to the Conservative Party. However, the deputation, like the Cabinet itself, was not agreed on exactly how the political levy ought to be tackled, with some favouring a more general, independent inquiry into the trade unions' political activities, while others thought that this too might be deemed provocative by the trade unions (Middlemas and Barnes, 1969: 292).

Baldwin himself evidently shared at least some their concerns, because a few days later, having secured the Cabinet's prior approval, he intervened early in the Second Reading debate on Macquisten's Bill, to call for peace in industry, and therefore a rejection of this legislative initiative. Baldwin explained that:

> We have our majority. We believe in the justice of this Bill, but we are going to withdraw our hand, and are not going to push our political advantage home at a moment like this. We are not going to fire the first shot, for we want to create peace, and create an atmosphere in which people can come together.
> (HC Debates, 5th series, Vol. 181, col. 840).

As Baldwin then emphasised a few days later, peace in industry could not be secured by legislation (HC Debates, 5th series, Vol. 182, col. 2445. See also Baldwin's comments in *The Times* 8 March 1925; Arthur Steel-Maitland, HC Debates, 5th series, Vol. 182, col. 820), while also claiming, in a separate speech at about the same time, that:

> By the natural evolution of our industrial life in England, we are confronted to-day, and shall be more and more, with great consolidations of capital managed by small concentrated groups, and by great organisations of Labour led by experienced and responsible leaders. That position must be accepted. It is the natural accompaniment of the large-scale production which is gradually becoming the predominant force in all the industrial countries of the world ... [These] ... organisations of employers and men, if they take their coats off to it, are far more able to work out the solutions of their troubles than the politicians. Let them put the State out of their minds and get down to it ... and seek and pursue peace throughout every alley and every corner of this country.
> (Quoted in Baldwin, 1926: 31, 34)

Towards the end of 1925, the (fourth) Marquess of Salisbury reflected upon Baldwin's stance over the Political Levy Bill, and proclaimed that no-one had done more than Baldwin to promote peace and goodwill in industry. Had Baldwin allowed the Bill to proceed, Lord Salisbury claimed, then there would have been no chance of securing such peace, or of fostering greater trust between the Conservative Party and the trade unions (*The Times* 7 December 1925). Baldwin himself subsequently informed King George V that: 'If there was one mission more than another which … it has been my dearest wish to fulfil, it was to lessen the misunderstandings which threaten industrial strife' (quoted in Williamson and Baldwin, 2004: 31).

The General Strike and its aftermath

However, other events were unfolding whose denouement would destroy the development of such trust for many years to come. Britain's coal industry had been suffering economically throughout the first half of the 1920s from increasing overseas competition, particularly from Germany and Poland, to the extent that, in 1925, the owners of Britain's coal mines sought to impose wage cuts on miners. Faced with the prospect of a coal strike for which it was not prepared, Baldwin's Government bought time by establishing an inquiry, chaired by Sir Herbert Samuel. This gave Ministers nine months in which to prepare, ideologically (in terms of political propaganda) and materially (in terms of arranging the maintenance of services and supplies), for an imminent strike by the miners. This duly ensued when the Samuel Report effectively endorsed the approach of the coal owners, by recommending cuts in wages and an increase in working hours, to ensure the competitiveness of the coal industry. The miners responded by going on strike, exactly as the Baldwin Government had anticipated, insisting 'not a minute on the day, not a penny off the pay'. Their strike, starting on 1 May 1926, was initially joined by various other industrial workers, in an unique display of working-class solidarity, although these other workers returned to work after nine days, whereupon the miners remained on strike until November that year.

Ultimately, though, this nine-day 'General Strike' was doomed from the outset, due to the careful preparations previously undertaken by Ministers and senior officials, the efforts of enthusiastic volunteers who were readily persuaded that they were helping to defend parliamentary democracy from a putative Bolshevik insurrection, and the vast resources at the Government's disposal. By contrast, the TUC was not nearly as well-prepared, but equally importantly, the trade unions would have been unable to support their members financially if they had remained on strike for much longer. Wiser heads among the trade union leadership also recognised that the longer the General Strike lasted, the more it would enable Conservative hard-liners to seize the political initiative by invoking draconian anti-trade union legislation, and even to 'smash the unions' once and for all. This last consideration derived from the manner in which Ministers insisted that this was definitely not a traditional trade dispute, but a politically-motivated attempt by industrial militants to coerce a democratically-elected government and the British people, an attempt which was deemed tantamount to treason. Moreover, when print workers refused to publish a *Daily Mail* editorial, entitled 'For King and Country', which bitterly denounced the strikers, the printers were strongly condemned by Ministers for denying freedom of speech and instigating a form of political censorship.

Although the General Strike was short-lived, and completely failed to prevent the imposition of wage cuts and longer working hours on the miners, it did seem to vindicate the dire warnings of right-wing Conservatives about the spread of Bolshevism from Russia, and the dangers posed by growing industrial militancy and syndicalism; the Reds were not merely 'under the bed', but slipping between the sheets. Thus did the Home Secretary, Sir William Joynson-Hicks, warn that the 'trade union question' would have to be dealt with sooner or later; the British people would have to decide whether their country was to be governed by Parliament and the Cabinet, or by a handful of trade union leaders.

In the aftermath of the General Strike, the pressure in the Conservative Party for trade union legislation could no longer be disregarded, even assuming that Ministers had wanted to discount it. Many Conservative backbenchers and rank-and-file members were incensed about this latest manifestation of industrial militancy, and would now brook no delay or denial by the parliamentary leadership over legislative action to curb trade unionism. Indeed, such was the strength of feeling among Conservative MPs and members that a former Party chairman, Sir George Younger, felt compelled to warn the Cabinet that failure to respond accordingly might lead to a split, with a 'die-hard' group breaking away to form a new party which might rival, or even replace, the existing Conservative Party, a concern which was reiterated by the then chairman, J.C.C. Davidson (Middlemas and Barnes, 1969: 447). Lest the Cabinet was still in any doubt about the strength of feeling in the Conservative Party following the General Strike, the annual conference that autumn heard numerous denunciations of the conduct of Britain's trade unions, and an associated demand for legislative action by the Cabinet, with one delegate instructing Baldwin to 'get on with it or get out', a demand which was greeted with enthusiastic applause.

Yet although Baldwin and his Cabinet colleagues all agreed that trade union legislation was now essential, there was less agreement over the precise form which this should take. Certainly, Harold Macmillan recalled that the Conservative Party itself was divided over the type of Bill which ought to be enacted in response to the General Strike (Macmillan, 1966: 225), for several Ministers wanted to avoid a Bill which was entirely repressive and vengeful, favouring instead legislation which would include some more constructive or conciliatory clauses. Indeed, Baldwin himself was reluctant to preside over a wholly negative or radical Bill, even though he was aware that such legislation would delight many backbenchers and constituency members. As he explained a few years later:

> I remember being pressed very hard … to pass drastic trade union legislation, and I resisted the whole time, I was pressed very strongly to introduce legislation before Christmas, and it would have been extraordinarily difficult for anyone in my position at that time, had he consented to introduce legislation before Christmas, to avoid introducing far more drastic legislation than was ever in my mind ....

> I felt that if the country had a little breathing space during Christmastime …
> we might come back in a better mood. Exactly what I anticipated occurred and,
> when we met in January, I found that the atmosphere was so much improved
> that it was possible to bring in a Bill … which at that time commended itself to
> the whole of the Members of the Government side of the House, even those who
> would have gone much further than did.
> (HC Debates, 5th series, Vol. 247, cols 417–18)

Certainly, the strongest support for a tough stance emanated from the constituency
Conservative associations, although here too there was a lack of unanimity over
specific measures. There were also some notable differences of opinion among
large employers, whose three main representative bodies – the Engineering and
Allied Employers National Federation, the National Union of Manufacturers and
the National Confederation of Employers' Organisations – were consulted by the
Cabinet Committee appointed to prepare the ensuing legislation.

Not surprisingly, some Conservatives were strongly inclined to enact
comprehensive legislation, in order to tackle various aspects of trade unionism
which they found objectionable. For such Conservatives, the General Strike had
starkly shown the degree of power which the trade unions had acquired, and the
extent to which they – and therefore the country itself – were vulnerable to the
machinations of militants who were willing to promote industrial conflict in order
to attain radical political goals. It was considered absolutely intolerable that the
government and the country could be 'held to ransom' in this manner by politically-
motivated extremists in the trade unions, and the Conservative Government would
therefore be guilty of a gross dereliction of duty if it failed to take decisive action
to tackle the more irresponsible and pernicious aspects of trade unionism which
had developed.

However, other Conservative Ministers – including Baldwin himself, apparently
(see Dilks, 1977: 308; Middlemas and Barnes, 1969: 449; Young, 1952: 124) –
and MPs would have been content merely with a simple Bill to prohibit general
strikes (indeed, one backbencher attempted, unsuccessfully, to introduce a Private
Members' Bill to this effect) and limit picketing. Such Conservatives were
anxious to avoid the impression that they were out to 'smash the trade unions'
as vengeance for their involvement in the General Strike, and as such, were
concerned that draconian or repressive legislation would alienate the moderate,
responsible trade unionists whose trust, or even direct support, the Conservative
Party needed to attract. In a letter to Baldwin, the (fourth) Marquess of Salisbury
suggested that it might be unwise for the Cabinet 'to do more than declare General
Strikes, and perhaps strikes aimed at the community, illegal, and strengthen the
law against picketing leading to intimidation', because 'unless combined with a
policy of reconciliation on Partnership lines, we may easily leave things worse,
and not better', while Davidson (the Party Chairman) similarly urged the Minister
of Labour, Arthur Steel-Maitland, to avoid legislation which was overly repressive
and thus appeared to represent 'an *attack* on the trade unions', and, instead,

imbue the Bill with some more constructive or progressive elements (quoted in Middlemas and Barnes, 1969: 447). More conciliatory or prescient Conservatives also seemed tacitly to believe that the bulk of the trade union movement had been suitably chastened by the General Strike, and would be highly unlikely to engage in such irresponsible and unconstitutional behaviour again.

It might well be asked why, therefore, the Conservatives still favoured a Bill to outlaw general strikes? As we have noted, there was unanimous agreement in the Party that *some* legislation should be enacted, and such a Bill was thought to be the most straightforward and least contentious. Indeed, if the trade unions were unlikely to resort to a general strike again, then they ought not to be too outraged at a Bill to prohibit such strikes, whereas a more comprehensive Bill, curbing such features as the political levy or closed shop, would probably cause long-lasting, possibly irreparable, damage to relations between the Conservative Party and the trade unions. Such a scenario caused considerable consternation to those Conservatives who, believing that the trade unions had probably 'learned their lesson' from the failure of the General Strike, wanted to offer an olive branch to the unions, and wean them away from syndicalism towards constitutionalism.

Yet the ensuing 1927 Trades Disputes and Trade Unions Act seemed to signify a victory for Conservative hard-liners, because its main provisions were to:

- outlaw general strikes, defined as strikes intended to coerce the government by imposing hardship on the community;
- outlaw strikes which were not in connection with a trade dispute, and in which those taking part were not directly involved;
- prohibit trade unions or other such bodies representing civil servants from affiliating to the TUC or any political party;
- render it unlawful for local (or other such public) authority employees to be required to join a trade unions as a condition of obtaining or retaining employment;
- replace 'contracting-out' of a trade union's political levy with 'contracting-in';
- place strict limits on the conduct of picketing.

Of course, the first two provisions were closely related, because a general strike intended to coerce the government would not be a legitimate trade dispute involving one group of workers pursuing industrial action against their employer over terms and conditions of employment in a particular occupation or industry. Similarly, the prohibition of strikes by workers who were not themselves employed in the industry affected effectively outlawed secondary or sympathy action in support of other workers, which would itself also prevent another general strike. This, of course, was at a time when neither public ownership of key industries nor the Beveridgian welfare state had been enacted, and so the issue of whether a strike by a group of workers (such as those in a nationalised industry or, say, the NHS) constituted a genuine trade dispute or a strike against the government or *inter alia* the community had not yet arisen.

However, even at this juncture, there were a sizeable number of civil servants whose involvement in strike action would almost certainly raise precisely this issue, for if they were, ultimately, government employees, then a strike for higher pay would *ipso facto* be a strike against the government and/or the wider community. More controversially, perhaps, the Act also debarred such workers from membership of any trade union which was deemed to have political objectives, by virtue of affiliation to the TUC and/or a political party, which, in this particular context, meant the Labour Party. The rationale was that such membership was totally incompatible with the obligation of civil servants to be politically impartial in the performance of their professional duties. The clear implication was that the loyalty of a civil servant in terms of faithfully serving the state in the performance of their professional duties, regardless of the party in government, would be seriously compromised if their trade union was affiliated to a political party; they could not then claim to be politically neutral.

Meanwhile, the clauses concerning local authority employees were intended to weaken the trade union closed shop, whereby union membership was compulsory, and where refusal to join – or expulsion from – a trade union could result in dismissal from employment. Although such compulsion meant that the closed shop became a constant target for many Conservative critics of trade unionism, the Party's leadership often shied away from an outright ban, partly because employers themselves sometimes claimed that maximum union membership made collective bargaining easier, partly because of a reluctance to interfere directly in the internal affairs of the trade unions, and partly because of likely problems pertaining to enforceability of outright prohibition, whereby the closed shop was likely to be driven 'underground'. Thus it was that the 1927 Trade Disputes and Trade Unions Act confined itself to banning the operation of a closed shop in local government

As to the issue of the trade unions' political levy, it is perhaps worth noting that the Minister of Labour was sceptical about the wisdom or necessity of replacing 'contracting-out' by 'contracting-in', not least because he feared that it would be widely interpreted as a highly partisan act, both by virtue of interfering in the internal affairs of the trade unions, and because it would financially damage the Party's main political opponents. Again, concern was expressed that such an apparently partisan measure might alienate moderate trade unionists – the very people whose trust or support the Conservative Party wished to attract (NA CAB 27/326, L. (26), 9th meeting of the Cabinet's Legislation Committee, 22 November 1926). Steel-Maitland's lack of enthusiasm for this particular aspect of the Trade Disputes Bill reaffirms the earlier point that a number of Ministers would have been content with legislation which confined itself to prohibiting general strikes, and limiting picketing. However, they were unable to resist the immense pressure in the Conservative Party for a more comprehensive Bill following the General Strike.

Although the 1927 Trade Disputes Act was inevitably denounced by the trade unions as a spiteful and vengeful Tory attack on the working class and its representative institutions, it was actually a somewhat diluted version of the original Bill, for a few contentious clauses and proposals had been excised from the first draft version. For example, it had originally been intended that strike ballots would be made compulsory, but this proposal was abandoned following objections from a number of employers, who explained to Ministers that quite apart from a host of logistical and organisational problems about conducting ballots prior to a strike – at what stage in negotiations would a ballot be conducted?; who would phrase the question?; who would ensure that ballot papers were completed in secret?; what size majority would be required to endorse a strike, and would it be a majority of those voting, or a majority of all members of the trade union involved?; who would finance the costs of a postal ballot, government or trade unions themselves?; would a ballot then have to be organised subsequently to enable members to decide whether to end a strike? – a 'yes' vote in a strike ballot would strengthen the hand of trade union negotiators *vis-à-vis* employers, because the former could then claim that they had the backing of (or were under pressure from) their members to drive a hard bargain (NA CAB 27/326, L (26) 6th conclusions, Appendix A, 26 July 1926; see also Neville Chamberlain's diary entry for 15 August 1926, in Self, 2000: 364).

In fact, this might also been seen as a potential weakness for trade union negotiators in such circumstances, because they would have less room to manoeuvre or exercise their discretion in agreeing a compromise with employers. Indeed, at a meeting with senior employers' representatives, Ministers were advised that trade union leaders 'are, generally, the more moderate men', whereas behind them were often 'young men anxious to get place and position, and whose policy is to advocate extreme measures. They are the men who have local influence ... [and who] ... largely control the effect of the ballot', and as a consequence, many employers 'fear a secret ballot ... would not make for industrial peace', although the then Chancellor, Winston Churchill, could not conceal his dismay at hearing employers advance such arguments, and was 'not prepared to accept this view' (NA CAB 27/326, L. (26), 6th conclusions, Appendix A, 26 July 1926). Ultimately, though, quite apart from the practical problems of conducting strike ballots, it was acknowledged that the result might be to empower ordinary trade unionists, or perhaps the militants on the factory floor, in a manner which would result in more, not fewer, strikes, and also strikes of a longer duration.

This perspective was clearly rather at odds with the common claim by Conservative backbenchers or rank-and-file members that ordinary workers and trade union members were moderates who were cruelly manipulated or coerced by their more militant or politically-motivated leaders into taking strike action. Those most intimately involved in industrial relations, however, strongly suggested otherwise, and feared that strike ballots would actually result in more frequent, and longer-lasting, industrial disputes, a concern which was to be cited by Conservative Ministers of Labour throughout the 1950s and early 1960s when they too were rejecting perennial demands from Conservative MPs and conference delegates for such ballots.

Consequently, at the next meeting of this Ministerial committee, the Attorney-General conceded that it would be impossible to insist on compulsory secret ballots in the face of opposition from employers themselves, a conclusion with which other Ministers somewhat reluctantly concurred. In effect, a proposal which most, if not all, Conservatives probably supported in principle, was omitted from the Trades Disputes Act, partly because of the likely problems pertaining to the practicability of such a measure, partly because the likely outcome of such ballots would probably not be that commonly envisaged, and partly because it was acknowledged that invoking a statutory obligation to conduct a pre-strike ballot would be bitterly resented by the trade unions as unwarranted interference in their internal affairs (NA CAB 27/326, L (26) 7th conclusions, 2 August 1926).

Another measure excised from the original Trade Union Bill was a proposal to reform Section 4 of the 1906 Trades Disputes Act, whereupon a trade union engaged in an unlawful or unauthorised strike would no longer enjoy legal immunity for torts while pursuing such industrial action. As with the issue of strike ballots, it was acknowledged that while there was widespread support in the Conservative Party – and, on this particular issue, among many employers – for such a reform, and that the principle of amending the 1906 Act was sound, it would be 'inexpedient' to persevere with such a measure. This was partly because such a reform would be construed as an attack on the trade unions generally – thereby alienating moderate and responsible trade unionists – and partly because it might also yield the return at the election of a [Labour] government committed to restoring the relevant Clause (although this particular line of argument hardly seems convincing, for it could just as readily be advanced against any change in the law). It was also argued, though, that the issue of amending the 1906 Act was somewhat obviated by the fact that the current Bill would itself render certain types of industrial action (general and sympathy strikes) unlawful, and thus immune from legal immunity anyway (NA CAB 27/326, C.P. 237 (26), First Report of the Cabinet's Legislation Committee, 28 June 1926; C.P. 406 (26) Third Report of the Cabinet's Legislation Committee, 23 December 1926).

In spite of the inevitable hostility and bitter denunciations which the 1927 Trade Disputes Act attracted from the trade unions, therefore, it appears to have been a somewhat less draconian law than originally envisaged, and certainly disappointed those Conservatives who felt that the final version did not go far enough. For them, the 1927 Trades Disputes Act represented the absolute minimum of what they deemed necessary, and as such, constituted something of a missed opportunity. For other Conservatives, though, including Stanley Baldwin himself, the Act struck a reasonable balance between tackling the most objectionable or dangerous aspects of trade unionism, but without being so repressive or vindictive that it would permanently alienate more moderate trade unionists.

Indeed, the Trade Disputes Act was immediately followed by Conservative efforts to seek something of a *rapprochement* with the trade unions, and to foster a more constructive or conciliatory relationship, including the renewed advocacy of partnership between the 'two sides of industry'. Baldwin himself, in the year that the Trade Disputes Act reached the statute book, expressed his hope that employers and trade unions would soon be able to develop a more harmonious relationship, thereby banishing industrial warfare to the past (*The Times* 14 June 1927). In similar vein, the Minister of Labour, Arthur Steel-Maitland, in a speech to the Movement for Industrial Peace, claimed – even as the Trade Disputes Bill was wending its way through Parliament – that there could be no lasting business efficiency without co-operation between the two sides of industry (*The Times* 2 December 1926), a point also emphasised by [the fourth] Lord Salisbury (*The Times* 28 January 1928).

In fact, some Conservatives went further than just urging partnership between capital and labour, by also recommending closer links between the State and the economy. The most prominent advocate of this approach was Harold Macmillan, who, in 1927, co-authored with a number of younger, similarly 'progressive' Conservative MPs, a booklet entitled *The State and Industry*, which called for a more active role for the state in economic affairs, along with partnership between government and the two sides of industry (Macmillan et al. 1927). This approach was depicted as a middle way between unfettered *laissez-faire* individualism and socialist state-controlled collectivism, whereby government would take responsibility for overall strategic co-ordination of the economy, while leaving day-to-day industrial activity under the jurisdiction of management and employers. Macmillan and his co-authors even alluded approvingly to a mixed economy, entailing a combination of private and public ownership.

With regard to trade unionism, Macmillan's 'middle way' envisaged that union leaders, along with senior industrialists and government Ministers, would meet regularly to discuss economic priorities and problems; in effect, a form of liberal corporatism. Two years later, Arthur Bryant's *The Spirit Of Conservatism* echoed much of Macmillan's perspective, proclaiming that 'the 19th Century gulf between Labour and Capital is a thing of the past', and was now being superseded by a new era of industrial partnership and co-operation, both between the State and the economy in general, and between the trade unions and enlightened employers in particular (Bryant, 1929: 96, 131).

Several of Macmillan's parliamentary colleagues also advocated industrial partnership during the 1930s, with one Minister of Labour, Sir Henry Betterton, claiming that there were no differences in industry which could not be reconciled if there was commitment and good will on both sides (*The Times* 13 April 1932). Similarly, Neville Chamberlain warned that industry and economic progress would be 'crippled' if the relationship between employers and workers was characterised by mutual suspicion rather than co-operation (*The Times* 29 April 1937). Meanwhile, 1934 heard Stanley Baldwin assert that the trade unions were now an integral element of contemporary industrial life (*The Times* 15 February 1934), while the following year, he declared that without the trade unions and their role in collective bargaining, there would be absolute chaos in British industry (*The Times* 5 May 1935).

It was in 1937 that Harold Macmillan published *The Middle Way*, a substantial book which developed many of the themes originally explored 10 years earlier in *The State and Industry*, and which effectively foreshadowed much of the approach which Macmillan himself would pursue or preside over during his subsequent premiership from 1957 until 1963. In particular, *The Middle Way* developed Macmillan's views about the need for a new approach to economic management and industrial organisation, one which would constitute 'a half-way house between a Free Capitalism and complete State Socialist planning', and thereby provide an attractive and realistic alternative to either 'a leap forward into the twenty-first century or retreat into the nineteenth'. This 'new synthesis of Capitalist and Socialist theory' would facilitate a 'peaceful evolution from a free capitalism to a planned Capitalism', and as such, would be perfectly 'in accordance with the traditional English principles of compromise and adjustment' (Macmillan, 1937: 185–6).

What Macmillan envisaged was an economic system in which most of industry would remain predominantly privately owned – although some public ownership was countenanced – but where state-sponsored institutions would co-ordinate or plan industrial production, in order both to minimise the former propensity for boom and slump or over-production followed by under-consumption, and to strengthen social stability and harmony. Specifically, Macmillan proposed the establishment of a National Economic Council comprising representatives from all sectors of the economy – finance, industry, export trade, etc. – along with representatives from employers' organisations and the trade unions, and also Ministers and officials from the Government's own 'economic' Ministries. The overall purpose would be to exchange information and discuss problems with a view to developing 'a comprehensive plan for national guidance'. Macmillan envisaged that the participants – providing 'the best intelligence of the nation' – would then 'conduct their operations in accordance with this policy', with each cognizant of what the other 'stakeholders' (to use early twenty-first-century terminology) were doing, and how their own activities would contribute to the agreed objectives. Consultation would promote co-ordination which, in turn, would yield improved economic and industrial confidence, especially with regard to taking longer-term decisions over such vital issues as investment, and, ultimately, greater social and political stability (Macmillan, 1937: 290–91). However, it was to be another 25 years before Macmillan's vision of a National Economic Council was finally realised, as we will note in chapter five.

More immediately, though, an early initiative in the pursuit of industrial partnership was signified by the 1928–29 Mond–Turner talks, entailing a series of discussions between a group of enlightened employers, led by Sir Alfred Mond (Chairman of Imperial Chemical Industries, ICI), and senior TUC figures, most notably Ben Turner, Ernest Bevin and Walter Citrine. Although it is widely accepted that these talks produced little of substance, the fact that they took place at all, particularly so soon after the General Strike, was significant, for it showed the extent to which more moderate or enlightened leaders on both sides of industry were willing to seek closer dialogue and co-operation, which at least boded well for the future (see, for example: Lovell and Roberts, 1968: 103–11; Macdonald, 1976: 114–15; Pelling, 1976: 188; Renshaw, 1982: 111–13), and which seemed to vindicate Conservative proponents of industrial partnership.

The impact of the Second World War

Nonetheless, Macmillan's conviction about the efficacy of industrial partnership, and the associated incorporation of trade union leaders into the highest echelons of decision-taking, was reinforced by the experience of the Second World War, when the (Conservative) leader and Prime Minister of the wartime Coalition Government, Winston Churchill (having replaced Neville Chamberlain in May 1940), appointed Ernest Bevin, the leader of Britain's then largest trade union, the Transport and General Workers' Union (TGWU), to the post of Minister of Labour. This would undoubtedly have met with the full approval of the Conservative politician, Leo Amery, for he was convinced that in the context of the war effort: 'The time has come when the organisation and influence of the Trades Union Congress cannot be left aside. It must … reinforce the strength of the national effort from the inside' (HC Debates, 5th series, Vol. 360, col. 1149). Of course, part of the reason for the Conservative leadership's determination to seek an alliance with the trade unions during the war was the manner in which the hitherto 'reserve army of labour', as evinced by the mass unemployment of the 1930s, had been superseded by a scarcity of labour, particularly in the spheres of industrial production where it was most urgently needed. Indeed, 'it was manpower, not finance, that set the financial limit to the national effort', whereupon: 'The status of labour, and therefore of the trade unions, was transformed' (Lovell and Roberts, 1968: 145).

Although the Second World War obviously constituted exceptional circumstances, the appointment of Bevin as Minister of Labour – in which post he was also vested with an extensive range of powers, some of which he abrogated from the Home Office – was still a remarkable achievement in view of the bitterness engendered between some Conservatives and the trade unions during the General Strike (during which Churchill himself had reportedly made some highly inflammatory remarks) and the consequent Trades Disputes Act. Yet 14 years later, the leader of Britain's then largest trade union was appointed, by Churchill, to a Ministerial post which was to prove absolutely vital to the war effort. Indeed, as one study of British labour history has noted:

> Bevin's Ministry of Labour took over the Treasury's traditional role as the most important economic department. From that vantage point, he did as much as

any single person to win the war. In so doing, he left an indelible imprint on the post-war settlement.
(Marquand, 1999: 77)

In similar vein, a major study of the history of the TUC refers to 'Bevin's achievement as the Churchill of the proletariat in the Workers' War', while also noting that 'the Second World War transformed the TUC into more of an Estate of the Realm than at any other time in its history' (Taylor, 2000: 273, 76. See also, Middlemas, 1979: 270–71).

In his role as Minister of Labour, Bevin ensured that trade unions were widely represented on a plethora of committees and other consultative forums established to co-ordinate industrial activity and the allocation of labour during the war. This naturally provided Bevin and other senior trade union officials with unprecedented and intimate involvement in numerous aspects of domestic politics and public policy, an involvement which was to be maintained, to a very considerable extent, after the war. As early as 1940, a senior TUC official was declaring that: 'Organised labour will henceforth be satisfied with nothing less than full partnership in the state. The war has brought out more clearly than ever before the country's dependence upon the mass of working people' (Price, 1940: 173). Churchill certainly acted as if this was true, for when he replaced Chamberlain as Conservative leader and Prime Minister of the Coalition Government, he sent 'emphatic and precise' instructions to the various government departments about the importance of maintaining the closest possible consultation and dialogue with the TUC, to the extent that the war-time leader of the TUC, Walter Citrine, later recalled that: 'We had very little to complain about after this, with officials falling over themselves to demonstrate their desire for co-operation' (Citrine, 1967: 31–2).

It was in this context that the TUC suddenly enjoyed extensive representation on numerous Whitehall committees, in addition to the close links established between the Ministry of Labour and the trade unions under Bevin's stewardship. For example, the TUC was represented on such bodies as the National Joint Advisory Council (soon replaced by the smaller Joint Consultative Committee, but with equal representation for the trade unions and employers on both bodies), the Central Production Advisory Committee and the Reconstruction Joint Advisory Council, as well as a National Arbitration Tribunal to adjudicate in the case of serious or damaging industrial disputes, and whose decisions were final and binding. Trade unions were also represented on various sectoral or departmental bodies, such as the Advisory Committees to the Minister of Supply, and the Ministry of Food. They also enjoyed representation on the (Board of Trade's) Central Price Regulation Committee (for fuller discussion of trade union representation on such bodies during the war, see: Brooke, 1992: *passim*; Bullock, 1967: *passim*; Lovell and Roberts, 1968: 144–54; Middlemas, 1979: chapter ten; Pelling, 1976: 210–21; Price, 1940: chapter six).

As a senior Cabinet Office official noted at the beginning of 1945, 'Departments have brought the TUC far more whole-heartedly and extensively into counsel during this war than at any other time' (NA PREM 4/8212, Rowan to Churchill, 9 January 1945). The scale of this incorporation has been noted by Allen, for whereas the trade unions were represented on just one governmental committee in 1931–32, they were represented on 12 such bodies by 1939, and this then increased to 60 by 1948–49 (Allen, 1960: 34). It should also be noted that during the Second World War, 46 joint industrial councils were established, each staffed by equal numbers of employer and trade union representatives, in accordance with the principles and recommendations originally emanating from the Whitley Committee, which had been established to advise on industrial relations issues during the First World War.

However, perhaps more importantly, there was a qualitative, as well as quantitative, dimension to this increased trade union participation, for as Samuel Beer has noted, 'mere representation on committees, or even the opportunity to consult with high civil servants and ministers, was not the essential advance. The important thing was the change in attitude', for on a wide range of important economic and social issues, Ministers and mandarins did not merely consult with the trade unions, they 'negotiated with representatives of the organized working class' (Beer, 1969: 213, 214), the point here being that 'negotiation' strongly implies, or reflects, a certain parity of power, and therefore the need to engage in a bargained exchange relationship.

Indeed, by this time, there was some exasperation among some senior Whitehall officials that Walter Citrine was not only 'always prone to claim that the TUC have a right to representation on … bodies', but that 'the TUC should be consulted' on *who* should be the TUC's representative, even when a Minister had already decided on the person (s) they wished to appoint (NA PREM 4/8212, Barlow to Rowan, 9 January 1945). Even Bevin himself was occasionally irked by the extent to which Citrine – 'Bevin and Citrine never liked each other personally' (Addison, 1977: 45) – seemed to expect that he or the TUC should be consulted on, or involved in, every inquiry or policy initiative throughout the war, even when either the urgency or specific nature of an issue made this impractical or inappropriate (see, for example, NA PREM 4/8212, Bevin to Citrine, 4 July 1941; Bevin to Churchill, 3 October 1941; Bevin to Attlee, 2 January 1942).

For the purposes of this particular study, there are four further aspects of the trade unions' political incorporation and involvement, during the Second World War, which are of particular significance. Firstly, there was their general acceptance of much greater state regulation, or even direction, of industrial affairs and employment, in order to ensure the maximum efficiency and co-ordination of the war effort. It was in this context that the trade unions accepted the introduction, in July 1940, of Order 1305, which outlawed strikes during the war, and imposed a system of compulsory arbitration in those cases where management and workers could not reach an agreement through the normal process of collective bargaining. It was also deemed illegal to engage in industrial action in defiance of the recommendations arising from such arbitration. Yet it is notable just how infrequently Order 1305 was invoked – just 109 prosecutions – with Bevin's biographer noting that up until the beginning of 1944, fewer than 2,000 workers had actually been convicted for engaging in industrial action in defiance of the Order. This was not due entirely to the self-restraint exercised by the trade unions, because sundry industrial disputes still occurred during this period, mostly unofficial strikes, but also to Bevin's own reluctance to instigate legal proceedings against fellow trade unionists (Bullock, 1967: 266–9. See also Barnes and Reid, 1982: 160; Macdonald, 1976: 126; Taylor, 1993: 18–20). However, it was also evident to those most closely involved that there were limits to how far Order 1305 could effectively be applied, because ultimately, continued defiance – including refusal to pay any fines imposed – would imply imprisonment of those involved, yet imprisoning workers at a time of serious labour shortages, in the midst of a major war, would be absurd, quite apart from the damage which would have been caused to relations with the trade unions in general. In many respects, therefore, Bevin envisaged that Order 1305 would have a largely symbolic impact, serving to persuade the trade unions just how dire the situation was, and thereby eliciting voluntary self-restraint deriving from patriotism.

Secondly, notwithstanding the enactment of such an ostensibly draconian initiative as Order 1305, Bevin was determined to defend, as far as practicably possible in the exceptional circumstances, the principle of voluntarism in industrial relations and trade unionism. As he explained to Churchill himself, 'on matters which are the subject of collective agreement between organised workers and employers', the Government 'relies upon organisations of employers and of workers to act as trustees for the avoidance of disputes and the settlement of wages', and this form of industrial self-government was 'even more important ... under War conditions' (NA PREM 4/8212, Bevin to Churchill, 24 March 1943).

Meanwhile, although the TUC's General Council published, in 1944, its own Interim Report on Reconstruction, reaffirming a long-standing commitment to extending public ownership, and greater regulation of those industries which remained privately-owned, it also insisted that:

> ... in all circumstances Trade Unions should retain their present freedom from legal restraints upon their right to frame policy and pursue activities in support of that policy... As voluntary associations of work people, they must, in their policies, interpret the wishes of work people and their actions must be designed to protect in advance work people's common interests. Otherwise, though they may continue to exist as organisations, they will cease to be Trade Unions.
> (Quoted in Lovell and Roberts, 1968: 151)

Although there was clearly a tension between extending the economic and industrial role of the state and retaining the independence and autonomy of the trade unions, it was, perhaps, a tacit awareness of this inconsistency which prompted the General Council's trenchant insistence on (continued) voluntarism.

Thirdly, but following on from the last point concerning voluntarism, there was the manner in which collective bargaining was devoutly defended against Treasury and Ministerial attempts at imposing wage controls. The various war-time shortages of labour effectively entailed a marked increase in the bargaining power of the trade unions, and for this very reason, some Ministers, along with the Treasury, were convinced that some central control of wages was necessary, particularly as other aspects of economic and industrial activity were now subject to unprecedented state intervention and regulation. Bevin, though, was adamant that free collective bargaining was a sacrosanct principle of trade unionism, and that the patriotism of industrial workers and the trade unions would ensure that wage claims would be reasonable and responsible; the trade unions would exercise voluntary self-restraint, and thereby refrain from unduly exploiting their more advantageous market position and stronger bargaining power (see, for example, Bullock, 1967: 84–92).

Fourthly, through their aforementioned membership of sundry committees, the trade unions made a signal contribution to the plans and preparations – some of which were commenced as early as 1941 – for post-war reconstruction. Indeed, it was an inter-departmental committee, established by the Department of Health in May 1941, and chaired by Sir William Beveridge, which transmogrified into an inquiry concerning social insurance and related services, and to which the TUC was the first body to submit evidence and detailed proposals. The consequent Beveridge Report, published in 1942, was to provide much of the framework (and intellectual justification) for the 'cradle-to-grave' welfare state which was established during the latter half of the decade (Taylor, 2000: 93).

Even before the end of the war, therefore, Conservative Ministers had acquired, or had reaffirmed, considerable respect for Britain's trade unions and the patriotism of the working class. As Walter Citrine, noted, as early as 1942:

> The influence of the trade unions has been enormously strengthened during the war, and at no period in British history has the contribution which the organised workers have made to the success of their country been more widely and readily recognised.
> (Citrine, 1942: 48)

Yet there was one particular source of continual tension between the trade unions and the Conservative Party throughout the war, namely the fact that the 1927 Trades Disputes Act remained on the statute book. In particular, there were repeated calls by some trade unions for a reform or relaxation of those clauses which forbade civil service unions from affiliating to the TUC, and initially, in response to these, there were occasional intimations from Churchill that aspects of this legislation might be reviewed, depending on how the trade unions conducted themselves in the meantime (*The Times* 31 March 1940; Conservative Party Archives, Bodleian Library, Oxford University [hereafter CPA], Conservative Research Department [hereafter CRD], 2/7/23, Churchill to Gibson, 11 March 1941 and Churchill to Anderson, 25 April 1941). However, it also became clear that even this conciliatory gesture would cause considerable consternation in the Conservative Party, irrespective of the otherwise more constructive approach being urged towards the trade unions during the war (CPA CRD 2/7/23, Petherick to Stuart [Chief Whip], 8 August 1943; Stuart to Barrington-Ford, 12 September 1943; Letter signed by more than 100 Conservative MPs to Churchill, 30 September 1943; NA CAB 65/26, W.M. (42), War Cabinet, 57th conclusions, 5 May 1942; W.M. (43), War Cabinet, 113th conclusions, 9 August 1943; Citrine,1967: 242). Consequently, near the end of the war, Churchill suggested that 'this question is one which should be submitted to the electorate, and that their verdict will govern its treatment in the new Parliament' (CPA CRD 2/722, Churchill to Citrine, 10 March 1945), a response which perhaps reflected Churchill's understandable confidence at the time that he and the Conservative Party would win a resounding victory in the first post-war general election, in which case they would be able to claim that there was little support among the electorate for amending the 1927 Trades Disputes Act.

Apart from this specific bone of contention, the emphasis in Ministerial war-time policy proposals and speeches was, as in the 1930s, on the vital role of responsible trade unionism in the workplace, and the necessity for industrial partnership. As Viscount Cranbourne argued, there had to be a true partnership between the two sides of industry if the British economy was to prosper after the war. Moreover, he added, now that Britain had established political democracy, it should not be thought that the country could not achieve industrial democracy too (*The Scotsman* 23 October 1943). Certainly, the war effort ensured that many Conservatives were 'quite determined not to return to the economic and social policies prevailing between the wars', not solely on grounds of decency and humanitarianism – vitally and intrinsically important though these qualities were – but also to ensure the future viability of the Conservative Party itself: 'if it is to remain alive and kicking, it must adapt itself to the changes in a changing world. Dogmatic parties would die as surely as the dinosaur' (Cazalet-Keir, 1967: 142, 143).

Winston Churchill himself, on more than one occasion, readily acknowledged the vital and constructive role played by the trade unions during the war. For example, in March 1943, he informed the House of Commons that 'We have had a very great success in this war in getting along without great stoppages in industry, and we have done it very largely by our reliance on the great trade unions' (HC Debates, 5th series, Vol. 387, col. 1477), while at the end of the war, he reiterated that: 'We owe an immense debt of gratitude to the trade unions, and never can this country forget how they stood by and helped' (HC Debates, 5th series, Vol. 410, col. 1405). Indeed, Rab Butler seemed to go further when he spoke to the Central Council of the National Union of Conservative and Unionist Associations in October 1941, for he asserted that 'there must be great permanent changes after the war', and hence it was necessary for those involved in preparing for post-war reconstruction to 'approach all problems with a fresh mind.'

To facilitate such preparations, the Conservative Party established, at the request of the Central Council of the [extra-parliamentary] National Union of Conservative and Unionist Associations, its own Post-War Reconstruction Committee, which then established an Industrial and Finance sub-committee. At its inaugural meeting, in February 1942, this sub-committee agreed initially to prioritise three policy issues, one of which was industrial relations. When this topic was briefly considered at the second meeting, it was acknowledged that 'there could be no return to the pre-war divisions in industry', which therefore made it imperative that careful consideration was given to future relations in the workplace, including the means by which industrial workers might enjoy greater security of employment (CPA, CRD 2/28/12, Industrial and Finance Committee, minutes of 2nd meeting, 18 March 1942). Subsequent discussion of the position of workers in post-war industry also heard calls for closer consultation and dialogue between employers and employees (CPA, CRD 2/28/12, minutes of 6th meeting, 20 May 1942; minutes of 9th meeting, 9 September 1942; minutes of 11th meeting 14 October 1942), clearly presaging the Conservative Party's post-1945 emphasis on co-partnership in industry as a means both of making workers feel more valued and involved, and of explaining to them the rationale of management decisions, which would also help to counter left-wing propaganda which cast aspersions about the motives of employers and industrialists.

By the end of the Second World War, therefore, the status of the trade unions had been totally transformed, and few Conservatives seemed to envisage that there would – or could – be any turning back of the clock during the transition to peace and post-war reconstruction. Similarly, while various war-time committees were disbanded, their work now successfully completed, the principle of trade union representation in Whitehall had been firmly established, and on those (many) committees which continued to function, was often deeply entrenched. Furthermore, when new committees were established to address immediate post-war problems, it was virtually inconceivable that trade union representatives or officials would not be offered membership on these too.

Consequently, a correspondent from *The Times* pointed out, with only a little hyperbole, to the TUC's 1945 annual conference:

> You have no longer any need to thunder; you have only to whisper and Ministers tremble ... How very far away are those days when a few top-hatted, frock-coated gentlemen made a promenade of Government offices in Whitehall respectfully carrying resolutions passed by Congress, leaving them at the door, extremely happy if they saw a permanent secretary, and more handsomely flattered if by accident they stumbled across a Minister.
> (Quoted in Beer, 1969: 214)

The position and status of the trade unions had been greatly enhanced by their contribution to the war, both in terms of industrial production, and the involvement of senior union leaders – Bevin providing the most obvious example – at the very highest levels of decision-taking and policy making in Whitehall. This was to have profound implications after the war, not just for the trade unions themselves, but for the Conservative Party's attitude and stance towards them.

Conclusion

The 146 years from 1799 to 1945 witnessed British Conservatism evincing the whole gamut of attitudes and stances towards the trade unions, ranging from antipathy to acquiescence through to acceptance, although even the latter was characterised by anxiety or admonishment concerning specific aspects of trade unionism. Thus it was that this period of British history saw the Conservative Party (or its forerunner, the Tory Party) start by seeking to suppress the nascent trade unions, and end by claiming that strong trade unions were an essential component of a modern industrial society, to the extent that if they did not already exist, they would have to be created.

Of course, the path to Conservative acceptance of the trade unionism was by no means smooth, even though it was the Tories and subsequent Conservatives who enacted a number of liberal or permissive laws which greatly assisted or benefited the trade unions, most notably the repeal of the Combination Acts in 1824–25, the 1859 Molestation of Workmen Act, and the two labour laws passed by Disraeli's Government in 1875. Grateful though they doubtless were for such measures, the trade unions could subsequently refer to the blame which some Conservatives apportioned to them for the economic problems of the late 1880s and 1890s, and the Conservative Party's apparent lack of enthusiasm for reversing either the 1901 Taff Vale decision, which rendered trade unions liable to civil action when pursuing strike action, or the 1909 Osborne judgment, which challenged trade union political donations to the Labour Party. In both cases, the legislation to neutralise or supersede these two judicial decisions was enacted by Liberal Governments (led by Henry Campbell-Bannerman and Herbert Asquith respectively). Of course, trade union suspicion that the Conservatives were instinctively and irrevocably hostile to organised labour was confirmed by the Baldwin Government's introduction of the 1927 Trade Disputes Act, which entered union folklore as a vicious and vindictive piece of anti-trade union legislation, passed as spiteful Right-wing revenge for the previous year's General Strike. However, the Conservatives maintained, both at the time and on subsequent occasions, that the 1927 Act did nothing to prevent legitimate and responsible trade union activity. Furthermore, it was notable that even before this law had entered the statute book, a number of senior Conservatives were already holding out an olive branch to the trade unions, in the guise of advocating industrial partnership, whilst Harold Macmillan and some of his close parliamentary colleagues were proposing a closer partnership between the State and the 'two sides' of industry.

Although the trade unions were subsequently aggrieved that Conservative Ministers would not amend, yet alone repeal, the Trade Disputes Act in grateful recognition of the unions' signal contribution to the war effort, their vital role did foster an otherwise more constructive and positive attitude among senior Conservatives towards organised labour, as indicated by various fulsome speeches, although there was little in the Party's 1945 election manifesto to illustrate what this would actually mean in terms of actual policies, beyond the notable commitment to 'high and stable levels of employment'. It would require a term in Opposition, having lost heavily in the 1945 election, for the Conservative Party to develop policies commensurate with its more conciliatory and appreciative rhetoric *vis-à-vis* the trade unions. Indeed, failure to do so, some Conservatives feared, might consign the Party to a lengthy spell in the political wilderness. It would therefore be vital for the Conservatives to develop a philosophy and associated policies – and a more emollient discourse – which would convince the trade unions that they could genuinely trust the post-war Conservative Party.

Chapter 2
Preparing a Voluntarist Approach, 1945–1951

The Conservative Party's manifesto for the 1945 general election contained no reference to trade unionism or industrial relations, and although it did enshrine a commitment to 'high and stable levels of employment', it also expressed strong opposition to nationalisation (Craig, 1970: 89, 93–4). The phrase 'full employment' was carefully avoided, on the grounds that this could not be guaranteed all the time, due to changing or unforeseen economic circumstances: 'to pin our flag to the employment mast is going to be desperately dangerous' (CPA CRD 2/7/1, Hutchinson to Fraser, 22 July 1948). Apart from this commitment, there has been some debate about whether or not the Conservative Party's 1945 manifesto enshrined much that was different to the Party's stance on most domestic policy issues prior to the formation of the Coalition Government in 1940. Gamble has suggested that, due to the policy objectives for post-war Britain jointly developed by Ministers during the first half of the 1940s, albeit with the exception of nationalisation, 'the parties [Conservative and Labour] fought the election on virtually the same policies. The real division lay between the Conservatives' declared policies in 1945 and their actual policies in the interwar years' (Gamble, 1974: 29). Yet this interpretation of policy convergence and bipartisanship as early as 1945 has been challenged by Girvin, who maintains that there 'was little difference in substance between the domestic policies advocated by the party in 1945 and those in 1939 … Conservative domestic policy … only slightly modified the priorities of the 1930s', and as such, the Labour Party far more closely and successfully reflected the widespread public desire 'to break with the past' (Girvin, 1994: 127).

Doubtless these divergent interpretations derive from the different emphases ascribed to particular aspects of Conservative policy prior to 1940 and in 1945, but the really important issue, as far as this chapter is concerned, is the degree to which Conservative domestic policies developed between 1945 and 1951, especially with regard to trade unionism and industrial relations, and *inter alia* the Party's attempt to render itself more electorally attractive to voters who had not previously voted Conservative, or who had switched from the Conservatives to Labour in 1945.

The scale of the Labour Party's victory in the 1945 general election, and the apparent mandate this bestowed on its comprehensive programme of economic and social reform, was naturally a profound shock to the Conservatives, but prompted rather divergent conclusions about the significance of Labour's electoral success. A few right-wing Conservatives complacently assumed that the newly-elected

Labour Government, led by Clement Attlee, would soon become unpopular, as the cost of its policies and the concomitant scale of state intervention, became increasingly evident to voters. As the public recoiled against such profligacy and *dirigisme*, it was confidently anticipated that the electoral pendulum would swing back to the Conservative Party at the next general election. The clear implication of this perspective was that the Conservative Party needed to do little by way of policy modernisation, but, instead, adhere to their traditional stance of promoting sound money, low taxation, minimal welfare provision, individual liberty and eulogising private enterprise. This account clearly assumed that Labour's 1945 election victory was an aberration, and that once the electorate suffered the anticipated consequences of the Attlee Government's interventionist and expensive policies, so the virtues of traditional Conservative values and measures would became self-evident to those who had seemingly been seduced by Labour's 1945 pledges. The Conservative Party should therefore remain confident in its existing principles and policies, attack the Labour Government at every opportunity, and wait for voters to flock back to the Conservative fold in four or five years' time.

However, more prescient or progressive Conservatives wondered whether the election of an apparently radical Labour government might actually signify a more substantial or long-term shift to the left in British politics (See, for example: Hinchingbrooke, 1946; Hogg, 1945; Macmillan, 1946). If this was the case, then it was clearly incumbent on the Conservative Party to reconsider, if not its principles, then, at least, their application to post-war Britain, and how they could best be translated into contemporary policies (in more recent discourse, placing traditional values in a modern setting). Or as Rab Butler expressed it, alluding to Robert Peel's Tamworth Manifesto: 'As in the days of Peel, the Conservatives must be seen to have accommodated themselves to a social revolution' (quoted in Butler, 1971: 133).

In undertaking such a reappraisal, the post-1945 Conservative Party sought to attract the support or trust of four discrete sections of British society beyond its traditional or core supporters. Firstly, there was a conscious attempt at making the Party more attractive to floating or politically non-aligned voters, particularly those who certainly did not consider themselves to be socialists, but who were fearful that the return of a Conservative government would presage the dismantling of the welfare state, a return to the mass unemployment of the inter-war years, and renewed industrial strife and conflict between capital and organised labour.

Secondly, and in order to assuage similar anxieties, the Conservatives sought to reinvent – or re-brand – themselves in the latter half of the 1940s, in order to increase the Party's appeal to sections of the working class (discussed more fully below). Not only did this entail a strong emphasis on the Party's own support for 'high and stable levels' of employment, greater government regulation of the economy, welfare provision and unequivocal acceptance of trade unionism, it also prompted a highly selective interpretation or revisionist account of Conservative history, which downplayed its erstwhile espousal of individualism, *laissez-faire* economics and unfettered market forces, and instead insisted that the Party had always recognised a legitimate role for the state in industrial and social affairs, while also supporting responsible trade unionism: the Conservative Party 'has never been frightened of using the power of the state to improve social conditions, to organize economic effort, and to provide collective services' (Alport, 1946: 14). Certainly, support for a more interventionist role for the state had been urged by the Tory Reform Committee during the war, for while it was formed, in 1943, primarily to urge acceptance of the previous year's Beveridge Report, it soon 'developed into an organized faction, trying to change Conservative thinking about government management of the economy' (Gamble, 1974: 33. See also Hoffman, 1964: 40–41; Molson, 1945: 250). To this end, one of the Tory Reform Committee's founders (and an early chairman), Lord Hinchingbrooke, claimed:

> True Conservative opinion is horrified at the damage done to this country since the last [1914–18] war by 'individualist' businessmen, financiers and speculators ranging freely in a laissez-faire economy and creeping unnoticed into the fold of Conservatism to insult the party with their vote at elections ... and to injure the character of our people. It would wish nothing better than that these men should collect their baggage and depart. True Conservatism has nothing whatever to do with them and their obnoxious policies.
> (Hinchingbrooke, 1944: 21)

Similar sentiments were expressed by Anthony Eden, when he informed delegates at the Conservatives' 1947 conference that 'We are not a party of unbridled, brutal capitalism, and never have been. Although we believe in personal responsibility, and personal initiative in business, we are not the political children of the laissez-faire school. We opposed them decade after decade.' The same year heard Quintin Hogg (later Lord Hailsham) claim that the Conservative Party had, for a long time, been highly critical of *laissez-faire* capitalism because it entailed 'an ungodly and rapacious scramble for ill-gotten gains, in the course of which the rich appeared to get richer and the poor poorer' (Hogg, 1947: 51). Indeed, even before the end of the war, Hogg was insisting that:

> This twentieth century society demands a measure of control to prevent chaos. The price of ignoring this need is unemployment, cut-throat competition, unbalanced economy, unjust distribution of wealth, slums, ignorance, bitterness, squalor and in the end [class] war ... They [the working class] have no hostility to private profit as such. But they do not understand why law should give profits priority over their needs.
> (Hogg, 1944: 80–81)

The third section of British society whom the Conservatives were seeking to attract the support or trust of was that of trade unions themselves, most of whose members at this time were industrial workers. It was hoped that by publicly committing itself to a more constructive and conciliatory relationship with organised labour, the enmities of the inter-war years, particularly with regard to the 1926 General Strike, the consequent 1927 Trade Disputes Act, and the mass unemployment of the 1930s, could be superseded by more harmonious relations between the Conservatives and trade unions. The patriotism displayed by the trade unions as part of the war effort, followed by the scale of Labour's victory in 1945, persuaded many Conservatives that they had little to gain – but much to lose – by treating the trade unions as a 'class enemy'. If the Conservative Party was to prosper in the second half of the twentieth century, then it had to acknowledge 'the forward march of labour', and seek a *rapprochement* with the trade unions, particularly as trade union membership increased from 4.8 million in 1935, to 6.5 million in 1940 and thence to 9 million in 1950. The Conservative Party simply could not afford, electorally, to be openly hostile towards such a vastly expanded and numerous socio-economic constituency.

Certainly, the Director of the Conservative Research Department was among those senior figures in the Party who readily acknowledged that:

> Collective bargaining is now the accepted method of settling industrial wages in this country, and it implies organisation on both sides … In large-scale industry there is in fact no alternative to collective bargaining. If unions did not exist, it would be necessary to create some industrial leadership among employees. Unofficial strikes not withstanding … Trade unionism is making an important contribution to the orderly conduct of industry.
> (Clarke, 1947: 16)

It was not just that a Conservative government might not be able to govern without the co-operation of the trade unions, but that public fear of renewed 'class war' might be sufficient to prevent the Conservatives from being elected in the first place. As such, once Clement Attlee's Labour Government had, in 1946, repealed the 1927 Trades Disputes Act, there was a clear recognition in the Conservative Party that it would be 'disastrous' if the Conservatives gave the slightest impression that they intended 'to re-enact the 1927 Act' (CPA, Conservative Central Office [hereafter CCO], 503/2/21, Minutes of a special meeting between the [Conservative] National Trade Union Advisory Committee and Conservative Parliamentary Labour Committee, 26 July 1951). It was largely to allay such anxieties that the Conservative's backbench Parliamentary Labour Committee emphasised that:

> Organized labour has won its place as a full partner in the state to be consulted equally at governmental level … the trade-union movement has now firmly established itself as one of the three interests that support our industrial fabric, namely: labour, management and government. The Conservative party regards the existence of strong and independent trade-unionism as an essential safeguard

of freedom in an industrial society. It must be the purpose of a Conservative
government to strengthen and encourage trade-unions.
(CPA, Conservative Parliamentary Labour Committee, 'Report of the Trade
Union Problems subcommittee', Advisory Committee on Policy [hereafter
ACP] 3/1 (1951)13, 2 May 1951).

This too reinforced the revisionist account of Conservative history, for it was now
asserted that the Party had always been supportive of 'responsible' trade unionism,
and cited various statutory measures, as noted in the previous chapter, which
Conservative governments had enacted since the nineteenth century to place the
trade unions on a secure and legal footing: 'The Conservative party have always
been firm supporters of the trade-unions. They have, to their credit, a long record
of legislation designed to help the unions' (CPA CCO 503/1/9, 'The Conservative
Trade-Unionists Movement', 1 September 1948). Similarly, the Conservative
Party's 1950 manifesto emphasised how: 'We have held the view, from the days
of Disraeli, that the Trade Union movement is essential to the proper working of
our economy and of our industrial life' (Craig, 1970: 118). This revisionist account
even entailed audacious attempts at presenting the 1927 Trade Disputes Act in a
more positive light, with the assertion that it 'in no way curtailed the efficiency or
working of the Unions. It was passed to protect the working man against bad Trade
Union leadership [and] the public against a general strike' (CPA, CCO 503/3/2,
'Lecture Notes – The Conservatives and the Trade Unions', April 1947).

There was, however, occasional (and lamented) acknowledgement of 'the
continued existence within the party of opposition to trade-unionism in all its
shapes and forms', a residual sentiment which, of course, merely made it even
more imperative that the Conservative leadership illustrated its full support for
'responsible [non-political and moderate] trade-unionism in post-war Britain'
(CPA, CRD 2/7/44, Minutes of the inaugural meeting of the Central Trade Union
Advisory Committee, 8 March 1947). In this respect, Conservative progressives
were not only trying to win the trust of the trade unions themselves, but
simultaneously to educate some of their own un-enlightened Party colleagues,
particularly as their continued antipathy towards trade unionism would doubtless
be cited as evidence buy some trade union leaders that the Conservatives had not
genuinely changed their attitude towards organised labour.

Consequently, there were repeated assurances that the next Conservative
government would seek a close and constructive relationship with the trade
unions, and seek to tackle any problems on the basis of discussion and dialogue,
not legislative diktat. Indeed, within three months of the 1945 election defeat,
forward-thinking Conservatives were emphasising 'a need for publishing the
attitude of the Conservative Party towards Trade Unions' in order to 'make it quite
clear that we are not against them, but in favour of them' (CPA, CRD 2/7/41 (1),
Brooke to Pierssené, 29 October 1945).

In this context, even the Party's hostility towards the closed shop and
'contracting-out' of the political levy – both of which were subsequently restored

by the Labour Government's 1946 Trade Disputes Act (which repealed the 1927 Trades Disputes Act) – was rather muted. It was even suggested that 'the initiative for such changes [in trade union law] must come from the Unions themselves. A Conservative government would always be anxious to avoid interference in Trade Union matters' (Leather et al., undated but circa 1951: 7). Consequently, when one senior Conservative official suggested that the Party's 'propaganda' against the political activities of the trade unions ought to be made 'more militant', by highlighting both the administrative costs of operating a political fund, coupled with the amount spent on the salaries of union officials, he was sharply rebuked; not only were the accuracy and assumptions of the figures he cited refuted, it was also made clear that 'trying to appeal to the Trade Unionist vote by attacking the Unions' was an approach which Conservatives should 'deplore', for 'the more you attack the Trade Unions, the more whole-heartedly the weight of their whole organisation will be flung into the next General Election against us', and this would 'count for far more than any odd votes you pick up by attacking them' (CPA CRD 2/7/6, Clarke to Chapman-Walker, 5 April 1950).

This was a clear reflection both of the determination to avoid any pronouncements which might be construed by the trade unions as a signal that the Conservatives would launch a new legislative assault against them, and of the 'voluntarist' perspective, which insisted that Acts of Parliament could not in themselves foster more harmonious industrial relations; these could only emanate from those working in industry, deriving from a genuine desire to tackle problems in the workplace. Voluntarism was predicated upon assumptions about the efficacy of industrial self-government, and bottom-up or in-house initiatives for improving industrial relations. As such, a Conservative government would seek to avoid legislative intervention in both internal trade union affairs, and in relations between employer and employees, unless expressly invited to intervene by those directly involved. As we will note in the next chapter, this would leave Ministers heavily reliant on encouragement and exhortation when seeking to promote improvements in industrial relations and more responsible behaviour by the trade unions, thereby firmly resisting the adoption of statutory solutions. Thus did the Party's 1950 manifesto promise that a Conservative government would 'consult with the Unions upon a friendly and final settlement of the questions of contracting out and compulsory unionism, on both of which Conservatives have strong convictions of principle, and on any other matters that the Unions may wish to raise' (Craig, 1970: 119). A virtually identical pledge was offered in the 1951 manifesto *Britain Strong and Free*.

Fourthly, in offering a recasting of its principles, and a revised account of Conservative history which emphasised its Disraelian tradition of progressive social reform and the creation of 'one nation', the Party was hoping to render itself more attractive to academic and cultural elites, and opinion-formers. This reflected concern that the Conservatives were not viewed favourably by intellectuals, many of whom, Alport lamented, had previously 'been singled out by the Liberals, socialists and communists as being a most important element in the struggle to mould public opinion', while the Conservative Party had 'always underestimated the sort of people known as the intelligentsia'. Yet it was these people, namely 'the professional classes, school and university teachers, writers, scientists, economists', who were more readily 'captured by the Fabian Society and who today dominate the Socialist party'. If the Conservative Party continued to ignore them, then 'they will have no alternative but to gravitate towards the left as they did between the wars' (Alport, 1946: 21).

Although the attempt at appealing to floating and working-class voters on the one hand, and intellectuals on the other, might have suggested distinctive approaches to different audiences, Conservative advocates of a newer, more progressive, approach treated them as inextricably linked, for as Leo Amery argued, there 'can be no permanent revival of Conservatism without a positive alternative policy to the policy of the socialist left ... a clear and comprehensive restatement [of Disraeli's principles] in the light of present-day conditions' (Amery, 1946: 5).

Also urging clarification of Conservative principles were delegates at the Party's 1946 annual conference, who demanded a 'statement giving, in fuller detail, the principles and programme of the party'. It was in response to such demands that Winston Churchill established an industrial policy committee, whose membership comprised five members of the Conservative Front-Bench, namely Rab Butler (who also chaired it), Oliver Lyttelton, Harold Macmillan, David Maxwell-Fyfe, and Oliver Stanley, whilst Conservative backbenchers were represented by Sir Peter Bennett, David Eccles, Derrick Heathcoat-Amory, and James Hutchinson. As Ramsden has noted, 'the composition of the Committee as a whole ensured that things would move in a progressive direction' (Ramsden, 1980: 109), for most of these figures emanated from the progressive or 'one nation' wing of the parliamentary Conservative Party.

The Industrial Charter

What the industrial policy committee produced, in 1947, was *The Industrial Charter*, which largely provided the intellectual basis of the Conservative Party's approach to economic affairs, industrial relations and trade unionism for the next 17 years. Selling 2.5 million copies in the first three months of publication, *The Industrial Charter* has variously been described as 'the most important post-war policy document produced by the Conservatives' (Lindsay and Harrington, 1979: 151), 'an early milestone' in the Conservative Party's 'adaptation to post-1945 politics' (Taylor, 1994: 513), 'a decisive moment in Conservative post-war history' (Gilmour and Garnett, 1997: 34), and 'the most memorable concession a free enterprise party ever made to the spirit of Keynesian economics' (Howard, 1987: 135).

The Industrial Charter opened with a brief statement of 'economic values', which acknowledged the need to devise 'a system of free enterprise which ... reconciles the need for central direction with the encouragement of individual effort', and which would serve to eradicate unemployment while also maximising 'the security of our social and industrial system', while also seeking to improve the status of 'the worker ... as an individual personality' through governmental action (Conservative and Unionist Central Office, 1947: 3–4). This introduction was then followed by three substantive sections, the first of which provided a short critique of the problems and immediate objectives of basic industries in the immediate aftermath of the war.

However, it is the other two sections which are of real interest to us, in terms of the Conservative Party's attempt at articulating a new, more progressive, approach to trade unionism and industrial relations. The second section of *The Industrial Charter* included such issues as employment policy, and the trade unions. With regard to the former, it was asserted that the Conservatives were now fully committed to 'maintaining a high and stable level of employment' – the Party deliberately avoided the term 'full employment', doubtless fearing that this might prove impossible to achieve, and as such, offering something of a hostage to fortune – to which end a Conservative government would 'ensure that the demand for goods and services is always maintained at level which will offer jobs to all those who are willing to work' (Conservative and Unionist Central Office, 1947: 15, 16).

With regard to trade unionism, *The Industrial Charter* emphasised that 'the official policy of the Conservative Party is in favour of trade unions' and 'attaches the highest importance to the part to be played by the unions in guiding the national economy', which 'depends upon the participation of union officials at all levels'. It was also suggested that as many employees as possible ought to join a trade union, albeit on an entirely voluntary basis, and thereafter become actively involved in its affairs. This, it was envisaged, would ensure that the trade unions were genuinely representative, thereby countering 'the tendency for some unions to fall into the hands of a small clique because of apathy' (Conservative and Unionist Central Office, 1947: 21–2).

Yet this section of *The Industrial Charter* also made clear the Conservative Party's unhappiness over the 1946 repeal of the 1927 Trade Disputes Act, which now meant that some local authority or public sector employees would have to become trade union members as a condition of retaining their employment (the closed shop), whilst the restoration of 'contracting-out' of the political levy meant that some employees would effectively be contributing to the finances of the Labour Party either against their wishes and political allegiances, or even without realising it. It was therefore recommended that legislation be introduced to restore the status quo *ante* with regard to the two aspects, as well as to prohibit civil servants from belonging to trade unions which were affiliated to the Labour Party or the TUC.

It was the third and final section of *The Industrial Charter*, though, entitled 'The Workers' Charter', which, right from the outset, attracted the most attention, for it was here that the Conservative Party most explicitly sought to convince industrial workers that it was not inimical to their aspirations nor indifferent to their anxieties. As such, it was emphasised that Conservative policy was 'to humanise, not nationalise' industry, and to this end, it was proposed that employees should be provided with 'a reasonable expectation of industrial security [of employment], improved incentives to develop skills and talents, and thereby realise their full potential as individuals, and enhanced status for all employees, irrespective of how menial or manual their occupation was.

Such measures, it was explained, would constitute 'a series of standards in the field of industrial relations to which ... employers must conform. However, 'the Workers' Charter' was also adamant that such measures could only be effective if they were introduced primarily on a voluntary basis, for the 'conditions of industrial life are too varied to be brought within the cramping grip of legislation', which therefore ensured that 'such a charter cannot be made the subject of an Act of Parliament' (Conservative and Unionist Central Office, 1947: 28). Yet it was suggested that employers and companies who failed to meet the objectives and standards decreed in *The Industrial Charter*, for which parliamentary endorsement would be sought in order to imbue it with clear moral authority, 'will not be entitled to receive any share of the large range of contracts put out to tender by public authorities' (Conservative and Unionist Central Office, 1947: 29. See also: CPA, CRD 2/7/1, 'The Conservative's Target for Industry', May 1948), a threat repeated in the Party's 1950 manifesto (Craig, 1970: 119).

To its admirers in the Conservative Party, *The Industrial Charter* was 'the pioneer of "the middle way"' (CPA, CRD 2/7/1, Fraser to Clarke, 8 January 1948.), a route which Macmillan himself had pointed to on more than one occasion during the inter-war period (Macmillan et al., 1927; Macmillan, 1937). Indeed, one newspaper columnist, writing under the pen-name 'Crossbencher', observed that Harold Macmillan 'once wrote a political treatise called *The Middle Way*. This is the second edition' (*The Sunday Express* 15 May 1947), although one suspects that this was not intended as a compliment. Much more fulsome was the depiction offered by the Conservative MP John Boyd-Carpenter, who asserted that the principles and policies enshrined in *The Industrial Charter* provided the Party with a 'central position between the extremes of Manchester[1] and Moscow' (Boyd-Carpenter, 1950: 11). In similar vein, David Eccles sought to explain, in a speech to Conservative candidates adopted for the next general election, that the choice was not between Soviet-style Socialist planning and the economic *laissez-faire* favoured by the Conservatives' 'anti-planners', but between the centralised, top-down, planning promoted by Socialists, and the more 'constructive' Conservative approach which uses 'the methods of freedom in operating our plans'. Ultimately, Eccles emphasised, the objection was not to planning *per se*, but 'to the particular aims and methods of Socialist planning' (CPA CRD 2/7/29, 'Forward from the Industrial Charter', 26 January1948). Eccles too was attempting to depict *The Industrial Charter* as a moderate, 'middle way' alternative between the extremes of right and left.

------

1   An allusion to the 'Manchester School' of *laissez-faire* economics and the 'night watchman' state which had been prevalent for much of the nineteenth century among political elites and many commentators or opinion-formers.

Not surprisingly, Rab Butler was particularly effusive in his praise, characterising *The Industrial Charter* as a concerted attempt by the Conservative Party to 'counter the charge and the fear that we were the party of industrial go-as-you-please and devil-take-the-hindmost, that full employment and welfare state were not safe in our hands' (Butler, 1971: 146), and in so doing, serving 'to prove that the Conservatives were human' (CPA, ACP (54) 19th meeting, 18 June 1954). In this respect, one Conservative historian has emphasised that the objectives of *The Industrial Charter* were 'to weld together the Liberal tradition of free enterprise with the … Tory concept of interventionism' and, thereby provide the Conservative Party with 'a new Tamworth manifesto' (Ramsden, 1980: 110). Some proponents also explicitly cited Disraeli's *Sybil*, and the need to overcome 'two nations' or, in this context, 'two sides' of industry, by promoting a 'united effort in a common cause' (CPA, CRD 2/7/1, Michael Fraser, 'The Industrial Charter', December 1947). Meanwhile, one Conservative constituency activist was so enthused by *The Industrial Charter* that he deemed it 'the finest document ever produced by the party', and suggested that it might well 'produce an additional 3 million votes at the next election', while also urging the Conservative leadership to 'stand by for converts' (CPA, CRD 2/7/30 (1), Day to Butler, 12 May 1947).

Yet, for many on the right of the Conservative Party, *The Industrial Charter* constituted what backbencher Sir Waldron Smithers contemptuously described (at the Party's 1947 conference) as 'milk-and-water socialism'. Indeed, he subsequently penned a 22-page tract – entitled *Save England* – replete with portentous Old Testament references and quotations, denouncing *The Industrial Charter* for 'its compromises with socialism and communism', and declaring that 'acceptance or rejection of the charter by the party is a matter of life and death for Britain, and therefore the whole world' (CPA, CRD 2/7/29, Sir Waldron Smithers, *Save England: 'Industrial or Magna Charter': The Conservative Industrial Charter Attacked – On Principle*, July 1947). In similar vein, one disgruntled Conservative wrote to Central Office to complain that *The Industrial Charter* 'paves the way for the complete triumph of socialism and probably, sooner or later, the communist State' (CPA, CRD 2/7/30 (1), Cooke to Butler, 20 May 1947), a warning strongly echoed by the critics who claimed that it 'proves that the infiltration troops of Leftism, the "Progressive" Conservatives, have captured Central Office' and 'abandoned the idea of fighting Socialism in favour of gradual surrender to Collectivism under Conservative patronage' (CPA, CRD 2/7/29, Jackson to Butler, June 1947), and that *The Industrial Charter* enshrined 'far too much agreement with … Socialist principles' (CPA, CRD 2/7/30 (2), Marshall to Butler, 19 May 1947). Indeed, the Conservative Party Archives (at the Bodleian Library in Oxford) include three large files full of such paranoid proclamations and deranged diatribes submitted to Central Office, and often addressed directly to Rab Butler (CPA, CRD 2/7/29, CRD 2/7/30 (1) and CRD 2/7/30 (2), letters submitted on various dates in May–July 1947). Among this voluminous correspondence is a series of increasingly curt letters between Conservative Central Office and an aggrieved Party member, Commander Hyde Burton, written during May and June 1947.

Such was the evident exasperation of the Central Office recipients of Burton's invective against *The Industrial Charter* that, on one occasion, he was informed 'you cannot be serious', while on another, the General Director of Central Office confessed to David Clarke that 'I doubt whether he is susceptible to reason.'

Macmillan's response to such criticisms was characteristically and loftily dismissive, declaring that when the Conservative's right wing claimed that *The Industrial Charter* was not Tory policy, what they really meant was that 'they wish it were not Tory policy', emphatically adding that: 'Fortunately, their wishes cannot be granted' (Macmillan, 1969: 306). In similar vein, Rab Butler later recalled with evident glee how he, along with other 'progressive' Conservatives, 'managed in one way or another to upset the right-wing or country-squire element' in the Party (Butler, 1982: 96).

A further criticism of *The Industrial Charter* emanating from Conservatives such as Sir Waldron Smithers was that the whole exercise reflected the Party's apparent capitulation to intellectualisation, when the strength of Conservatism had hitherto derived in large part from its faith in instinct, intuition and tradition. Yet now, Smithers complained, the Conservative Party has succumbed to 'a dangerous and growing tendency in all political parties to be run by their "intelligentsia", men who are determined to enact their theories without regard to ... consequences' (CPA, CRD 2/7/29, Sir Waldron Smithers, *Save England*, July 1947). Similar concerns were expressed by the Conservative agent for the Worthing constituency, who regretted that 'the Political Education methods adopted by the Party' – such as promoting *The Industrial Charter* – entailed too much emphasis on targeting 'our intelligentsia' at the expense of 'our ordinary members' (*Conservative Agents' Journal*, No. 329, April 1948).

Such complaints prompted Alport to retort that while 'I do not suppose that the average voter in Worthing, who is remote from industry, is interested in the problems of industrial relations ... the outcome of the next election will depend on whether we are able to convince the factory worker' that we fully intend to pursue a constructive approach to industrial relations, for it was in 'the industries of Manchester and Birmingham ... urban, industrial areas' that the Conservative Party needed to win support in order to be returned to office (Quoted in *Conservative Agents' Journal*, 330, May 1948 and 333, August 1948).

Meanwhile, there was some ambiguity over the attitude of Conservative leader Winston Churchill, to the extent that Conservative politicians and historians have never been able to agree about Churchill's true feelings concerning *The Industrial Charter*, nor about how carefully he actually read the final draft. Harold Macmillan recalled being 'surprised at the attention he gave, not merely, as one might expect, to the drafting, but to the substance' (Macmillan, 1969: 32), yet Reginald Maudling (1978: 45) claimed that in his capacity as Churchill's speech-writer at the Conservative's 1947 conference, he was asked to include 'five lines explaining what the Charter says', implying that Churchill himself had not read it with particular care.

This led to the second ambiguity over Churchill's opinion of *The Industrial Charter*, for having read Maudling's summation of it in the draft of his speech, the Conservative leader declared: 'But I don't agree with a word of this', thus obliging Maudling to inform Churchill that the conference had already endorsed it. 'Oh well, leave it in', replied Churchill (Howard, 1987: 156). Subsequently, the eminent Conservative historian Robert Blake has argued that Churchill 'seems to have taken a good deal of persuasion to give his *imprimatur*' to *The Industrial Charter*, although Blake adds that Churchill was rather more interested in foreign affairs than domestic 'bread-and-butter politics' (Blake, 1985: 258; see also Norton and Aughey, 1981: 128). Yet Rab Butler had assumed that Churchill was favourably disposed towards *The Industrial Charter*, albeit 'not so much obtained as divined', due to the cordiality with which Churchill treated him at a Savoy dinner for the Leader's Consultative Committee (effectively the Conservative's shadow cabinet) in May 1947 (Butler, 1971: 145). Macmillan also discerned approval by Churchill for *The Industrial Charter*, on the grounds that in his speech to the 1947 conference, the Conservative leader 'gave firm support to the new Conservatism which always appealed to him sentimentally, since it seemed to be a return ... to the Tory democracy of which his father, Lord Randolph, had been the pioneer. This endorsement completed the struggle for the Charter' (Macmillan, 1969: 308).

However, antipathy and ambiguity were very much exceptions to the favourable reception which *The Industrial Charter* received from the bulk of the Conservative Party. A number of Conservatives considered it 'good ... to find that there are Progressives in the Party', fearing that they were 'in far greater danger of being sabotaged by our own right wing than of being defeated ... by the Socialists'. The danger facing the Party, such Conservatives warned, was 'to be held back by these reactionaries on our Right' (CPA, CRD 2/7/30 (1), Verity to Butler, 24 May 1947). A similarly delighted Macmillan explained that: 'Between the two wars there was always a progressive element in the party; but it never dominated the party. Now it has seized the control, not by force or palace revolution, but by the vigour of its intellectual and spiritual power' (*Tory Challenge* November 1947).

Such was the optimism which *The Industrial Charter* fostered among 'progressive' Conservatives that one of its authors, James Hutchinson, predicted that 'far-sighted Trade Unions will, in the near future, realise the Conservative Party to be their best friends' (CPA, CCO 503/2/21, Central Trade Union Advisory Committee, 2nd meeting, 12 June 1947). There was also optimism that *The Industrial Charter* would play a major role in the afore-mentioned objective of attracting 'floating' or non-aligned voters: 'it would have a definite effect upon the man sitting on the fence', for it 'supplied something that has been lacking within the Conservative Party for a long time' (CPA, CCO 503/2/21, Central Trade Union Advisory Committee, Minutes of 2nd meeting, 12 June 1947).

Macmillan's confidence about the recently-established dominance of the 'Tory progressives' was partly derived from the fact that *The Industrial Charter* was endorsed by an overwhelming majority – with only three votes against – at the

Conservative Party's 1947 conference. Having been duly endorsed, the principles enshrined in *The Industrial Charter* were reiterated two years later in the policy document *The Right Road for Britain*, which declared:

> Conservatives believe that the problems of industry are, first of all, human problems, and that continuous attention must be given to the personal relations between management and labour. The key to the proper working of British industry lies in humanising free enterprise, and not in nationalising it. Industrial relations must no longer be thought of in terms of two sides with interests which are permanently opposite and inevitably conflicting. Fundamentally, both management and labour have the same interest in the prosperity of their industry, and to this they must devote their attention in a spirit of co-operation and partnership. The spirit of partnership cannot be enforced by law.
> (Conservative and Unionist Central Office, 1949: 23).

The subsequent impact of *The Industrial Charter* has occasionally been disputed, with Nigel Harris among those claiming that it was largely ignored as a guide to policy when the Conservatives were returned to government [in 1951] (Harris, 1972: 77, 82, 145), while Taylor has argued that having become Minister of Labour, '[Walter] Monckton displayed no apparent interest in propagating the Conservatives' Industrial Charter ... was not even prepared to make any innovative moves by implementing the more tangible parts of the Industrial Charter' (Taylor, 1993: 84, 87). We would disagree with these dismissive judgements about the apparently limited impact or influence of this policy document, though, for it is evident that the principles enshrined in *The Industrial Charter* provided the intellectual paradigm for much of the Conservative Party's approach towards industrial relations and trade unionism throughout the 1950s. As Ramsden has noted, it deliberately avoided specific policy proposals in favour of 'a framework of philosophy and guidelines of administration rather than an immediate programme for the next Parliament' (Ramsden, 1977a: 422). Indeed, as we will note in the next chapter, Conservative industrial relations and trade union policy henceforth comprised three discrete – but inextricably connected and mutually reinforcing – tenets or themes, namely voluntarism, a socio-psychological critique of industrial conflict aligned to the insistence that 'industrial relations are human relations', and advocacy of industrial partnership or co-partnership, each of which are clearly discernible in *The Industrial Charter*.

Moreover, Conservative Ministers and Central Office officials variously cited *The Industrial Charter* when discussing industrial relations and trade unionism throughout the 1950s and early 1960s. For example, in 1954, James Douglas, a senior official in the Conservative Research Department emphasised the extent to which the Churchill Government's industrial relations policy 'had kept within the frame-work of the principles laid down by *The Industrial Charter* (CPA, ACP (54) 34, 'Industrial Relations', 11 June 1954; see also NA PREM 11/4314, Butler to Heath, 9 May 1960; CPA ACP (62) 94, 'A Tory Look at Industrial Relations', 29 January 1962).

Conservative Trade Unionists

Although *The Industrial Charter* was therefore a crucial component of the post-war Conservative Party's effort to reconstitute itself in order to attract increased working-class and trade union support, it was by no means the only innovation with regard to this particular objective. Also of signal importance was the creation of the Conservative Trade Unionists (CTU), a body intended to establish closer ideological and organisational linkages between the Conservative Party and organised labour.

The antecedents of the CTU can be traced back to 1918, when the Conservative Party established a Central Labour Advisory Committee to offer advice to the Party's leaders and officials on trade union affairs. Although originally confined exclusively to trade unionists, after 1927, its conditions of membership were relaxed in order to permit wage earners generally to join (a further subsequent relaxation of the membership rules permitted the wives of industrial workers to join too). However, the Central Labour Advisory Committee atrophied during the Second World War, after which, it was decided to revive it, but on a somewhat different basis.

Thus were Conservative Trade Union Councils (CTUC) created, as part of the Party's determination to establish links with the trade unions, and *inter alia* broaden the social bases of its electoral support after Labour's 1945 victory. Their appellation was soon changed however, to Conservative Trade Unionists, in order to avoid any misapprehension that they were a Conservative alternative or challenge to the TUC – a move which was itself symbolic of the Party leadership's desire to avoid offending the trade unions at this juncture. In establishing these Conservative Trade Union organisations, it was hoped to illustrate that there was no incompatibility between being a committed Conservative and an active trade unionist (CPA, CCO 503/3/2, 'Lecture Notes: The Conservatives and the Trade-Unions', April 1947).

However, the primary purpose of the CTU was to disseminate Conservative arguments and ideas in the workplace (and also in union branches and pubs), and thereby counter the propaganda of the left. It was envisaged that Conservative trade unionists would 'act as trained gossipers in their factories and works, so that they are constantly spreading Conservative ideas' (CPA, CRD 2/7/6, Sub-Committee on Political Education, 'Report of the Working Party on the Approach to the Industrial Worker', 20 July 1950; CRD 2/7/3, Conservative Parliamentary Labour Committee to Maxwell Fyfe, 3 July 1950; National Union of Conservative and Unionists Associations, 1952: 9).

Another key objective ascribed to the CTU was to counter the power and influence of the left by ensuring that Conservative or 'non-Socialist' trade unionists played a more active role inside the trade unions, through attendance at meetings, and possibly by standing as candidates in trade union elections (Rowe, 1980: 216–17. See also CPA CCO) 503/1/9, 'The Conservative Trade Unionists Movement', 1 September 1948). There was a concern among some senior Conservatives that because of the link between the trade unions and the Labour Party, some 'men vote Socialist because they are Trade-unionist, irrespective of their real political sympathies' (CPA CCO 4/3/125, Adamson [Conservative and Unionist Central Office] to TUAC Regional Secretaries, 13 March 1950. See also CCO 4/4/127, Woolton [Conservative Party Chair] to Conservative MPs, prospective parliamentary candidates, constituency chairmen and constituency agents, 9 November 1950). It was therefore envisaged that the involvement of more Conservatives in the trade unions would help to convince union members that they could, without any qualms or contradiction, vote Conservative.

At the same time, however, it was envisaged that this would similarly help to challenge preconceptions or prejudices among some Conservative constituency members concerning trade unionists, a point clearly alluded to by Sir Thomas Dugdale when he addressed a Regional Party meeting in Yorkshire in November 1950, on which occasion he felt obliged to emphasise that 'the typical Trade Unionist and his family are fundamentally good Britishers, and we must not try and deal with them as something out of the ordinary or peculiar … as something different and apart'. On the contrary, it was vital that Conservatives 'adopt a natural friendly attitude towards them … strive to recruit them as full members of our [constituency] Associations', and thus avoid segregating them, or adopting a 'patronising air towards them'.

Furthermore, the involvement of more Conservatives in the trade unions was deemed to be the best antidote to Communist involvement in trade unions; rather than seeking to prohibit Communists from being candidates in trade union elections or from serving as elected officials, it was argued that trade union members should simply refrain from voting for Communists. Such a solution would be greatly encouraged if more Conservatives put themselves forward as candidates in trade union elections, thereby not only offering members a greater choice, by enabling them to vote for non-left candidates, but also further illustrating that one could simultaneously be a Conservative and a committed trade unionist; the two were not mutually exclusive (CPA CCO 4/2/83, CTU Advisory Committee, 9th meeting, 14 July 1949).

Indeed, in this context, it was sometimes pointed out that prior to the Labour Government's recent replacement, via the 1946 Trades Disputes Act, of 'contracting-in' by 'contracting-out', only 2.4 million trade union members (out of the 5.6 million members of trade unions which operated a political fund) paid the political levy, which seemed to prove two vital points. Firstly, that the majority of trade union members had not endorsed their union's funding of the 'socialist' party, and secondly, that the subsequent increase in the number of trade unionists paying the political levy, following the 1946 Act's re-introduction of 'contracting-out', suggested that the Labour Party was being heavily bank-rolled by the apathy or ignorance of non-socialist trade union members (CPA, CCO 503/3/2, 'Lecture Notes: The Conservatives and the Trade Unions', April 1947). As such, it was envisaged that if more Conservatives became actively involved in their trade unions, not only would they illustrate that there was no incompatibility between being a Conservative and being a trade unionist, they would also be able to explain to fellow union members how the political levy operated, and encourage them to exercise their right to 'contract out' (See for example, CPA, CCO 4/5/363, Piersenné to Fraser, 26 March 1952).

This would, in turn, help the next Conservative government to avoid the need to legislate against the political levy, for such action would not only be incompatible with the 'voluntarist' approach to industrial relations and trade unionism, it would almost certainly, from the outset, provoke conflict with the trade unions, and thereby seriously damage the Party's professed commitment to conciliation and co-operation. Certainly, towards the end of its period in Opposition, there had emerged a strong body of opinion among those Conservatives most interested in trade union matters that the Party should not pledge to replace 'contracting-out' with 'contracting-in', partly because of the recognition that the trade unions were 'rather touchy' about what they saw as governmental interference in their internal and organisational affairs, and also because of a desire to avoid adopting a 'tit-for-tat policy'. Moreover, if the Conservatives pledged to restore 'contracting-in', the Party would be 'offering the Socialist Party a political stick for our own backs' (CPA, CCO 503/2/21, Minutes of meeting of the Conservative Parliamentary Labour Committee, 26 July 1951), and would probably reinforce the link between the Labour Party and the trade unions as they jointly attacked the Conservatives over this issue (CPA, ACP (51) 13, Conservative Parliamentary Labour Committee, 'Report of the trade union problems sub-committee', 2 May 1951). Ultimately, therefore, it was generally accepted that rather than seek to replace the 'contracting-out' aspect of the political levy, Conservatives should be encouraged to become actively involved in trade unions in their workplace, whereupon they could inform fellow workers of their right to 'contract out', and thereby serve to de-couple trade unionism from party politics.

With regard to this last point, Conservatives insisted that the objective of the CTU was not to convert trade unions *qua* institutions to Conservatism, but to tackle their susceptibility to left-wing domination, and ultimately de-politicise trade unions, whereupon they would focus fully on legitimate industrial matters, with particular regard to their members' terms and conditions of employment.

Clearly though, there were two tensions or inconsistencies here. Firstly, to suggest that the more active involvement of Conservatives in the day-to-day affairs and activities of the trade unions, coupled with the fielding of Conservative candidates in union elections, would de-politicise them, suggests a singularly skewed definition of what constitutes 'political' in terms of trade unionism. The implication is evidently that the propaganda of socialists and communists is political (or politically-motivated) whereas Conservative propaganda is not, as if the latter were merely an impartial presentation of the true facts or even simple common sense (indeed, Conservatives have often insisted that they are non-ideological, and that their philosophy is derived from, and merely reflects, 'common sense').

Secondly, there seemed to be an assumption that trade unions no longer needed to focus on political issues now that a Labour Government was actively delivering the goals which the trade unions had long campaigned for, most notably full employment and a comprehensive welfare state, as well as some public ownership. With the attainment of such policy objectives, it was intimated, the trade unions ought to turn their attention (back) to purely industrial and work-place matters. However, in many respects, nationalisation, governmental responsibility for the maintenance of full employment and the expansion of the welfare state all served to 'politicise' what might previously have been viewed as primarily economic or industrial matters, thereby rendering it much more difficult, if not impossible, to distinguish clearly between industrial and political issues. This was especially the case concerning industrial disputes in the newly nationalised industries or recently expanded public sector, where government itself was, in the last instance, the employer, and hence responsible for wages, along with other terms and conditions of employment.

Attracting the 'skilled worker'

Although the Conservatives were keen to increase their electoral support among industrial workers and trade unionists – as already noted above with regard to *The Industrial Charter* and the Conservative Trade Unionists organisation – it was the *skilled* working class especially which was the primary focus of the Party's parliamentary leadership and senior officials in Conservative Central Office. This derived from a strategic calculation that it was among skilled workers that a revulsion against Labour's egalitarianism goals and redistributive policies would increasingly manifest itself, as these workers witnessed the erosion of their wage differentials *vis-à-vis* semi-skilled or unskilled manual workers. Once these skilled industrial workers became disillusioned with Labour policies (if they were not so already), then the Conservative Party would be able to attract their support by promoting the Party's belief in pay differentials and economic rewards for talent, hard work and individual initiative or effort (CPA, CRD 2/7/6, Sub-Committee on Political Education, 'Report of the Working Party to the Approach to the Industrial Worker', 20 July 1950). In short, the Conservatives hoped to convince skilled workers that they would be better served politically and thus better-off financially, under a Conservative government than a 'socialist' Labour administration. This was to become a consistent theme of Conservative electoral strategy in subsequent decades, proving particularly effective in the 1979 election, when Margaret Thatcher's Conservative Party explicitly targeted skilled workers with promises of restored pay differentials, and was rewarded with an 11 per cent swing from the skilled working class, or 'C2s' as they became known.

However, this approach also meant that the Conservative Party would need to accept that it would probably not be able to secure the votes of more than 40 per cent of industrial workers, due to the slightly greater proportion of semi-skilled and unskilled workers among the working class as a whole. Indeed, it was alleged that as much as '30% of the working population is of mentality which will only respond to a "something for nothing" type of policy', and for the Conservatives to pledge 'the sort of policy which would satisfy the shiftless and idlers would be to antagonise the more self-reliant workers' (CPA, CRD 2/7/6, Sub-Committee on Political Education, 'Report of the Working Party on the Approach to the Industrial Worker', 20 July 1950).

Showing that the Conservatives are *not* 'the bosses' Party'

One other facet of the Conservative's efforts to win the trust and co-operation of the trade unions and (skilled) industrial workers during this period was the emphasis placed on the role and responsibility of employers, not merely in terms of the traditional Conservative emphasis on leadership in the workplace, but also in terms of minimising the damage done both to the Conservative Party's own image or reputation, and to good industrial relations, by bad employers. There was a recognition in some quarters of the Conservative Party that there existed 'a profound suspicion [amongst industrial workers] of the motives and intentions of our own Party, based partly on an identification of it with the employer' (CPA ACP 3/1, Conservative Parliamentary Labour Committee, 'Report on Ways and Means of Attracting the Vote of the Skilled Worker in Industry', 3 July 1950). Indeed, in 1949, one senior Conservative parliamentarian was suggesting that the Party's 'biggest problem in connection with industry is to live down the notion that we are the representatives of the bosses' (CPA CRD 2/7/37, Heathcoat Amory to Fraser, 25 May 1949). Consequently, during the preparatory period in Opposition, various Party officials emphasised the need to illustrate to industrial workers that the Conservatives were not 'the Party of the bosses', but were genuinely a One Nation party which sought to serve all sections of British society.

Certainly, there was concern about the damaging impact, both on good industrial relations and the credibility of the Conservative Party among industrial workers, of disreputable bosses, for: 'Bad employers create more Socialist voters than result from Socialist propaganda', to the effect that 'the whole effort of Conservative policy can be destroyed in a whole district by the action of a bad employer.' It was therefore deemed vital that employers, in both their attitudes and actions, adopted a more constructive approach to workplace leadership and management, and inspired admiration and enthusiasm, rather than animosity and enmity, among their workers. This was especially important when an employer was also known to be a Conservative, for they would often automatically be viewed with suspicion by many industrial workers on their payroll. In this context, intelligent and humane management would simultaneously improve industrial relations (in accordance with the prognosis and principles of *The Industrial Charter*) while also reducing some of the suspicion among industrial workers concerning the links between employers and the Conservative Party: 'The best service that employers can render the Party is to act so that their workers begin by saying "He's not a bad chap, even though he is a Tory" and end by saying "He's a good chap because he is a Tory"' (CPA, CRD 2/7/6, Sub-Committee on Political Education, 'Report of the Working Party on the Approach to the Industrial Worker', 20 July 1950; see also CPA CRD 2/7/39 (2), Watkinson to Butler, 6 July 1951).

It was therefore suggested that the Conservative Party should denounce, or distance itself from, bad employers, along with other individuals associated with the Party who were deemed to have proved unworthy of their public position or responsibility. For example, there was a recommendation that Conservative politicians should 'publicly condemn known examples of anti-social behaviour by industrialists, landlords, and wealthy individuals of all kinds, because such people are automatically labelled Conservative'. Furthermore, local Conservative associations were urged not to elect or select officials or local government candidates 'with bad records as employers, landlords, contractors or traders', whilst with regard to parliamentary candidates, it was recommended that not too many employers should be adopted because this 'fosters the idea of the Conservative Party being the bosses' party', although at the same time, it was argued that if more working men were adopted as candidates, they were likely 'to be distrusted by [their] fellows' (CPA, CRD 2/7/6, Sub-Committee on Political Education, 'Report of the Working Party on the Approach to the Industrial Worker', 20 July 1950).

Moreover, it was suggested that good employers could do much to reduce conflict and suspicion in the workplace by being more direct or honest with their employees about the company's economic affairs. In this respect, it was suggested that if workers were imbued with a better understanding of the costs and financial pressures faced by their employers, and the impact of these variables on profits, then excessive wage claims, and the damaging strike activity often invoked to secure such pay increases, would be correspondingly reduced; greater economic awareness by workers would enhance industrial realism and responsibility (CPA, CRD 2/7/39 (2), Watkinson to Butler, 6 July 1951; Leather et al., undated but circa 1951: 4). This is a major reason why such importance was subsequently placed on promoting industrial partnership and increased dialogue between management and labour.

Promoting the new approach

The task of winning the trust of (skilled) industrial workers and the trade unions was to be pursued at four discrete levels, these reflecting careful consideration of how the themes and arguments could best be disseminated to the target audience. Firstly, as briefly alluded to above, there was emphasis on the extent to which the Conservative Party had itself historically endorsed responsible trade unionism, and variously enacted legislation to grant statutory protection to particular union activities, including the right to strike. Not surprisingly, this benign account of the history of British Conservatism and trade unionism tended to gloss over or reinterpret the 1927 Trades Disputes Act, and highlighted, instead, the liberalising or permissive legislation mentioned in the previous chapter. At an even more general level, there were also various references to the role which nineteenth-century Conservatives had played in passing or promoting Factory Acts to improve the employment conditions of industrial workers (see, for example, Macleod and Maude, 1950: 74).

Secondly, but directly following on from this last point, Conservatives were encouraged to warn industrial workers that the main threat to free trade unionism actually emanated from the nationalisation and state control which were intrinsic to socialism; it was not Conservatism and trade unionism which were mutually exclusive and diametrically opposed, but socialism and trade unionism. The reasoning was that public ownership and control would both destroy the independence of the trade unions by rendering them mere adjuncts of the state. This scenario was explicitly linked to the affiliation of many trade unions to the Labour Party, which itself was formally committed to the extension of public ownership of major industries and utilities, yet this posed a grave danger for the trade unions: 'a strong, independent Trade Union movement … is gravely compromised by nationalization'. This was because state ownership would invariably destroy *free* collective bargaining and the right to strike, along with an ability to appeal to an independent higher authority which could arbitrate between the competing claims of workers and employers. Indeed: 'The further nationalization is extended, the greater … is the tendency for the state to achieve dominant power as an employer', for dissatisfied workers would increasingly be 'unable to "sack your boss" and go and work for another one' (Macleod and Maude, 1950: 77).

However, nationalisation was also deemed to exacerbate the problem of size and scale in industry, with the ensuing feelings of alienation and lack of self-worth experienced by employees; a nationalised industry 'must tend to greater centralization of control and more bureaucratic methods; the worker on the shop floor must be further removed from the highest authority in the industry' (Macleod and Maude, 1950: 77). Quite apart from the traditional ideological objections which many Conservatives harboured towards nationalisation, and the professed concern about the detrimental impact on the independence of the trade unions, this concern chimed neatly with the 'human relations' perspective, for if many industrial relations problems were derived from workers feeling that their day-to-day contribution was insignificant or unappreciated, due to the size of industry or the vertical remoteness of management, then nationalisation would greatly compound such feelings. Instead of heralding a new era of harmonious industrial relations, whereby workers' perception of being 'exploited' by profiteering capitalist employers was superseded by a sense of working for the wider community or national interest, nationalisation was likely to compound those industrial relations problems arising from the increasing size and scale of modern industry and the concomitant remoteness of management from the factory floor. In this respect, Conservatives expected the extension of public ownership to exacerbate feelings of alienation or anomie among industrial workers, although this might at least weaken their support for the Labour Party and socialism.

Thirdly, but inextricably linked to the earlier point about challenging the perception that the Conservatives were primarily the bosses' party, there were also clear suggestions about what sort of people ought to be adopted as Conservative parliamentary candidates in urban constituencies. When employers were selected, they ought to be exemplary ones in terms of their positive contribution to enlightened management and good industrial relations. At the same time, it was suggested that men with a military title should not ordinarily be adopted as Conservative candidates in industrial seats, 'as many working men will not vote for a Colonel on principle'. Also deemed to be unsuitable as Conservative candidates were young men who had recently graduated from university, for they would not yet have earned a living, and would thus be unlikely to attract the respect of industrial workers (CPA, CRD 2/7/6, Sub-Committee on Political Education, 'Report of the Working Party on the Approach to the Industrial Worker', 20 July 1950). Meanwhile, it was subsequently discovered that very few Conservative trade unionists sought nomination as parliamentary candidates, because 'they were content to leave this to those who had the necessary education' (CPA, CCO 4/5/94, Adamson to General Director [Central Office], 23 February 1953), a clear reflection of the deference which was formerly a key characteristic of working class Conservatism (Jessop, 1974; Mackenzie and Silver, 1968; Nordlinger, 1967).

Beyond the adoption of suitable (in terms of appealing to industrial workers) Conservative parliamentary candidates, it was also argued that that 'in dealing with the widespread feeling that our Party is a class party, care should be taken to ensure that both in its broadcasts and on the platform at some of the bigger public meetings, prominence should be given to speeches by speakers whose accent is not what is commonly known as "refined" … all the voices on Conservative platforms are generally of this sort' (CPA, CRD 2/7/37, Heathcoat Amory to Fraser, 25 May 1949).

Fourthly, there were also suggestions that the Party ought to make more effort not only to attract industrial workers and trade unionists into local Conservative associations, but to enable them to hold office at constituency level, and serve on committees. Meanwhile, Conservative women's branches were encouraged to attract the wives of these industrial workers and trade unionists, while the Young Conservative movement was urged to attract the sons and daughters of such workers. It was also suggested that the Young Britons could recruit their children, thereby fostering the involvement of industrial workers' whole families in their local Conservative party (CPA, CCO 4/4/127, Woolton to Conservative MPs, prospective parliamentary candidates, constituency chairmen and constituency agents, 9 November 1950). Such recruitment was intended to break down various barriers, not least of these being those perceived to exist between predominantly middle-class Conservative constituency associations which had hitherto experienced little direct contact with (skilled) workers or trade unionists, and who might therefore harbour preconceived or prejudiced ideas about them. Yet at the same time, it was envisaged that the involvement of such workers and trade unionists in the Conservative Party would equally serve to dispel some of the misconceptions which they might have about Conservative Party members.

Moreover, as with the Conservative Trade Unionists, the increased involvement of industrial workers and their families in local Conservative associations was intended to counter 'socialist propaganda' that Conservatism and trade unionism were mutually exclusive, and had diametrically opposed political interests. Instead, it was anticipated that by increasing the participation of industrial workers and trade unionists in local Conservative associations, so working-class membership of, or electoral support for, the Conservative Party would become normalised, thereby weaning at least some industrial workers away from the Labour Party and socialism.

Yet these exhortations from officials at Central Office about recruiting and promoting more industrial workers and trade unionists in the Conservative Party at local level were to little avail, largely due to a marked reluctance by the overwhelmingly middle-class local membership to incorporate sections of the working class. Part of this recalcitrance derived from the fact that local Conservative constituency associations have traditionally resisted perceived interference by Party headquarters in London – ironically, just as the trade unions resisted external interference in their internal affairs – but there is little doubt that part of this resistance also derived from social snobbery, whereby 'attitudes of social superiority continue to intrude themselves' (Nordlinger, 1967: 37). According to a Conservative Trade Unionists delegate speaking at the Party's 1952 conference, 'in some constituencies, we are tolerated ... in others we are cold-shouldered and looked upon as a necessary evil'. Such attitudes among the Conservative's grass-roots membership led the Party's Parliamentary Labour Committee to bemoan 'the class barriers which still exist inside some Conservative Associations', and which were hindering efforts to adopt more Conservative Trade Unionists as candidates in local elections in industrial constituencies (CPA, CRD 2/7/3, Conservative Parliamentary Labour Committee to Maxwell-Fyfe, 3 July 1950), a problem to which we will return in the next chapter with regard to the 1952 Keatinge inquiry.

Such attitudes did leave the Conservative's national leadership with a clear dilemma, one which it never satisfactorily resolved. On the one hand, ordinary trade unionists were apparently deterred from joining the Conservative Party, either because they were convinced that Conservatism and trade unionism were ideologically incompatible and thus mutually exclusive, or because they believed that the Conservatives were 'the bosses' party', whereupon industrial workers had no place in it. On the other hand, many local Conservative parties were reluctant to recruit or encourage the active involvement of trade unionists, either because they seemed to accept *a priori* that trade unionism was intrinsically hostile to, or at least incompatible with, Conservatism, or because they equated trade unionists with industrial workers, and who would therefore be 'out of place' in a local

Conservative association whose membership was overwhelmingly middle class or *petit-bourgeois*.

What about wages?

One other aspect of the Conservative Party's search for a more constructive and conciliatory approach to industrial relations and trade unionism while in Opposition concerned the question of pay determination; how would the next Conservative government attempt to prevent 'excessive' wage increases which would fuel inflation and/or undermine the new commitment to maintaining a 'high and stable' level of employment. One way would have been to accept the need, right from the outset, of an incomes policy, or at least some institutional forum for determining what constituted an acceptable or affordable pay increase each year. However, this was emphatically ruled out in favour of an unequivocal insistence on free collective bargaining (see, for example: CPA, CCO 503/3/2, 'Lecture Notes: The Conservatives and the Trade Unions', April 1947; One Nation Group of Conservative MPs, 1950: 77; CPA CRD 2/7/3, Conservative Parliamentary Labour Committee, 'Report of Trade Union Problems sub-committee', 2 May 1951; CPA, CCO 503/2/21, Minutes of meeting of the Conservative Parliamentary Labour Committee, 26 July 1951).

This stance owed much to Conservative recognition that organised labour would strongly resent governmental interference in wage bargaining; for the trade unions, free collective bargaining – 'free' in the sense of being free from state control – was sacrosanct and inviolate, notwithstanding the fact that it was the government which ultimately determined pay levels and increases in the recently nationalised industries and expanded public sector. In the context of the trade unions' commitment to free collective bargaining, senior Conservatives readily acknowledged that any attempt to invoke either an incomes policy, or any other means of regulating wages, would not only provoke widespread trade union resentment and resistance, it would also jeopardise the Conservative Party's commitment to securing the trust of the trade unions as the prerequisite of establishing a more harmonious relationship when the Conservatives were next in government. Indeed, failure to secure such trust might well militate against the election of a Conservative government in the first place.

Consequently, the non-interventionist approach which was being promoted by senior Conservatives *vis-à-vis* trade union activities and internal affairs was to be accompanied by an equally non-interventionist approach to pay determination, the nationalised industries and public sector notwithstanding. In both instances, it was hoped that responsible behaviour by the trade unions could be secured through consultation, dialogue and exhortation; it could not be attained as a result of legislative interference or Ministerial imposition of controls or statutory limits on wages.

For similar reasons, the Conservative Opposition also ruled out schemes for compulsory arbitration in the case of wage disputes which resulted in strike action. Not only would such compulsion antagonise the trade unions, it would also be viewed by them as a restriction on the right to strike when wage negotiations broke down. Besides, more prescient Conservatives also realised that the introduction of compulsory arbitration would effectively embroil governments in pay bargaining and industrial conflict resolution. Not only might this make the Government a target for aggrieved trade unions in the case of a serious pay dispute, it would also, more generally, inadvertently deter the development of industrial self-government, whereby employer and employees, or management and trade unions, worked more closely together to solve problems and resolve disputes. Indeed, in the case of a pay dispute, either 'side' might be deterred from actively seeking an amicable settlement in the expectation that recourse to compulsory arbitration would yield a more favourable or generous outcome. As such, compulsory arbitration was, paradoxically, quite likely to result in more industrial disputes over pay.

The most that the Conservative Party was prepared to pledge with regard to pay determination, according to *The Industrial Charter*, was that the Ministry of Labour 'should keep the two sides of every industry informed both about the general economic situation of the country' and about the situation in each particular industry, in the hope that 'wage levels may be kept in proper relationship to productivity' (Conservative and Unionist Central Office, 1947: 12). This, of course, neatly accorded with the more general premise that closer dialogue and exchanges of information would not only foster greater trade union trust, both in employers and the Conservative Party, but would consequently yield more responsible behaviour, particularly with regard to voluntarily restraining their pay claims, or linking them to increased productivity. The attainment of such moderation and maturity would then vindicate the Conservative leadership's voluntarist approach with regard to industrial elations and trade unionism, and in so doing, help to marginalise or neutralise the Party's right-wing critics.

Conclusion

The shock of losing the 1945 general election, and the sheer scale of Labour's victory, galvanised more progressive Conservatives into accommodating the Party to a changed ideological and political landscape. The Second World War had seemingly resulted in a left-ward shift in British politics, the intellectual climate and public opinion, whereupon collectivism and governmental regulation of economic affairs were imbued with much greater credence and credibility due to the experience of the war effort, and the evident success accruing from state intervention during the first half of the 1940s. Of course, citizens wanted to see war-time restrictions removed as soon as practicably possible, but the result of the 1945 general election strongly suggested that there was little public appetite for a return to the *laissez-faire* economics and minimalist welfare of the inter-war years.

Consequently, more prescient and progressive Conservatives readily acknowledged the need for the Party to adapt itself to the new realities and public expectations of post-war Britain. The Conservatives not only needed to adapt themselves by modernising their principles and policies, but convince the electorate that they had changed, and that they could genuinely be trusted to maintain 'high and stable' levels of employment, a comprehensive welfare state and work constructively with the trade unions. If they could not achieve this transformation, then the fear of more progressive Conservatives was that Labour might be in power for a generation, not because the British people actually wanted extensive state intervention or interference in their lives, but because they feared that a Conservative government would herald the return of mass unemployment, increased poverty, and class conflict manifesting itself through confrontation with organised labour and the trade unions.

It was to obviate such fears and anxieties that the more progressive 'One Nation' Conservatives who increasingly dominated the higher echelons of the Party after 1945 worked tirelessly to redefine Conservatism by accommodating it to post-war realities and changed circumstances. Yet in so doing, they not only repudiated the Party's erstwhile association with *laissez-faire* economics and anti-trade unionism, in order to convince non-Conservatives that the Party was now an entirely new political entity which they could now trust, they also insisted that the Conservative Party actually had a long and proud tradition of social reform and pro-trade union legislation, with the Disraelian era readily cited as exemplification of this. Ultimately, what was deemed to be new was the dominance which the paternalistic 'One Nation' Conservatives had obtained in the Party after 1945, which strongly implied that those who still revered free markets and were hostile towards organised labour would be marginalised. The paternalism which had characterised nineteenth-century Conservatism at particular junctures would henceforth become the permanent and defining feature of post-war Conservative politics; the heirs of Disraeli and Randolph Churchill had seemingly acquired hegemony in the Party, and would henceforth seek conciliation with the industrial working class and their representative institutions, namely the trade unions. To this end, *The Industrial Charter* was to constitute their mid-twentieth-century equivalent of Robert Peel's Tamworth Manifesto.

As Charles Hill, observed: 'The health and strength of Conservatism depends on its capacity to attract and to hold the reluctant vote … it was between 1945 and 1950 that the Conservatives first gave convincing evidence that they were a national party' (Hill, 1964: 9–10). Their success in so doing delivered victory to the Conservatives in the 1951 general election – albeit narrowly, with Labour actually polling about 250,000 more votes – thereupon heralding 13 successive years in office, throughout which time the Party leadership faithfully adhered to the principles enshrined in *The Industrial Charter*, to the extent that Ministers resolutely refused to introduce legislation to curb trade union activities or regulate their internal affairs. Instead, the emphasis was to be on conciliation, dialogue, and exhortation as the means of modifying trade union behaviour and practices, while employers were repeatedly encouraged to treat their workers with more respect, or even as partners, in order to foster more harmonious industrial relations. Consequently, the 1950s were to prove a golden age for constructive relations between British Conservatism and trade unionism, a relative cordiality which had never previously been experienced, nor has been attained ever since.

Chapter 3
Voluntarism in Practice, 1951–1960

The perspective enunciated in *The Industrial Charter*, and subsequently reiterated through various speeches pertaining to trade unionism by Conservative politicians while in opposition, therefore provided the framework and ethos of the Party's approach to industrial relations and trade unionism throughout the 1950s. As Winston Churchill himself affirmed in a speech prior to the 1951 general election: 'The Conservative Party has no intention of initiating any legislation affecting trade-unions should we become responsible in the new Parliament' (*The Times* 10 October 1951). This declaration seemed to signify a shift away from the previous pledges to reform specific features of trade unionism recently permitted by the 1946 Trades Disputes Act, most notably the affiliation of civil service trade unions or associations to the TUC, the operation of the closed shop in public or local authorities and the 'contracting-out' aspect of the political levy. Indeed, so anxious was the Conservative leadership to avoid antagonising the trade unions that, at the end of 1951, when a Conservative parliamentary candidate publicly claimed that the newly-elected Churchill Government was in favour of once again replacing 'contracting-out' with 'contracting-in', he was swiftly rebuked by Central Office, being told that he must have confused his own personal wishes with official policy, and bluntly advised to be more careful about his public comments in future (CPA, CCO 4/4/314, Adamson to West, 6 December 1951).

Consequently, in accordance with the critiques articulated in *The Industrial Charter* and *The Right Road for Britain*, and emphasised in numerous speeches by senior Conservatives from 1947 onwards, the Party leadership refused to countenance legislation to curb the trade union activities or practices, most notably the closed shop and unofficial strikes, of which many in the Party most disapproved. According to Rab Butler, 'a quite deliberate policy of appeasement was adopted. Winston Churchill still had unpleasant memories of the General Strike to live down' (Butler, 1971 164), while John Biffen later recalled that 'the important thing in the 1950s was to live down the bad, black days of [inter-war] Britain' (Biffen, 1968: 43). Consequently, the emphasis was on leaving 'the two sides of industry' generally, and the trade unions in particular, to modify their behaviour, and adopt more responsible practices. The prevalent view among senior Conservatives throughout this period was that 'politics should be kept out of industry' (CPA, ACP 3/4 (54), 'Industrial Relations – Draft Report', 11 June 1954. See also NA, LAB 43/280, Douglas to Carr, 30 July 1956), thereby enabling 'employers and trade-unionists [to] be left to settle these matters through their negotiating machinery or through free [collective] bargaining' CPA, CRD 2/7/6, PLC (54) 1, 'Some Background Facts concerning Industrial Relations', 15 February 1954).

Conservative Ministers, especially those at the Ministry of Labour, consistently stated that legislation itself could not procure more harmonious relations in the workplace but might actually exacerbate suspicion and distrust among employees, especially if any laws were enacted which appeared to favour employers. A constant refrain of senior Conservatives throughout this period was that 'industrial relations are human relations' and, as such, not amenable to legislative prescription. According to Robert Carr, for example, 'it is upon voluntary agreement in industry that we must depend for good industrial relations ... good industrial relations cannot be enforced by laws' (HC Debates, 5th series, Vol. 568, col. 2127). Meanwhile, Walter Monckton, Minister of Labour from October 1951 to December 1955, explained to his colleagues that the Conservative Party's 'established policy [is] to leave the regulation of their relationships and the determination of terms and conditions of employment to employers and workers, normally acting through their collective organisations', thereby 'supporting the basic principles of industrial self-government' (NA CAB 134/1273 IR (55) 10, Memorandum by Minister of Labour: Survey of Present Situation, 25 July 1955. See also Ministry of Labour, 1957: 16). Elsewhere, Monckton's Parliamentary Private Secretary (PPS), Harold Watkinson, when giving evidence to the Party's Keatinge inquiry on its relationship *vis-à-vis* trade unions (see below), reiterated that the pursuit of better industrial relations should entail government Ministers 'adopting a conciliatory and not a party political attitude' (CPA, CCO 4/5/67, Evidence presented by Harold Watkinson to the Keatinge inquiry, 18 June 1952). Ultimately, senior Conservatives insisted that: 'If trade-union organisation is to be reformed ... success will ... depend on the movement coming from within the unions themselves. Little can be done from above' (CPA CRD 2/7/6, Douglas to Sherbrooke, 23 June 1953. See also CPA CCO 4/7/429, Poole to Baxter, 11 September 1956). Incidentally, this stance was wholly shared at the highest levels within the Ministry of Labour, whose permanent secretary during the first half of the 1950s, Sir Godfrey Ince, explained that: 'The State recognises that the improvement of human relations in industry is a matter primarily for industry itself' (Ince, 1960: 133).

Of course, what strongly underpinned Ministerial determination to refrain from invoking industrial relations or trade union legislation during the 1950s was the recognition that any recourse to the statute book would fatally damage the trust of organised labour which the Conservative Party was carefully cultivating. Alienating organised labour in this manner would, in turn, merely serve to strengthen the bond between the trade unions and the Labour Party, while also rendering moderate trade unionists more susceptible to the propaganda of the left. In this respect, practical, political and electoral considerations were inextricably combined, for as a Central Office official emphasised, 'as a government, we shall have to work with the trade-unions ... the more you attack the trade-unions, the more wholeheartedly the weight of their organisation will be flung into the next election against us, and this will count for far more than any odd votes you pick up by attacking them' (CPA, CRD 2/12/5, Chapman-Walker to

Clarke, 4 April 1950). Or, as Monckton himself noted, legislative intervention or prescription in relationships between employers and employees was likely to prove 'politically inexpedient and ineffective in practice' (NA CAB 134/1273 IR (55) 10, 'Memorandum by Minister of Labour: Survey of Present Situation', 25 July 1955. see also PREM 11/3570, Bishop to Macmillan, 17 May 1961).

As such, when, during the 1959 election campaign, Iain Macleod was asked whether a re-elected Conservative Government would legislate against the political levy, he firmly discounted any prospect of such legislation, 'for such a measure would stir up deep and bitter controversy throughout the trade union movement'. It was precisely to avoid such bitterness or antagonism that, immediately following the Conservative Party's victory in the 1951 general election, Churchill appointed Walter Monckton as Minister of Labour, with the clear instruction to do his best 'to preserve industrial peace' (Quoted in Birkenhead, 1969: 2676), for he was 'determined that there should be no industrial strikes during his term as Prime Minister' (Woolton, 1959: 279–80).

The Churchill Government's voluntarist approach was underpinned by the extent to which, for most of the 1950s, much of the trade union leadership was itself on the right of the labour movement, and thus itself keen to marginalise the left and combat communism within the trade unions (discussed below). This right-wing trade union leadership variously made ritualistic denunciations of the Conservatives in public, and rejected sporadic suggestions for an incomes policy to secure wage restraint (see next chapter), but in private, there was often a relatively good rapport and tacit understanding of each other's stance. Many senior Conservatives during the early 1950s were pleasantly surprised at the 'responsible' character and 'realism' of this coterie of senior right-wing trade union moguls – indeed, one writer has characterised them as a 'TUC junta' (Taylor, 2000: 124) – who themselves echoed Conservative denunciations of the irresponsible left-wing elements within the trade unions and on the factory-floor, who were deemed culpable for many (if not most) of the unofficial strikes which occurred during this period. For example, a motion condemning unofficial strikes and denouncing the 'small minority of undisciplined and subversive individuals' fomenting industrial conflict for their own political purposes was comfortably passed at the TUC's 1955 annual conference, with a number of right-wing trade union leaders having spoken enthusiastically in support of the motion. Just three months earlier, the chair of the TUC, Charles Geddes, had warned the trade unions that if they failed to do more to curb unofficial strikes and inter-union disputes, then 'there would be complete justification for the Government stepping in' (*The Yorkshire Post* 23 June 1955).

Consequently, Lord Woolton, the Conservative chairman, could inform the Party's 1954 conference that since returning to Office in 1951, 'we have been gratefully impressed by the statesmanlike way in which so many trade union leaders have sought to gain their legitimate ends' (See also the One Nation Group of Conservative MPs, 1954: 8). Indeed, so cordial were relations during this period that various trade union leaders regularly dined with Churchill at 10 Downing

Street (Taylor, 1993: 81), whereupon Churchill's doctor observed that 'their response to his advances is interesting. They know when they dine with him at No 10 it will do them no good in the Labour Party. But they cannot help liking him' (Moran, 1965: 395). Trade union leaders also dined regularly with Churchill's first Minister of Labour, the ultra-conciliatory Walter Monckton (Taylor, 1993: 82), further indicating not only the Conservatives' efforts at securing the trust of Britain's trade unions, but the willingness of many senior trade union officials to respond positively to such overtures during the early 1950s.[1] For example, in spring 1955, Tom Williamson, General Secretary of the General and Municipal Workers Union (then Britain's second largest trade union), met with Monckton to report the concern of moderate trade union leaders about increasing irresponsibility among some trade unionists, and the need for a reassertion of authority and discipline. Although specific measures to achieve this were not canvassed, Williamson did inform Monckton that if the Conservatives were re-elected in the imminent general election, they would probably be able to count on considerable co-operation from the TUC if they subsequently proceeded to address this problem. Williamson's pledge convinced Monckton that it was 'doubly important for us to keep on good terms with the moderate elements in the TUC' (NA PREM 11/921, Monckton to Eden, 21 April 1955). To this end, Monckton even invited Vincent Tewson, General Secretary of the TUC, and other 'suitable' members of the TUC's General Council, for drinks at the Savoy (in a private room, to avoid publicity) in order to conduct informal talks (NA PREM 11/921, Monckton to Eden, 10 June 1955).

Meanwhile, moderate trade union leaders also appear to have been occasionally invited to parties hosted by Churchill, at which informal soundings were taken by Conservative Ministers, as was the case when, at one such soiree, Charles Geddes confided to Harold Macmillan about how concerned he and other moderate union leaders were concerning communist activity inside certain trade unions (discussed below), particularly with regard to fomenting unofficial or 'wildcat' strikes (NA PREM 11/921, Macmillan to Eden, 10 June 1955). Indeed so cordial were some of the contacts between Conservative Ministers and some senior trade union leaders that the latter reportedly became 'very sensitive about the accusation of being "Tory stooges"' (NA PREM 11/1402, Macmillan to Eden, 14 July 1956).

---

1   Monckton later advised one of his successors at the Ministry of Labour, Edward Heath, 'to cultivate the moderate union leaders by giving them meals individually as soon as possible' (Heath, 1998: 194), advice which Heath evidently heeded, for he and George Woodcock, newly-appointed General Secretary of the TUC, 'used to be seen dining together behind a screen at the Carlton Club', where Heath also sometimes dined with Woodcock's Deputy, Vic Feather (Campbell, 1993: 111).

The socio-psychological critique of industrial conflict: 'industrial relations are human relations'

What significantly underpinned the Conservative leadership's voluntarist approach to industrial relations throughout this period, and reinforced Ministerial reluctance to invoke legislation against particular trade union practices – especially with regard to strikes – was the professed belief among some senior Conservatives that much industrial conflict was attributable less to 'Reds under the bed' (notwithstanding the concerns of moderate union leaders about communist activity in their unions) than to feelings of alienation among ordinary employees. To the extent that left-wing elements or militants did foment conflict in industry, they were only able to do so, it was suggested, because of the existence of such alienation in the first place, which communists and their fellow travellers were able to exploit; 'agitators can hardly make much headway unless they can find latent grievances to work on' (CPA, ACP 3/10 (63) 105, 'Report of the Industrial Relations Committee', 8 May 1963).

Such alienation, it was suggested, partly derived from the growing size and scale of modern industry and the workplace, for this entailed a widening gulf between management at the top and the employees on the factory floor. Consequently, individual employees found it increasingly difficult to comprehend the significance or value of their own particular day-to-day contribution to the enterprise in which they worked, so that a sense of alienation also fuelled a concomitant loss of self-esteem and self-worth. On numerous occasions, Anthony Eden lamented the tendency for modern industrial workers to be reduced, in effect, to a mere 'cog in the wheel' (*The Times* 4 November 1946; *The Times* 21 March 1947), as 'the functions performed by ... individuals have been steadily broken down, divided up and simplified', to the extent that due to 'the gap between the top and bottom of the industrial structure ... the parts are now so small and the whole so large that they are often mutually incomprehensible' (Fraser, 1948: 2). This was deemed to exacerbate the feelings of alienation and low self-esteem which many workers now experienced, and which often underpinned much of the conflict which occurred between management and labour. In order to ameliorate such feelings, Walter Monckton suggested, in a speech to delegates at the Conservative's 1954 National Union conference, that:

> The policy of management ought to be based on the recognition that a man is not a tool, not a machine, but a complex human personality. A man brings more to his work in his factory than the work of his hands. He brings there a part of his life, and he ought to be able to enjoy rights and satisfactions in that working life just as much as he does in his life a citizen.

This reinforced the need for the Conservatives to develop 'a new political approach to the vital problems of human relationships throughout our complex industrial structure' (Leather et al., 1951: 2).

However, alongside the nature of the work undertaken on a daily basis, it was recognised that security of employment also had an important impact on the attitudes of many workers, for as a senior Conservative Research Department official noted, the 'more irregular a man's employment, the greater is the temptation for him to develop irregular habits', whereas 'regular employment and wages tend to develop self-respect and other qualities valuable both to the worker himself and to his employer'. Too often, however, 'the manual worker is picked up and dropped again by industry to suit the circumstances of the moment', and the fact that he is also 'paid by the hour ... tends to emphasise the fundamental insecurity of his position'. Such a situation 'does not accord well with our idea of the common interest of workers and management' (Fraser, 1948: 15).

Other Conservative proponents of the human relations approach also drew attention to this aspect, pointing out: 'Many of the difficulties now being experienced are the result of distrust of the motives of the Conservative Party, and fears of recurrent mass unemployment', a distrust which was 'of long standing', and thus in need of 'patience and persistence' in the application of Conservative principles and policies 'before it can be dispelled' (CPA, CRD 2/7/6, Sub-committee on Political Education, 'Report of the Working Party on the Approach to the Industrial Worker', 20 July 1950). In this respect, it was acknowledged that 'the memory of unemployment in the inter-war years is a spectre that can only be exorcised with the passage of time', and by 'the strengthening of mutual confidence between management and employees in conditions of at least fairly full employment' (CPA, CRD 2/7/14 (IRC 21), 'Problems of Social Balance in Industry', 15 November 1955). Of course, this rather begged the question of just how long it would take for this legacy of distrust to be eradicated, but this was not the sort of question which senior Conservatives could – or would have wanted to – place a time limit on.

The advocacy of industrial partnership

As noted in the previous chapter, more progressive or 'one nation' Conservatives were convinced that an important means of ameliorating the feelings of alienation and lack of self-worth which many workers apparently experienced – and which were routinely exploited by communists for their own political ends – while also pursuing the afore-mentioned 'strengthening of mutual confidence between management and employees', was to promote a stronger sense of 'partnership' in industry and the workplace. This, it was envisaged, would provide much of the answer to the question of how the contemporary industrial worker was 'to be helped to comprehend the social importance of his job and so of himself' (CPA, CRD 2/7/14 (IRC 21), 'Problems of Social Balance in Industry', 15 November 1955).

Conservative advocacy of industrial partnership certainly did not presuppose any equality between employers and employees – managerial authority remained sacrosanct: 'we do not intend any Sovietisation which would transfer the authority of management to a committee' (CPA, CRD 2/7/32, Greenwell to Buler, 5 January 1948; see also CPA, CRD 2/7/1, Hutchinson to Fraser, 22 July 1948) – but it did envisage increased communication between management and labour, which also neatly accorded with the human relations perspective. If there was more frequent and extensive dialogue between the 'two sides of industry', it was anticipated that much of the mutual suspicion would be overcome, sources of anxiety eradicated, and workers would be likely to develop an appreciation both of the value of their own role to the enterprise's success, and of the rationale underpinning various managerial decisions. Robert Carr believed that, where management made a conscious effort to keep the workforce informed about what was happening in the company, then smoother and more constructive industrial relations invariably ensued (HC Debates, 5th series, Vol. 568, col. 2127), a view shared by Anthony Eden, Churchill's successor as Conservative leader and Prime Minister (Eden, 1947: 428–30. See also Clarke, 1947: 29). Throughout the latter half of the 1940s and into the 1950s, senior Conservatives consistently called for an end to 'us and them' attitudes between management and labour; what Eden once referred to as 'the 'Maginot line' mentality in industry' (Quoted in Conservative Research Department, 1956: 10), and what Sir William Robson Brown termed 'a form of inverse apartheid' (HC Debates, 5th series, Vol. 636, col. 1931). To this end, it was lamented that: 'some employers have been ... slow to realise that the old autocratic relationship of master and man is ... outdated' (Leather et al., 1951: 4).

It was also believed that fostering a spirit of partnership, trust and co-operation between management and labour in the workplace would further undermine the influence of the left in the trade unions. Certainly, Harold Watkinson, was confident that if employers provided their employees with an honest and straightforward account of the company's financial and commercial situation, they would dispel the false notions about the 'bloated profits of capitalism' which were propagated by Communist agitators in the trade unions (quoted in *The Times* 20 October 1950. See also CPA CRD 2/7/39 (2), Watkinson to Butler, 6 July 1951). At a wider level, it was also envisaged that industrial partnership would provide workers 'with a practical insight into the working of the free enterprise system' (CPA, ACP (55) 39, I.R.C 18, 'Co-Partnership – 1955', 21 October 1955. See also CPA, CCO 4/2/83, Douglas to Kaberry, 14 November 1955). Either way, it was envisaged that co-partnership schemes would provide 'a very good basis for more harmonious industrial relations', especially when pursued by 'an enlightened management' (CPA, CCO 4/2/83, 'Co-Partnership – 1952', 10 March 1952), and in this respect, would greatly assist the Conservative leadership in its determination to avoid industrial relations legislation, while simultaneously countering left-wing propaganda. However, as originally noted in *The Industrial Charter*, it was reiterated that co-partnership schemes were often a consequence, rather than a cause, of good industrial relations: 'they follow good industrial relations, rather than create them. They are the coping stone which in many cases may properly be put upon a sound foundation of good industrial relations' (CPA, CCO 4/2/83, 'Profit Sharing, Co-Partnership and Joint Consultation', 14 November 1955).

One specific scheme which was occasionally mooted within the general ambit of co-partnership was that of employee share-ownership, which some Conservatives claimed would facilitate 'the most complete identification of the worker with the fortunes of his firm', for they would not only share in its profits, but in its ownership too. This would do much to foster better industrial relations, because it would 'help to create a loyal team spirit in the firm', while simultaneously serving to 'raise the status of the employee by treating him as a partner' (CPA, CCO 4/2/83, 'Co-Partnership – 1952', 10 March 1952). However, in accordance with the prevailing voluntarist ethos, and the recognition that trust and co-operation between management and workers could not be enforced by Acts of Parliament, Conservative proponents of industrial partnership insisted on the need for such schemes to be developed freely and pragmatically, in accordance with each workplace's or industry's own particular context and organisational structure. Co-partnership was 'a plant of delicate growth and not ... just a bit of mechanism' and, as such, any hint of compulsion would prove fatal (CPA, CRD 2/7/7, Heathcoat Amory to Fraser, 28 February 1952).

Consequently, while Conservative policy was to welcome industrial partnership schemes, and to reiterate the general case for them at opportune moments, the emphasis remained on leaving management and labour 'free to adopt the arrangements best suited to their individual circumstances' (CPA, IRC/18, 4/2/83, 'Co-Partnership – 1955', 21 October 1955), or as Rab Butler suggested to the mid-1950s' Cabinet Committee on Industrial Relations, 'the government's policy should be to continue to express support for co-partnership schemes in principle, wherever a company decides that it its own circumstances are favourable to their introduction. But we should certainly take no steps to make such schemes compulsory' (NA CAB 134/1273, I.R. (55) 8, Memorandum by the Chancellor of the Exchequer, 'Co-Partnership', 21 July 1955), because 'any attempt to force them on people ... is likely to do more harm than good' (CPA CRD 2/7/7, Douglas to Fox, 26 June 1956). As such: 'The proper role of the state in encouraging such schemes would appear to lie in the direction of advice and encouragement', although 'guidance on co-partnership ... in general might also be made available via the Ministry of Labour... [which] ... would appear to be the appropriate vehicle' (CPA, IRC/18, 'Co-Partnership – 1955', 21 October 1955. See also, CPA CRD 2/7/3 PLC (54) 1, Conservative Parliamentary Labour Committee, 'Some Background Facts Concerning Industrial Relations', 15 February 1954). Clearly, in accordance with the twin perspectives of voluntarism and human relations in industry, the notion of state-imposed industrial partnership would have been an oxymoron, and would have alienated both employers and the trade unions.

Refusing to legislate for strike ballots

Elsewhere, the combined impact of the 'human relations' perspective, the advocacy of industrial partnership, and the Conservative leadership's determination to develop a constructive working relationship with the trade unions, ensured that Ministers consistently dismissed perennial calls from some Conservative backbenchers and conference delegates for legislative action to curb strikes, particularly unofficial stoppages (i.e., those not authorised by the trade union leadership itself). One particular demand was for strike ballots to be made obligatory prior to the pursuit of industrial action, but the Conservative leadership in general, and Ministers of Labour in particular, repeatedly rejected this demand, invoking voluntarist and 'human relations' principles, and noting some of the practical problems which were likely to arise from the imposition of statutory strike ballots.

Indeed, Monckton melded both of these strands when he informed the Cabinet that such a proposal 'would be resisted [by the trade unions] as an interference with the right to strike and as an interference with the union's management and regulation of its own affairs'. Moreover, he elaborated, 'provision for a secret ballot would not, of course, help to prevent unofficial strikes which are *ex hypothesi* against the will and authority of the unions'. Given that Monckton was unwilling to invoke strike ballots, it was not surprising that he also emphatically ruled out legislation to render unofficial strikes illegal, because this would raise 'difficult questions of penalties and enforcement', for penalties invoked against the unofficial strikers themselves might mean fining, or, ultimately, imprisoning, tens of thousands of workers – a 'dangerous' scenario – while the alternative would be to impose sanctions 'against the funds or officers of the unions whose authority is being flouted' (NA PREM 11/921, CP (55) 25, Memorandum by the Minister of Labour: Current Industrial Relations Problems, 2 June 1955. See also: CPA CRD 2/7/8, Dear to Pickthorn, 20 August 1956; CPA, CRD 2/7/6, 'Secret Ballots before Strike Action', 2 August 1956; CPA, ACP (59) 74, 'Trade-Union Reform', 4 June 1959). Indeed, during the mid-1950s, these arguments formed the basis of a pro forma issued by Conservative Central Office's Labour Department, in response to the letters regularly sent by impatient grass-roots Conservatives demanding legislation *vis-à-vis* strikes (See the correspondence in CPA, CRD 4/7/429, particularly the replies sent by Oliver Poole, the Conservative Party Chairman). Such arguments were quite apart from those which maintained that, however much Conservatives deplored such industrial action: 'The right to strike is a fundamental freedom and an essential foundation of Trade-unionism with which we would not interfere' (CPA ACP (51) 13, Conservative Parliamentary Labour Committee – Report of Trade-Union Problems Sub-committee, 2 May 1951).

This voluntarist stance was reaffirmed at the very first meeting of a Cabinet committee on industrial relations (chaired by Rab Butler), established in the summer of 1955 – but disbanded just ten months later, having effectively ruled out legislative solutions to the sundry industrial relations problems it considered – at which it was agreed that legislation to prohibit unofficial strikes 'would be impossible to enforce', and as such, 'that it was unnecessary to pursue this proposal any further' (NA CAB 134/1273, IR (55), Minutes of 1st Meeting, 22 June 1955. See also: CPA CCO 503/2/21, Conservative Trade-Unionists' National Advisory Committee, Conclusions of Special Meeting with Conservative Parliamentary Labour Committee, 26 July 1951). Similarly rejected, partly to avoid antagonising the trade unions, and partly because of envisaged problems regarding enforceability, was the proposal for a 'period of reflection' (or 'cooling-off period') prior to strike action. When this idea was mooted in the Cabinet committee on industrial relations, Monckton was adamant that 'you cannot legislate for responsibility, and I am sure that a legal requirement imposing statutory timing on the calling of strikes would only raise the usual awkward problems of enforcement'. Ultimately, Monckton reiterated, 'the best we can hope for is for the Trade Unions to discourage precipitate action' (NA CAB 134/1273, I.R (55) 3, Memorandum by the Minister of Labour, 28 July 1955).

However, there does seem to have been something of an inconsistency in Conservative explanations of the incidence of strike activity during this period, for whereas the afore-mentioned 'human relations' perspective maintained that much industrial conflict was either an enduring legacy of the insecurity once experienced by workers in previous decades – which continued to fuel suspicion towards the Conservative Party, and which would thus only be overcome with time and patience – or derived from workers feeling that they were unappreciated cogs in a large, impersonal industrial machine (neither of which would be amenable to legislative solutions), some in the Party, including the otherwise emollient Monckton, now argued that strikes could be attributed, at least partly, to the attainment of full employment, which had fostered 'an irresponsible attitude towards workers' discipline' for there was 'a greater inclination to strike because the workers felt that they were not at risk and could, if necessary, obtain other employment' (NA CAB 134/1273, I.R (55), Minutes of 2nd Meeting, 28 July 1955).

Yet this alternative prognosis did not prompt any abandonment of the voluntarist approach, nor did it lead many Ministers to question the efficacy of full employment, even though the ineluctable logic of this account seemed to be that permitting higher unemployment would serve to weaken the bargaining power of industrial workers and trade unions. This was not an option which senior Conservatives were willing to countenance at this juncture, and it would certainly have been incompatible with the rest of their approach towards industrial relations and trade unionism in the 1950s. Instead, official Conservative policy remained that tackling trade union irresponsibility, particularly with regard to strike activity, required a painstakingly patient approach to winning the trust of industrial workers and trade unions, coupled with a tireless Ministerial campaign of education and exhortation to persuade trade unionists of the need for greater responsibility and moderation. With trade union legislation, higher unemployment and incomes policy (to curb wage increases) all ruled out at this time, Ministers were obliged to rely almost entirely on the power of persuasion to convince industrial workers and trade unions to modify their attitudes and behaviour, and thereby minimise strike activity.

This stance was fully upheld by Iain Macleod, who succeeded Monckton at the Ministry of Labour in November 1955, and who immediately insisted that by their very nature, unofficial strikes – which constituted the vast majority of industrial stoppages – were unlikely to be affected by legislation (HC Debates, 5th series, Vol. 568, col. 1285). In fact, Winston Churchill himself had previously endorsed this perspective, maintaining that the disadvantages of introducing compulsory strike ballots would greatly outweigh any advantages which might accrue (HC Debates, 5th series, Vol. 522, cols 835–6), a stance maintained by Churchill's successor, Anthony Eden (NA PREM 11/1029, Eden to Monckton, 29 July 1955). Meanwhile, when Oliver Poole (Conservative Chairman) received a letter from a Party member who claimed to be so frustrated with the Cabinet's refusal to legislate for compulsory strike ballots that he had joined the People's League for the Defence of Freedom to protect liberty and democracy from trade union tyranny, Poole patiently explained – as he did with a steady stream of similarly disgruntled Conservative Party members who wrote to him at Central Office during 1956 and 1957 – that 'such legislation would in practice be virtually unenforceable and probably quite ineffective', and consequently, the best means of securing better industrial relations would be 'if more trade unionists played the full part to which they are entitled in the affairs of their union' (CPA CCO 4/7/429, Poole to Dixon, 17 August 1956). One does not imagine that the recipients of these replies would have been particularly pacified by Poole's emollience, however.

As for the routine backbench and annual conference demands for the introduction of statutory strike ballots, Macleod informed delegates at the Conservatives' 1956 conference that there was no evidence that ordinary trade union members were any less militant than their leaders, and therefore he did not accept the premise that ballots would necessarily yield any reduction in strike activity overall (On this point, see also, CPA, Advisory Committee on Policy [hereafter ACP], 33rd meeting, 30 April 1958). Indeed, following a strike by London bus drivers in the early summer of 1958, Macleod noted that it was the trade union leaders and officials who had endeavoured to end the dispute, while the rank-and-file had sought to prolong it: 'Beyond doubt, a secret ballot would have resulted in a continuation of the stoppage' (CPA, CCO 4/7/417, Macleod to Poole, 16 August 1958).

However, during the next few years, as the TUC's right-wing 'junta' was superseded by a number of rather more left-wing trade union leaders – most notably Frank Cousins, who actually became leader of Britain's then largest trade union, the Transport and General Workers' Union (TGWU) in 1956 – a somewhat different line of argument was advanced against the introduction of compulsory strike ballots, namely that: 'Owing to the apathy of the rank-and-file, secret ballots would tend to be influenced disproportionately by militant elements' (NA PREM 11/3570, Bishop to Macmillan, 17 May 1961. See also, CPA CCO 4/7/429, Poole to Cockshut, 17 August 1956).

Either way, therefore, the logic was against the introduction of compulsory strike ballots: either ordinary trade union members were often more militant than their leaders, in which case, they might use such ballots to vote in favour of strike action, possibly against the advice or recommendations of their union leaders, *or* rank-and-file members were more moderate, but also, as a consequence, less active in their union's affairs, whereupon the outcome of strike ballots would often effectively be determined by left-wing elements who were more active and well-organised, and who would almost certainly vote in support of strike action whenever presented with the opportunity to do so.

One of the most consistent Conservative backbench critics of the trade unions – particularly with regard to strike activity – and *inter alia* of the Party leadership's voluntarist industrial relations strategy, was Thomas Iremonger, whose concerns were such that he was specially permitted to express them to a meeting of the CTU's National Advisory Committee early in 1957, even though he was not himself a member. Iremonger would have left disappointed, though, for having listened to his peroration about the industrial disruption fomented by militants and shop stewards in Britain's trade unions, and heard him reiterate his demands for legislative action, the Committee's ensuing discussion of the relevant points led to 'the unanimous view that legislation was undesirable … the Trade-union Movement could solve its own problems through the existing machinery'. One member of the CTU's National Advisory Committee even described some of Iremonger's statements as 'dynamite, and unless care was taken, harm could be done to the Party'. The only practical measure which Conservatives could take to tackle trade union militancy and left-wing domination was 'to get more and more Conservative Trade-unionists to take office' (CPA CCO 503/2/22, Conservative Trade-unionists' National Advisory Committee, conclusions of the 48th meeting, 14 February 1957).

A further rationale offered by the Conservative leadership for refusing to introduce legislation during the 1950s was that such action might alienate 'moderate' trade unionists, and provide succour to the left. Monckton warned that, unless Conservatives 'carry with us the responsible elements, who are at present in the majority, we run the risk of uniting the whole trade-union movement against us' (NA PREM 11/921, Monckton to Eden, 2 June 1955). Certainly, as a sub-committee of the Conservative's [backbench] Parliamentary Labour Committee had previously noted, while compulsory pre-strike ballots were 'an attractive idea on the face of it … it would be most unlikely to work in practice, and is, therefore, not a matter upon which it would be worth incurring the inevitable opposition of the trade-unions' (CPA, ACP (51) 13, Conservative Parliamentary Labour Committee, 'Report of Trade-Union Problems Sub-committee', 2 May 1951).

One other legislative initiative occasionally mooted with regard to strikes – or the threat of such industrial action – which was also routinely rejected by the Ministers most closely involved with Conservative industrial relations policy during the 1950s, was that of a compulsory 'cooling-off' period prior to the commencement of a stoppage. Monckton insisted that empowering the Government, via the Ministry of Labour, to prohibit strike action for a specified period of time in order to provide for 'a period of reflection', would be highly unlikely to reduce the incidence of unofficial strikes. Indeed, he feared that if the official trade union leadership were prevented, by a compulsory cooling-off period, from calling a strike, then this might actually result in *more* unofficial strikes, due to 'workers with a sense of grievance [being] tempted to take the law into their own hands'. Not only would 'a legal requirement imposing statutory timing on the calling of strikes' probably have little effect on promoting genuine industrial harmony, it would also – as with other proposals for statutory curbs – 'raise the usual awkward problems of enforcement'. Again, therefore, tackling the problem was 'best left to responsible trade-union leaders', for 'you cannot legislate for responsibility' (NA CAB 134/1273, I.R. (55) 3, Memorandum by the Minister of Labour, 'The Possibility of Introducing a Legal Requirement for a Period of Reflection Before the Taking of Strike Action', 22 July 1955; CAB 134/1273, I.R. (55), 2nd Meeting, 28 July 1955; See also NA PREM 11/1029, Eden to Monckton, 29 July 1955).

Ministers were similarly reluctant to tackle strikes by extending the legal liability of strikers, particularly those engaged in unofficial industrial action. Again, it was the Minister of Labour who provided the most robust rebuttal of such a proposal, pointing out that the trade unions would reject such a proposal outright, in which case, any attempt at enacting it regardless would seriously damage industrial relations, both between the Conservative Government and the trade unions, and also between employers and the unions. Indeed, with regard to the latter relationship, it was noted that many employers were themselves sceptical about the efficacy of such a policy. Once again, the envisaged problems of enforceability reinforced Ministerial caution, with Monckton emphasising that if the Government sought to extend the legal liability of trade unions or their members for certain kinds of strike action, this would 'place both the Attorney-General and myself in the dilemma of having to choose between large scale prosecutions or turning a blind eye to breaches of the law' (NA, CAB 134/1273, I.R. (55) 5, Memorandum by the Minister of Labour, 'Extension of the Liability of Strikers to Legal Proceedings', 22 July 1955).

One further factor which reinforced the reluctance of senior Conservatives, especially successive Ministers of Labour, to pursue industrial relations or trade union legislation throughout the 1950s was that most large employers, many of whom were represented by the British Employers' Federation (BEF), were also opposed to legislative remedies. They shared the official Ministerial perspective that 'legislation on strikes was neither practical nor desirable', and that the best means of securing better industrial relations was for both the Government and employers to continue developing a 'friendly partnership with the TUC'. This would, it was noted, have the added advantage of enhancing the position of moderate trade union leaders, and thereby marginalising the minority of militants and communists. As such, the BEF fully endorsed the Conservative Government's determination to avoid, as far as practicably possible, 'any head-on collision with the TUC' (NA PREM 11/921, Note of a Meeting between the Minister of Labour

[Walter Monckton] and representatives from the British Employers' Federation',
7 June 1955).

Ultimately, therefore, the stance of those Ministers most closely involved
with Conservative industrial relations policy during the 1950s was that 'there is
virtually no legal or constitutional action which can be taken to improve industrial
relations, and to diminish the frequency and gravity of strikes'. Instead, the
prevailing view – and certainly the departmental ethos or in-house philosophy
of the Ministry of Labour during this period – was that peace in industry and
responsible trade unionism could not be secured by statutory prescription. Instead,
the only practical and realistic approach was 'to rely on the gradual and organic
growth of good relations in industry' (NA CAB 21/4459, Burke Trend [Cabinet
Secretary], 'Briefing Notes for Committee of Industrial Relations', 25 July 1955;
NA PREM 11/921, Butler to Eden, 24 June 1955). Thus did Monckton, having
submitted several discussion papers to the 1955–56 Cabinet committee on aspects
of industrial relations, admit to being 'conscious that the conclusions reached do
not so far suggest great scope for positive action' (NA CAB 134/1273, I.R. (55)
10, 'Memorandum by the Minister of Labour: Survey of Present Position', 25
July 1955). Nonetheless, Rab Butler, the chair of this committee, subsequently
suggested that in spite of the failure to develop concrete proposals, Ministers had
partaken in 'a most useful discussion', one which paved the way for 'a number of
interesting studies which I hope we may be able to combine into a steady policy
for the gradual improvement of industrial relations' (NA PREM 11/921, Butler to
Eden, 24 June 1955). A more nebulous or non-committal conclusion it is hard to
imagine.

Social security payments to strikers

One other measure variously demanded by right-wing Conservatives in response to
concern over strike activity was the curbing of social security payments to workers
engaged in strike action. During this period, an employee who had temporarily
withdrawn their labour, by virtue of taking part in a strike, was entitled to claim
National Assistance (what is now called Income Support) in respect of their
dependents, namely their marital partner – assuming they themselves were not
in paid employment – and children. Only in very rare cases involving extreme
hardship, though, was a striker permitted to claim such assistance for themselves.

This did not deter sporadic right-wing outrage – often encouraged or echoed by
sensationalist newspaper reports seeking to promote a moral panic (see, for example,
The Daily Mail 19 March 1957) – that the state was effectively encouraging or even
rewarding workers who took part in strike action. This, in turn, was thought to
promote or prolong strike activity, because workers could withdraw their labour
secure in the knowledge that either they, or their families, would not suffer undue
financial hardship. Of course, such a view also reflected right-wing misconceptions
about how 'generous' social security payments actually were.

However, rather than introduce or extend curbs on the right of strikers to claim social security, Ministers opted to illustrate to right-wing critics, and also the wider public, just how limited the scale of the alleged problem actually was, both in terms of the number of claimants and the sums of money actually paid out. For a start, it was noted that National Assistance was not generally paid for the first fortnight, and hence, given the short duration of most strikes, very few of them entailed social security being paid to the strikers or their dependents. Indeed, it was noted that of the 671,000 workers involved in strike action during 1955, for example, social security payments were paid to fewer than 20,000 of them, and in the vast majority of these cases, the recipients were family members, not the strikers themselves. Moreover, of the total of £98 million expended in National Assistance payments during the same year, only £155,000 was paid to strikers of their dependent families. In a riposte to their right-wing critics, the Minister of Labour, in tandem with the Minister of Pensions and National Assistance, tartly suggested that: 'In view of the relatively trivial nature of these figures, it is clear that the present practice can have little, if any, effect on ... trade disputes.'

Moreover, any attempt to curb such payments, quite apart from yielding only minimal savings, would nonetheless cause considerable financial hardship to the wives and children of men on strike, and would therefore 'be hotly contested by the trade unions', while also creating considerable 'bad feeling'. As such, the Ministers whose Departments were most closely involved in this particular policy issue were adamant that 'no change should be made in the present law and practice' (NA PREM 11/1988, Macleod and Boyd-Carpenter to Eden, 31 August 1956), a stance endorsed by the Prime Minister himself, who suggested that more should be done to present the public with the true facts, and thereby counter misleading headlines and misinformation in certain newspapers. Meanwhile, the occasional suggestion by right-wing Conservatives that income tax refunds should be withheld from workers pursuing strike action which had not been endorsed by a secret ballot, was denounced as 'thoroughly unsound and untenable', for one could not invoke 'the precedent of altering income tax law to discriminate against people whose activities a Government may happen to disapprove of ... [after all, even] ... rape and manslaughter do not incur this type of penalty' (CPA, CRD 2/7/8, Dear to Pickthorn, 20 August 1956).

Playing down the incidence and impact of strikes

In addition to insisting that legislation was highly unlikely to curb strike activity, some Ministers also argued that the scale of strike activity in Britain was rather exaggerated (See, for example: NA PREM 11/921, 'Notes for Mr Eden – Industrial Relations', 17 March 1954; CPA, CRD 2/7/6, PLC (54) 1, 'Some Background Facts concerning Industrial Relations', 15 February 1954; CCO 4/8/358, Hailsham to Krisky, 13 November 1958). This was clearly a manifestation of the Conservative leadership's efforts at managing the issue and the policy agenda within the Party, and also of further resisting right-wing demands for legislative action to curb strike activity. To this end, a 1955 internal Party study argued that over their lifetime, the average employee in most industries was unlikely to lose more than one day's work due to strike action, with the median worker (based on strike statistics since 1945) likely to lose just one day in 70 years due to involvement in an industrial stoppage. In arguing that strikes were 'not a common trouble and are relatively short lived' in most cases, it was suggested that 'we seem to have got very near to the irreducible number of strikes', to the extent that the incidence of strike activity – 'relatively little industrial warfare' – did not 'seem to provide adequate grounds for any widespread review of our policy on industrial relations' (CPA, ACP (55) 40, 'Industrial Relations – a Progress Report', 21 October 1955; see also CPA, CRD 2/7/6, 'Notes for Mr. Eden: Industrial Relations', 17 March 1954). Such claims were lent considerable credence by the official statistics covering this period, and which were, understandably, readily cited by senior Conservatives rejecting ritual backbench and conference demands for legislative action against the trade unions, as illustrated by Table 3.1.

Table 3.1   Strike activity in Britain 1946–56

Year	Number of strikes starting that year	Number of workers involved in strikes (000s)	Total working days lost due to strikes (000s)
1946	2,205	529	2,158
1947	1,721	623	2,433
1948	1,759	426	1,944
1949	1,426	434	1,807
1950	1,339	303	1,389
1951	1,719	379	1,694
1952	1,714	416	1,792
1953	1,746	1,374	2,184
1954	1,989	450	2,457
1955	2,419	671	3,781
1956	2,648	508	2,083

Source: Labour Gazette

Although these statistics illustrate a gradual increase in the incidence of strikes during the mid-1950s, the increase was certainly not deemed sufficient to warrant any change in the Conservative leadership's extant voluntarist industrial relations policy and concomitant refusal to invoke statutory pre-strike ballots. Furthermore, while 1954 witnessed more strikes than the previous year, Ministers could point out that these involved only one-third as many workers. Similarly, the higher incidence of strikes in 1956 nonetheless involved fewer workers than had been involved in strike activity the previous year, and entailed fewer working days had been lost too. In short, Ministers seeking to resist pressure for trade union legislation would naturally offer the most positive interpretation possible ('spin' in today's political parlance) of the official strike statistics: if they could not point to a reduction in the total number of strikes, then they would look for evidence either that fewer workers had been involved, or that the strikes were of shorter duration, for example.

The same attempt at agenda-management and playing down the scale of the problem also resulted in strike statistics being placed in an international context, whereupon senior Conservatives drew similarly sanguine conclusions. In this respect, it was noted that strike activity in Britain was 'noticeably better than that of most other countries in the world', with American and French workers, for example, losing about seven and five times as many working days respectively compared to their British counterparts, due to strikes, as indicated by Table 3.2.

Table 3.2   Days lost (per 1,000 employees) due to strike action in main industries.

Country	1947	1949	1951	1954	1957	Average (1947–57)
USA	1,450	2,290	920	890	630	1,381
France	3,350	890	500	210	490	1,013
Belgium	1,370	530	350	290	2,350	888
Italy	N/A	1,730	800	700	480	806
Ireland	1,290	1,110	810	250	350	725
Japan	740	620	740	400	520	698
Denmark	790	15	5	30	10	216
UK	190	140	130	190	620	205
W. Germany	N/A	35	180	150	80	102
Netherlands	140	190	40	35	5	75
Sweden	55	10	220	10	20	74

Source: International Labour Office.

Furthermore, during the early summer of 1957, the Conservative leader and Prime Minister, Harold Macmillan, commissioned an internal inquiry by senior civil servants, to ascertain the costs to the British economy of strike activity. Comprising senior officials from the Treasury, the Ministry of Labour, the Home Office, the Board of Trade, the Ministry of Power, the Ministry of Transport and the Ministry of Agriculture, Fisheries and Food, their ensuing report maintained that Britain's strike record was not as poor as was commonly assumed, for not only had the post-war period been largely 'free from widespread and protracted stoppages', the amount of working time lost due to industrial disputes since 1945 was less than it had been in the 1930s, and 'has been trivial compared with the 1920s'. The officials' report also noted that most of the serious industrial disputes which had occurred since 1945 had *not* been about pay claims, for 'the vast majority of wage settlements are achieved peacefully', although whether these were inflationary was a separate issue. In view of the relatively limited number of serious industrial disputes, and the practical problems which were likely to accrue from subjecting them to legislation, the report re-affirmed the Cabinet's own voluntarist approach by insisting that 'the scope of action by the Government in this whole field is limited' (NA PREM 11/1821, Note by Officials, 'Industrial Disputes', undated, but circa July 1957).

When he conveyed the findings of this report to his Cabinet colleagues, Macmillan drew particular attention to the observation that the economic damage caused by strikes 'seems to be less than is commonly believed', largely because most strikes were confined to a relatively small number of industries, and were usually of relatively short duration. Indeed, on the basis of the report, Macmillan argued that 'we should try to correct the view which has recently gained ground among the public and the Press that it is the Government's duty in the interests of the national economy to prevent strikes at almost any cost'. Instead, he suggested, 'we ought to emphasise the economic damage of cost inflation rather than the economic damage of stoppages of production' (NA PREM 11/1821, 'Memorandum by the Prime Minister – The Economic Cost of Industrial Disputes', 30 July 1957).

The largely short-term nature of most strikes was itself deemed a justification by senior Conservatives for their refusal to countenance legislation on this issue, because most strikes would have ended by the time employers had instigated legal action against those involved. Furthermore, if such legal action continued to be pursued after a return to work, it would almost certainly re-ignite the conflict which prompted the strike in the first place. Yet even if legal action was swiftly invoked at the outset of a strike, it was quite likely to exacerbate problems, and make it more difficult to secure a prompt and amicable solution to the dispute. Indeed, trade union or employees' anger at an employer who hastily sought legal redress through the courts might actually serve to supersede the original grievance which had initially prompted the strike, and render industrial disputes rather lengthier and more bitter than they would otherwise have been. Cognizance of such factors meant that many employers were broadly supportive of the Conservative Governments' reluctance to introduce strike legislation during the 1950s.

In refusing to countenance legislation on aspects of trade unionism that most Conservatives deemed highly objectionable, such as unofficial strikes and the closed shop, Conservative Ministers again placed considerable emphasis on exhorting trade unions to behave more responsibly, and 'put their own house in order' in order to eradicate alleged malpractice. Not only was prescriptive or punitive legislation deemed inappropriate to the attainment both of more harmonious industrial relations and securing the trust of the trade unions – indeed, such legislation was almost certainly likely to prove counterproductive – it was also maintained that achieving improved industrial relations and responsible trade unionism was likely to take time, and require patience by Conservatives. Certainly, Monckton was emphatic that 'there is no panacea for these ills and, in particular, the scope for remedial action by the government is limited', for ultimately, what was needed was to foster 'a sense of national responsibility and of internal discipline among the rank-and-file of the trade-union movement', yet the 'educational task involved is a long-term one, and can only be tackled by the unions themselves' (NA PREM 11/921, CP (55) 25, 'Memorandum by the Minister of Labour: Current Industrial Relations Problems', 2 June 1955. See also CPA CCO 4/7/429, Poole to Brightman, 7 November 1956).

Toleration of the closed shop

For many Conservative critics of contemporary British trade unionism, probably the most objectionable feature was the 'closed shop', whereby union membership was compulsory, to the extent that refusal to join a trade union, or expulsion from a union on disciplinary grounds, invariably resulted in loss of employment.[2] For such Conservatives, the closed shop was not merely repugnant on the grounds of individual liberty – denying employees the right to choose for themselves whether or not they wished to belong to a trade union – it was also deemed objectionable because of its infringement on management's right to manage, for in some cases, a trade union, rather than an employer, could effectively determine if someone was to be employed, depending on whether or not they belonged to a trade union.

Yet in spite of such objections, the 1951–60 Conservative Governments refused to invoke legislation to curb the closed shop, and as with unofficial strikes, this disinclination to legislate was derived from both political and practical considerations. Politically, Ministers emphasised that for the Conservatives to legislate against the closed shop would not only constitute a breach of their voluntarist approach to industrial relations, but that such action would seriously damage, probably irreparably, their tireless efforts in seeking to win the trust of the trade unions. However, Conservative adherents to the voluntarist approach also insisted that seeking to outlaw the closed shop would almost certainly prove impracticable in terms of enforceability, for any attempt at prohibition was likely to drive closed shop arrangements 'underground', where compulsory union membership schemes would continue to be enforced in clandestine secrecy (CPA, ACP 3/6 (59)74, 'Trade-Union Reform', 25 November 1959). Not only was this likely to compound the potential for abuse and victimisation by, virtue of removing such activities from public scrutiny and opprobrium, it also risked bringing the law into disrepute, due to the difficulties of enforceability. For the self-proclaimed Party of law-and-order, passing such legislation would clearly be a grave mistake.

An indication that Conservative objections to the closed shop might not actually result in legislative action had been discernible in *The Industrial Charter*, whose criticism was relatively muted, merely suggesting that while: 'It is right that the unions ... should aim to organise all workers in unions so that they are fully representative', maximum trade union membership was 'best' when it was achieved on a 'voluntary' basis (Conservative and Unionist Central Office, 1947: 21–2).

---

2   A point clearly revealed by the high-profile 1964 *Rookes* v. *Barnard* judgment, which is discussed in chapter five.

However, quite apart from the issue of compulsion and denial of liberty, and the practical difficulties of trying to outlaw compulsory trade union membership schemes, the closed shop posed two particular dilemmas for the Conservative Governments during the 1950s (and beyond), quite apart from the issue of how statutory prohibition could be enforced anyway. Firstly, senior Conservatives were cognizant that many employers were broadly amenable to the existence of the closed shop, because 100 per cent trade union membership facilitated effective collective bargaining; if all employees were members of a specific trade union, then employers only needed to conduct negotiations with one set of union officials, whereupon agreements reached would be applicable to all members of that union. From an employer's perspective, this was much more efficient than having to conduct negotiations concerning terms and conditions of employment with a range of trade unions, or even individual non-unionised employees. Recognition of the extent to which the closed shop was often favoured by, and beneficial to, large employers further encouraged caution among senior Conservatives, regardless of their objection to the closed shop in principle. Industrial order, it seems, was ultimately prioritised over individual liberty.

The second particular dilemma which the closed shop posed for Conservative Ministers throughout this period was that they were keen to secure maximum trade union membership in order to overcome the influence of the left, which was widely believed to be responsible for fomenting industrial unrest in the workplace. Many Conservatives assumed that moderate trade unionists, by virtue of not being ideologically or politically motivated, were less inclined to become regularly or actively involved in trade union affairs, or even to join a union. This, though, unwittingly aided the left, which was often able to exercise a degree of influence out of all proportion to its relatively small numbers of adherents and fellow travellers. In ruling out compulsory strike ballots for the reasons delineated above, senior Conservatives tended to temper their ideological antipathy to the closed shop by acknowledging that the greater the number of employees who joined a trade union, the more the left could be out-manoeuvred and out-voted, and thereby marginalised. Put another way, tolerating the closed shop was often tacitly accepted as the lesser of two evils when the alternative might well have been to witness key trade unions fall into the hands of the more active and better-organised left. This was a particularly salient consideration during the 1950s, when there was growing concern about Communist involvement in some trade unions.

Tackling Communism in the trade unions

For many Conservatives, particularly those on the right of the Party, many strikes and other manifestations of industrial unrest were attributable to Communist infiltration of Britain's trade unions, with left-wing elements deemed to foment trouble in the workplace as part of a strategy to sabotage capitalism and/or promote a more revolutionary consciousness and outlook among the industrial working class. For Conservatives of this cast of mind, strikes were often evidence of 'Reds under the bed', which made the right even more frustrated at the Party leadership's refusal to adopt a tougher stance against such subversives in the trade unions. This concern with perceived Communist activity in the trade unions increased during the mid-1950s in tandem with an intensification of the Cold War and heightened fear of the alleged Soviet threat to the West (for a general overview of Communist and anti-Communist activities in the trade unions, see Stevens, 1999). Such fears were certainly lent credence by the Soviet Union's brutal suppression of anti-Communist protests in Hungary in 1956, but were also given a direct domestic focus that summer by elections for both a new President, and a new General Secretary of the Amalgamated Engineering Union (AEU), as well as to fill a vacancy which had arisen on the General Council. The concern was that even if the Communist candidates for these two posts were defeated, the election of a Communist candidate to the General Council would give the Communists virtual control of this executive body.

The following year also heard allegations of ballot-rigging and other irregularities by Communists in the Electrical Trades Union (ETU), which was voting, towards the end of 1957, to fill a vacancy on its executive committee. However, the Ministry of Labour concluded that there was 'little or no evidence of the truth of the various allegations', although it did suggest that the ETU's election rules needed to be amended to eradicate the potential for abuse in the future. Such a change would be for either the ETU's executive committee itself, or the union's members, to pursue, and as such, it was adjudged wise for the Government to 'do nothing and say nothing that will hinder them from doing this', although if they (or the TUC) failed to take such action to do so – or were prevented from so doing due to obstruction or intimidation by Communists within the ETU – then it might become necessary for the Cabinet to consider what the Government could do to remedy the situation (NA CAB 129/90, C (57) 294, Memorandum by the Minister of Labour, 'The Electrical Trades Union', 16 December 1957).

Ultimately, though, Conservative Ministers, especially Ministers of Labour, tended to view the problem somewhat differently to some of their backbench colleagues and the Party's extra-parliamentary activists. Not only did they insist that direct governmental action against Communists in the trade unions was not practicable, but also that many on the right tended, if not to exaggerate the scale of problem, to misunderstand its nature and significance. The Conservative leadership's more nuanced understanding of the nature of Communist involvement in the trade unions was not due solely to the fact that senior Conservatives, particularly the Minister of Labour, dealt with industrial relations on a regular basis, greatly assisted by their departmental officials, but also because these Ministers were routinely briefed by the security services about Communist activity in the trade unions, although much of the information gleaned in this manner was deemed so confidential that it was not disseminated beyond the Cabinet, which itself was sworn to secrecy.

For example, during the spring of 1956, the Prime Minister, Anthony Eden received a report from the security services which claimed that contrary to popular opinion, the Communist Party 'has not yet adopted a policy of promoting strikes or fostering industrial unrest', but was primarily concentrating on securing election to senior positions in key trade unions. This, however, posed something of a problem for the Conservative leadership, because if the Communist Party was acting as 'a legitimate political Party' by openly seeking election through trade union ballots, then Ministers could not legitimately 'take much effective action, overtly, against it', nor could 'Government agencies … be covertly used to counter the threat' of Communist candidates being constitutionally elected. Instead, the most realistic approach was to ensure that 'responsible' trade unionists were alive to the Communist 'threat', and that they thus organised themselves to counter it (NA PREM 11/1238, Brook [Cabinet Secretary] to Eden, 30 May 1956; see also CPA, CRD 2/7/6, Douglas to Sherbrooke, 23 June 1953).

However, this certainly did not mean that senior Conservatives adopted an entirely passive or fatalistic stance with regard to countering communism in the trade unions. They might not have felt able to take overt action, but there were certainly indirect means of seeking to counter the apparent threat from Communist elements within the unions. This primarily entailed supporting anti-Communist organisations which were formally independent of the Conservative Party but which shared many, if not most, of its beliefs and values, most notably a commitment to capitalism and private enterprise. In this context, senior Ministers warmly welcomed the formation, in spring 1956, of the Industrial Research and Information Service (IRIS), founded by two former senior trade union officials. Although it was primarily concerned with publishing a regular news-sheet for trade union members, and offering an advice service for them, it was envisaged that this would *inter alia* assist the development of 'a healthy, militant (sic), well-informed and responsible trade unionism'. The pursuit of such an objective 'will involve a good deal of anti-Communist work, both direct and indirect'. What particularly heartened senior Conservatives about this new body was that because its founders had themselves been trade unionists, and intended to maintain regular contact with current union leaders and officials, IRIS would 'have an advantage over other anti-Communist bodies such as the Economic League, Common Cause and Aims of Industry which are tainted with the "bosses' gold"' (NA PREM 11/1238, Brook to Eden, 2 May 1956).

Another means by which Conservative Ministers sought indirectly or covertly to neutralise the Communist threat was to support – or encourage others to support – anti-Communist candidates in trade union elections. The advance of Communism within the trade unions was largely attributed to the apathy of many ordinary trade unionists, which thereby enabled Communists to inveigle their way into positions of authority and power within the trade unions, and exercise a pernicious influence greatly in excess of their actual numbers – a mere one in 500 trade union members were actually deemed to be Communists – or popular support. Yet while the Communists were undoubtedly small in numbers, they were often far more effectively organised and highly-disciplined than other trade union candidates and parties (NA CAB 130/115, Memorandum by the Security Service – 'Industrial Unrest 1953–1955: The Role of the Communist Party', 27 March 1956).

It was in this context that Ministers envisaged a valuable role for the Conservative Trade Unionists organisation (as discussed in the previous chapter), for even when this body did not directly field candidates in union elections, it could play a vital part in challenging Communist propaganda, and alerting moderate trade unionists to the dangers posed by far-left infiltration. Indeed, on one occasion, the Conservative Trade Unionists' Advisory Committee itself cautioned *against* any campaign for legislation *vis-à-vis* the political levy, on the grounds that workplace campaigns encouraging workers to exercise their right to 'contract out' also afforded the CTU 'perhaps their best opportunity for disseminating Conservative propaganda within the unions' (CPA CCO 4/8/365, Kaberry to Glyn, 8 March 1960).

In addition to these two methods of countering the perceived Communist threat within the trade unions, Conservative Ministers, particularly the Minister of Labour, held various meetings with those whom they themselves regarded as right-wing trade union leaders, This did not mean that such union leaders were actually Conservatives – politically and ideologically, most, if not all, of them of them were staunchly pro-Labour – but within the trade union movement, they bitterly opposed the Communists, and were therefore willing to talk with moderate Conservatives in order to discuss ways of defeating communism within the trade unions. One such meeting took place in the summer of 1956, when Iain Macleod met with Sir Vincent Tewson and Tom Williamson, to consider how Communists in the trade unions could be defeated. Although Macleod considered this particular meeting to have been generally inconclusive, he did glean that specific evidence of cheating by Communists in union elections would probably be far more effective in boosting support for moderate candidates than any number of anti-Communist speeches by Ministers. The acquisition of such evidence, Macleod noted, was something which the security services might be able to assist with, whereupon, this evidence might then discretely be passed on to anti-Communist trade union leaders to utilise in union election campaigns (PREM 11/1238, 'Communism and the Trade Unions – Memorandum by the Minister of Labour and National Service, 5 July 1956. See also PREM 11/1238, Brook to Eden, 28 April 1956; CAB 130/115, Note of the 2nd meeting of the Ministerial Committee on Communism and the Trade Unions, 6 September 1956).

One final measure which was mooted by the Minister of Labour during the mid-1950s, in the context of concern over Communist involvement in the AEU elections, was that employers be encouraged to allow trade union ballots to be conducted during work time and in the work-place. The rationale was that whereas voting in other forums might boost Communist candidates, due to the often lower levels of involvement in union affairs by moderates, work-place ballots would ensure a much higher turn-out, thereby ensuring that the majority of moderate trade union members actually voted, and thereby contributed to the defeat the Communist candidate(s). Indeed, Macleod claimed that 'if we can get enough people in the unions to vote, then all our troubles can be overcome' (NA PREM 11/1238, 'Communism and the Trade Unions – Note by the Minister of Labour and National Service, 11 June 1956). However, once again, there was an insistence that this could not be achieved through legislation or compulsion, but only through encouragement and exhortation.

Opposition to the Conservative leadership's approach

Apart from the antipathy of a few backbench Conservative MPs and sundry constituency delegates at annual conference, who invariably demanded a tougher approach to trade unionism by the Party's leadership, in the guise of legislative curbs on strike action and/or the closed shop, ballots for leadership elections and the prohibition of Communists, there were two other discrete sources which evinced a definite lack of enthusiasm for, or even criticism of, the Government's approach to trade unionism during the 1950s. In both cases, this divergence from the official Party line was articulated through reports or publications which the Party leadership immediately sought to play down or distance itself from.

The Keatinge report

The first of these was the 1952 Keatinge Report, which contained the findings of an internal Party inquiry conducted during the Conservatives' first year in Office, following their victory in the October 1951 general election. This inquiry was undertaken by an 11-member committee – including its chair, Sir Edward Keatinge, himself a former Conservative MP – consisting of Conservative trade unionists, Party officials, and one Conservative MP. Its remit was to 'consider, in the light of experience, the Party's policy in regard to Trade Unionists in the past, and assess the extent to which this policy has produced results', while also recommending means by which the trade unions might be freed 'from political domination', and to 'win over the votes of Trade Unionists and their families to the Conservative Party' (National Union of Conservative and Unionists Associations, 1952: 4). The impetus for conducting such an inquiry was a recognition within Conservative Central Office that the Party's success in securing greater support and membership from non-socialist trade unionists had been rather disappointing, which was partly due to confusion, or even ignorance, in the Party about the role and activities of the Conservative Trade Unionists.

The Keatinge inquiry, held nine meetings during the summer of 1952, these hearing wide-ranging evidence from Conservative MPs, Conservative trade unionists, the Young Conservatives, members of local, regional and national Conservative organisations and the Labour Department of Conservative Central Office. A questionnaire was also sent to the Chair of each Conservative Constituency Association, enquiring about their relationship or contacts – if any – with local Conservative trade unionists. The Keatinge committee also established four regional sub-committees, which then conducted hearings from a wide range of Conservative officials and Party members in their particular region.

Ultimately, though, the Keatinge inquiry confirmed what the parliamentary leadership had already known or strongly suspected, namely that there existed a strong (and misguided) affinity between trade unionism and the Labour Party or socialism – for most Conservatives, one and the same thing – even though about 40 per cent of trade union members had not voted for Labour in the 1951 election. Nonetheless, 'fear of intimidation, entrenched Socialism [and] widespread apathy' were deemed to be the main reasons for the limited involvement or impact of Conservative trade unionists inside Britain's trade unions. However, precisely because of the long-standing and deep-rooted nature of these problems, there were unlikely to be any 'sudden and spectacular results' with regard to overcoming such obstacles. The Conservatives' mission to wean industrial workers and trade unionists away from the Labour Party and socialism would therefore require 'a combined and prolonged effort from the Party, at all levels' (National Union of Conservative and Unionists Associations, 1952: 6).

Yet if the involvement of Conservative trade unionists in trade union affairs was partly deterred by the ideological antipathy by the 'host' institutions, much the same, the Keatinge report ruefully acknowledged, could be said with regard to the limited involvement of trade unionists in local Conservative constituency associations. Here, it was noted, the mode of Conservatism often subscribed to among constituency members was one which was intrinsically suspicious of, if not antipathetic towards, trade unionism, even of a Conservative variant. This problem was compounded by the extensive role played by local employers in many Conservative constituency associations, particularly in urban or industrial areas, for these employers were often unenthusiastic about encouraging the active involvement of trade unionists – even if they were Conservatives – whom they employed. Such suspicion or antipathy was deemed a key factor in deterring Conservative constituency associations from adopting trade unionists as parliamentary candidates (National Union of Conservative and Unionists Associations, 1952: 12). Certainly, there was some concern at the very highest levels in the Party that some 'ill-informed Conservatives [were] telling Trade Unionists that their place within the Party was not in their Ward Organization, but only on the Councils of Trade Unionists', thereby 'completely putting the Trade Unionists into an entirely separate compartment' (CPA, CCO 503/1/1, W.T.M. to Hare, 21 May 1952). Consequently, when the Keatinge Report was published, Walter Monkton, and his PPS, Harold Watkinson, were 'extremely anxious that no undue publicity should be given to the report', and suggested that parts of it might be better disseminated 'by word of mouth to whatever body was charged with examining it' (CPA, CCO 503/1/2, Hare to Errington, 29 October 1952). In fact, very little was subsequently heard of the Keatinge inquiry and its report, even within the Conservative Party itself.

A Giant's Strength

The second example reflected a hardening of opinion against the Conservative leadership's constructive and conciliatory approach to trade unionism towards the end of the decade, with 1958 witnessing the publication of *A Giant's Strength* by the Inns of Court Conservative and Unionist Association. Extrapolating its title from a line in Shakespeare's *Measure for Measure* (Act II, Scene II) – 'O, it is excellent to have a giant's strength, but it is tyrannous to use it like a giant' – this 86-page critique of contemporary British trade unionism argued that the time had now come 'to question the validity of certain assumptions that have come to be very nearly articles of faith to trade unionists', although this assertion was immediately followed by an insistence that such questioning was to be pursued 'with no sense of animosity towards the unions' (Inns of Court Conservative and Unionist Association, 1958: 13).

In spite of this apparently placatory caveat, *A Giant's Strength* argued that having often been subject to tyranny and denial of liberty in their formative years, the trade unions had now acquired so much power that they themselves were capable of behaving 'tyrannically' and denying the liberty of individuals, to the extent that it was now essential to address 'the problem of restraining the overmighty subject so that his power is not used, either intentionally or accidentally, as a means of oppression' (Inns of Court Conservative and Unionist Association, 1958: 14).

In the case of British trade unionism, the irresponsible or tyrannical exercise of power manifested itself at two discrete levels, the national and the individual, although these were by no means mutually exclusive. At the national level, trade union power had become problematic because of the damaging impact of strikes and restrictive practices on the British economy, for strikes disrupted production and exports, and also led to lost orders in the future, as potential purchasers of British goods and raw materials decided to look elsewhere due to lack of confidence that they would be produced or delivered on time because of industrial stoppages. Meanwhile, restrictive practices prevented the modernisation necessary to improve the productivity or efficiency of industry, and thereby reduced the competitiveness of the British economy. Although it was acknowledged that restrictive practices were frequently derived from an understandable fear among workers that new technology or working methods would result in the loss of their jobs or skills, it was emphasised that if industries – or the economy in general – failed to remain competitive by increasing productivity or improving efficiency, then the ensuing decline in trade, exports and profitability would result in job losses anyway.

With regard to the individual level, *A Giant's Strength* highlighted the threat to individual liberty arising from the operation of the trade union closed shop, and thus the potential loss of livelihood suffered by workers whose employment was terminated, or job applications were rejected, as a result of their refusal – on grounds of conscience or principle – to join a trade union for which membership was deemed compulsory.

Due to the extent and impact of these problems, *A Giant's Strength* was adamant that voluntarism and industrial self-government would no longer suffice, for governmental action was now imperative. However, it was also readily acknowledged that tackling these problems would require a mix of policy solutions; blanket statutory prohibition or prescription would not, in itself, be an adequate or appropriate response. With regard to strikes, it was proposed that the 'privileges' enjoyed by trade unions and/or their members due to the protection afforded by the Trade Union Act 1871, the Conspiracy and Protection of Property Act 1875 and Trade Disputes Act 1906, should not apply unless a strike had been preceded by an independent tribunal inquiry into the facts and circumstances pertaining to the dispute *and* a period of 14 days had subsequently elapsed following publication of the tribunal's report. It was also proposed that in order to continue enjoying these 'privileges', trade unions should be required to register with the Registrar of Friendly Societies.

With regard to restrictive practices, *A Giant's Strength* recommended that allegations of such cases should be referred to a Restrictive Practices Court (or similar such body) to ascertain whether the action was commensurate with the public interest, with the burden of proof residing with the workers or trade union involved. However, *A Giant's Strength* did acknowledge that restrictive practices sometimes derived from perceptions of job insecurity among workers, and as such, Ministers were encouraged to enact relevant proposals originally enshrined in *The Industrial Charter*, most notably those pertaining to contracts of employment.

Nonetheless, it was probably inevitable that the punitive or legislative aspects of *A Giant's Strength* would attract the most headlines and publicity, whereupon senior Conservatives hurriedly disassociated themselves from it, insisting that: 'Neither the Government, nor the Conservative Party ... believe in any of the suggestions made for reform of trade unions law', and as such, it was emphasised that '*A Giant's Strength* ... is not in any way official policy. It was not published by any Conservative organisation, but by an outside publisher' (CPA CRD 2/7/8, 'Notes for Sir Eric Errington's Speech at Aldershot', 10 March 1959; see also CPA ACP (59) 74, 'Trade Union Reform', 4 June 1959).

The Conservatives therefore ended the 1950s as they had begun them, by insisting that improved industrial relations could only be attained through the development of trust between employers and employees, which required more (or better) communication and dialogue, as well as a genuine sense of industrial partnership, between management and labour. None of this was amenable to governmental legislation, and any attempt at invoking statutory measures would, it was maintained, poison industrial relations, and alienate the trade unions with whom senior Conservatives had tried so patiently to establish a close working relationship. To those in the Conservative Party who did demand legislation against the trade unions, particularly in the form of compulsory ballots, or, for example, prohibition of Communist candidates in union elections, Ministers not only insisted that laws and bans would not produce the desired results, but that those in the Party who continually called for such measures were too far removed from day-to-day industrial reality to comprehend fully the issues involved. Ministers who dealt with industrial relations issues and the trade unions on a regular basis – especially Ministers of Labour – therefore claimed to possess a much deeper and nuanced understanding of the problems, and thus of the inappropriate or unworkable nature of apparent solutions proposed by those on the Conservative backbenches or at Party conferences, many of whom seemed to be motivated by a visceral hatred of trade unions, rather than a careful consideration or appreciation of industrial reality, and the need for policies which were practicable, and therefore pragmatic.

Conclusion

The 1950s were remarkable for the degree of cordiality which existed between senior Conservatives and many trade union leaders, especially during the first half of the decade. Throughout this time, Ministers refused to accede to perennial backbench and conference demands for legislation to address aspects of trade unionism which many Party members found especially objectionable, most notably the closed shop, and unofficial strikes. There was also a strong disinclination by Ministers to amend the 1946 Trades Disputes Act in order to replace 'contracting-out' of the political levy with 'contracting-in'. Indeed, much to the frustration of some of the Party's MPs and extra-parliamentary members, the Conservative Governments of the 1950s did not introduce *any* legislation pertaining to the activities or internal affairs of the trade unions.

Instead, throughout the decade, the stance adopted by Ministers, particularly those who served at the Ministry of Labour, and who could therefore claim to have a better understanding of industrial relations problems, was that legislation could not produce more harmonious relationships between employers and employees, or management and labour. Better industrial relations could only be achieved through developing trust and greater understanding between the 'two sides' of industry, whereupon each would develop an appreciation of the concerns and motives of the other, and whereby industrial workers would feel more appreciated and valued, rather than feeling that they were merely small insignificant cogs in a large impersonal machine. This was not a scenario which could be conjured up by passing Acts of Parliament, but only through patiently promoting greater dialogue and improved communication between employers and workers, to the extent that a genuine sense of industrial partnership would be attained. Much of the responsibility for achieving such a partnership was deemed to rest with enlightened managers.

Senior Conservatives hoped that the practical manifestation of this 'human relations' approach – which clearly reflected the ethos of *The Industrial Charter* – would, in turn, lead to a steady reduction in the incidence of strikes and other forms of damaging industrial action, as workers became more trusting and understanding of managerial decisions, and of the need to forgo 'excessive' pay rises if their company could not afford them due to profit margins or other commercial considerations.

Similarly, Ministers and many Conservative officials, both in Central Office and the Conservative Trade Unionists organisation, consistently maintained that industrial relations legislation would alienate or antagonise trade unions and their members during a time when senior Conservatives were doing their utmost to pursue a constructive and conciliatory approach towards organised labour, and show that the Party was not anti-trade union. This approach was underpinned by repeated Ministerial insistence that legislation to tackle objectionable aspects of trade unionism, such as unofficial strikes or the closed shop, would be impracticable and unenforceable. Instead, more responsible trade unionism would only be realised if the Conservatives could win the trust of trade union leaders, and thereby render them more amenable to persuasion and exhortation to 'put their own house in order'. Even when the trade unions failed to respond in kind, Ministers refused to abandon their 'voluntarist' stance, merely reiterating that legislation would not actually tackle the problems anyway, although towards the end of the decade, Ministerial exhortations to the trade unions were increasingly tinged with a degree of frustration or exasperation, and this impatience was to increase further in the early 1960s.

Chapter 4

In Defence of Free Collective Bargaining, 1951–1960

As noted in chapter two, the Conservatives did not develop a wages policy between 1945 and 1951, because the voluntarist policy adopted in Opposition *vis-à-vis* trade union organisation and behaviour was matched by an equal commitment to free collective bargaining in the sphere of wages and salaries. Just as the activities of trade unions were deemed to be for the unions and their members themselves to determine, so too, Conservative Ministers insisted, were the terms and conditions of employment to be settled jointly by management and trade unions, without interference by government. Thus did the Party's 1951 election campaign emphasise that a Conservative Government would retain and strengthen the British practice under which wages and conditions are negotiated by representatives of employers and employed, a commitment which was reiterated on numerous occasions, such as three years later, when a Treasury paper asserted that 'the principle of collective bargaining, unfettered from the outside, is the foundation of industrial relations [in Britain], questioned by neither party in industry, nor any party in state' (NA T 227/261, 'Draft White Paper on Full Employment and Price Stability', 18 June 1954).

At the time, this was widely seen as a natural reflection of the Conservative's traditional view that governments ought not to interfere in what were essentially economic decisions, yet in many other respects, as we have noted in the previous two chapters, the Conservative Party of the late 1940s and 1950s had effectively abandoned the *laissez-faire* model of capitalism in favour of a regulated variant. Ironically, therefore, wage determination was one of the only areas of economic affairs where the Conservative Party continued to insist upon a predominantly non-interventionist approach, maintaining that it was 'entirely in line with Conservative policy that employers and trade unionists should be left to settle these matters through their negotiating machinery or through free bargaining' (CPA, PLC (54) 1, 'Industrial Relations', 15 February 1954). This endorsement of free collective bargaining logically entailed a firm rejection of compulsory arbitration too, in favour of 'a system of voluntary arbitration ... encouraged by the Minister of Labour' (CPA, ACP 1 (51)13, 2 May 1951).

Of course, none of this meant that the Conservative Governments were unconcerned with what was happening on the wages front. On the contrary, as the Attlee governments had previously discovered, an interventionist role for the state, coupled with a political and electoral commitment to full employment, ensured that any government was compelled to take an interest in what was happening with regard to pay determination. Throughout the 1950s therefore, Conservative

Ministers found themselves simultaneously insisting that pay determination was not the responsibility of government, whilst exhorting, with increasing urgency, trade unions and their members to exercise restraint and moderation in order to minimise inflation and maximise employment.

Even during its very first year in Office, the Conservative Government was imploring the trade unions to exercise wage restraint, in the context of a strong upwards trajectory in prices and incomes, occasioned by the combined impact of a sharp increase in import costs following the outbreak of the Korean War in 1950, and the end of the previous Labour Governments' 1948–50 wage freeze. Nonetheless, Ministers fully acknowledged that it 'would be impracticable to prevent claims for wage increases from being put forward' (NA CAB 128 (52), 51st conclusions, 8 May 1952), and Walter Monckton, as Minister of Labour, was certainly convinced that 'there is no prospect that the trade unions would accept any general wages standstill', although he was reasonably confident that 'there is evidence of support from responsible trade union leaders for a policy of wage restraint' (NA CAB 128 (52), 57th conclusions, 29 May 1952). Such confidence reflected a widespread faith amongst many senior Conservatives and Departmental officials, particularly within the Ministry of Labour – during this period in the persuasive power of education and exhortation to modify trade union attitudes and behaviour. It was commonly assumed that if the economic facts of life were carefully and consistently explained to the trade unions, they would respond by practising more responsible collective bargaining.

Fortunately for the new Conservative Government, the prices and incomes explosion rapidly dissipated, and in so doing, seemed to vindicate the faith of Ministers like Monckton that the Conservatives could expect considerable co-operation and moderation from the trade unions, and also that wage increases were often a response to price increases, which encouraged a Ministerial perspective that the key to securing voluntary pay restraint was to persuade employers to curb prices. What also reinforced this somewhat sanguine approach was that from early 1952 to the middle of 1954, 'the world trade situation was extraordinarily favourable for Britain' (Dorfman, 1973: 79).

Rejecting alternative options

This Ministerial insistence on the maintenance of free collective bargaining as the primary method of pay determination was not solely due to their conviction that the trade unions could be persuaded, through reasoned argument and the presentation of economic facts, of the need for moderation and responsibility in pay determination, but also because the three alternatives to this policy were deemed unpalatable or impracticable, namely deflation (and *inter alia* higher unemployment), incomes policies or trade union legislation. Free collective bargaining was the default policy for the vast majority of Conservative Ministers throughout the 1950s, and although they became increasingly frustrated during the second half of the decade at the apparent failure of the trade unions to practise wage restraint in the manner exhorted by the Government, the Cabinet invariably concluded that free collective bargaining was the best, or most practicable, method of determining pay, and other terms and conditions of employment, when compared to the three alternative policy options which were variously canvassed within the Party.

One option which was occasionally mooted, mainly by Conservative neo-liberals and monetarists, was that of deflation, entailing significant cuts in public expenditure and/or higher interest rates, whereupon the ensuing increase in unemployment would reduce the bargaining power of the trade unions, and thereby yield lower wage settlements. This is certainly the option most commonly associated with Peter Thorneycroft, who, during his mid-1950s role as President of the Board of Trade, explained to the Prime Minister, Anthony Eden, that: 'The solution in my view must be to reduce the total demand on our resources right across the board. The prime need is to reduce the total of monetary demand, rather than to attempt to restrain demand in certain selected fields, a process which would only leave the money to be spent elsewhere.' In urging a significant reduction in Government expenditure, in tandem with a credit squeeze in the private sector, Thorneycroft readily acknowledged that 'it will certainly involve a definite increase in unemployment' (NA PREM 11/1324, Thorneycroft to Eden, 6 January 1956). However, such an option was anathema to most Cabinet Ministers during this period, committed as they were to maintaining 'high and stable' levels of employment, forging a harmonious relationship with the trade unions, and thus banishing the bitter memories of the mid-1920s and 1930s. Certainly, most senior Conservative Ministers at this time were absolutely determined to avoid a return to high unemployment, especially Harold Macmillan (Conservative leader and Prime Minister from 1957 to 1963) who never forgot the plight of his own constituents in Stockton-on-Tees during the Great Depression of the 1930s. Reginald Maudling, who served as a President of the Board of Trade and, later, Chancellor during Macmillan's premiership, recalled that, 'his [Macmillan's] experience in Stockton ... so moulded his subsequent approach to economic affairs' (Maudling 1978: 103).

Throughout his 1957–63 premiership – and indeed, during his tenure as Chancellor immediately prior to entering 10 Downing Street – Macmillan therefore refused to countenance a deliberately deflationary policy which would fuel unemployment, a stance shared throughout the 1950s by most of his Ministerial colleagues. As Iain Macleod's biographer notes: 'The political imperative of this period, when folk memories of the 1920s and 1930s were potent and the majority of voters were working class, was to keep the numbers registered as unemployed below half a million' (Shepherd, 1994: 133). The Conservative Party had, after all, in *The Industrial Charter* and sundry other policy statements, committed itself to maintaining 'high and stable' levels of employment, and such pledges further militated against the switch to a deflationary economic policy.

Meanwhile, just after the Conservative Party's 1951 election victory, the Director of the Economic Section within the Cabinet Office, Robert Hall, had suggested that the level of unemployment which would be necessary 'to put a really effective stop on wage increases' would be 'economically wrong as well as politically disastrous', and as such, he was confident that 'no government in the UK would be likely to push unemployment as far as this' (NA T 229/409, Hall to Bridges, 19 November 1951; NA T 229/402, Hall to Bridges, 28 November 1951). This stance was further endorsed by the Conservative Party's [extra-parliamentary] industrial research committee, which had been established after the 1955 election victory in order to investigate various aspects of industrial relations. The committee claimed that if unemployment was allowed to rise beyond three quarters of a million 'under a Conservative administration ... great and lasting harm would be done to the Conservative Party', for such a figure was 'probably a fair estimate of the maximum unemployment the country is prepared to stand'. Anything higher, and 'the Conservative Party is likely to get badly concussed. It might indeed sustain a shock from which it would have great difficulty in recovering' (CPA, ACP 4 (56)41, 2 February 1956).

The second option potentially available to the Conservative Governments with regard to wages and inflation during the 1950s was recourse to an incomes policy, on the basis that reaching agreement with the trade unions and employees over somewhat lower wage increases would yield a corresponding reduction in inflation. Yet this option was also rejected by Conservative Ministers, partly on the grounds of principle, namely that in a liberal democratic society, governments had no business in seeking to determine wages and salaries, and partly on grounds of impracticability, it being assumed that an incomes policy would be unenforceable, unless the state abrogated to itself draconian powers and punitive sanctions deemed incompatible with a liberal democracy. Any incomes policy was 'liable either to make radical inroads into the essential liberties of a free society or in practice to prove unfair, and in the final analysis unworkable' (CPA, ACP 4 (56)41). Instead, as the Conservative's backbench parliamentary labour committee emphasised, 'the Government should, so far as it can, keep out of industrial negotiations ... employers and trade unionists should be left to settle these matters' themselves, with the Government merely making available conciliation and arbitration services when the two sides of industry wished to secure independent third party involvement to reach a settlement (CPA, CRD 2/7/3, PLC (54) 1, 'Some Background Facts Concerning Industrial Relations', 15 February 1954). It was also suggested that the trade unions were highly unlikely to agree to a period of wage restraint unless corresponding limits were imposed on profits and dividends (NA CAB 134/1273, IR (55), 2nd meeting, 28 July 1955).

The third option which Ministers might conceivably have contemplated was the introduction of legislation to curb the activities of the trade unions, particularly unofficial or wildcat strikes, as demanded each year by a handful of Conservative MPs and conference delegates. Yet as we discussed in the previous chapter, this option was also firmly rejected during the 1950s, for not only would trade union legislation have destroyed the tireless efforts of Conservative Ministers in pursuing a constructive relationship with the trade unions and winning their trust, it too would have faced practical problems in terms of enforceability. What could Ministers really do, for example, if unofficial strikes were outlawed, but some trade unions and their members engaged in such action regardless? Would the Government really want to see thousands of trade unionists sent to prison, thereby incurring the likely wrath of the whole trade union movement, and quite possibly, a shift in public opinion against the Conservative Party? In short, the assumption of most Conservative Ministers was that the likely repercussions of trade union legislation would probably prove more damaging, both to industrial relations and to the British economy, than the trade union behaviour they were seeking to eradicate in the first place. The Cabinet thus shared the view of the Conservative's backbench labour committee, which insisted that: 'Any suggestion of special government intervention, whether this be in the form of secret ballots or of imposed wages policy, would not only be rejected by both sides [of industry], but would itself lead to major industrial unrest' (CPA, PLC (54)1, 'Industrial Relations', 15 February 1954).

Yet in rejecting the above three options – deflation/higher unemployment, incomes policy and trade union legislation – the Conservative Governments of the 1950s were left with no other option than continued reliance on a policy of exhortation, albeit increasingly desperate as the decade progressed, whereby trade unions were encouraged to exercise wage restraint voluntarily. For their part, Ministers sought repeatedly to explain the economic facts of life to trade union leaders and their members, in the hope that they would then appreciate the need for moderation and responsibility when pursuing pay increases. As Clem Leslie, the Head of the Treasury's Economic Information Division, explained:

> Full employment without price stability in a nation which lives by overseas trade is a long-term impossibility, but if the collective wisdom, moderation and good sense of employers and trade unionists, enlightened by a clear awareness of the issues at stake, can be brought to bear upon the problem, it will be solved ... [It] is the duty of government to ensure that the problem in its full significance and gravity is understood throughout the country. This is the best means of ensuring that the collective wisdom and restraint of the Community will furnish in practice the remedies which no administrative formula ... can provide.
> (NA T 227/261, 'Draft White Paper on Full Employment and Price Stability', 18 June 1954)

As such, right from the outset, in the months following the Conservative Party's 1951 election victory, the Chancellor held regular meetings with the TUC's Economic Committee to explain the necessity for moderation and responsibility in wage bargaining, whilst urging also that, as far as possible, pay increases should be more closely linked to increased productivity (NA T/229/405, Economic discussions with the Trade Union Congress, various dates 1951–52).

Moreover, the first three years of post-war Conservative rule was accompanied by an apparently improving economic situation, as indicated by Table 4.1. Price increases declined dramatically during this short period, from 9.2 per cent in 1951 to three per cent in 1953 (and down to just two per cent the following year), while earnings also evinced an initial downward trend, for having increased by 10.2 per cent in 1951, the increase in 1953 was 5.4 per cent, albeit rising the following year.

Table 4.1   Prices and earnings 1951–59 (% increase per annum)

	Prices	Earnings
1951	9.2	10.2
1952	9.1	7.5
1953	3.0	5.4
1954	2.0	7.4
1955	4.4	9.0
1956	4.9	7.3
1957	3.7	5.8
1958	3.1	2.3
1959	0.5	5.1

Source: Taylor, 1993: 385

The initial trend in earnings suggested a remarkable degree of voluntary self-restraint by the trade unions in the early part of the decade, and seemed to suggest that the conciliatory stance adopted by senior Conservatives since the end of the Second World War had elicited a similarly benign attitude on the part of many trade unions leaders, particularly those who constituted the TUC's right-wing 'junta', as acknowledged in the previous chapter.

This certainly appeared to be the case in the context of some of the major speeches at the TUC's annual conference in 1952. For example, Arthur Deakin explained that trade unionists had:

a clear duty to act with a full sense of responsibility ... not to make unreasonable demands, and to do all we can to avoid interruptions of work ... It is of the utmost importance to keep our industries going with full employment and with steadily rising productivity at the lowest possible production costs.

These sentiments were clearly echoed at the same conference by Sir Lincoln Evans, leader of the Iron and Steel Trades Confederation, who argued that the trade unions had an obligation:

to maintain economic stability and avoid unemployment ... We know that wage levels do affect prices and we are only misleading our people by encouraging them to believe that all the increases we demand can be met out of profits because that simply is not true ... Those who possess power must accept responsibility

... We want to maintain economic stability and avoid unemployment, but if we price ourselves out of world markets, we automatically create unemployment.

However, such 'realism' did not imply any trade union willingness to contemplate a formal incomes policy in order to ensure continued wage restraint. Instead, the unions remained fully committed to free collective bargaining, albeit responsibly pursued.

The Economic Implications of Full Employment

However, from the mid-1950s onwards, the issue of wages acquired a renewed significance, for as Table 4.1 also illustrates, earnings increased by 9 per cent in 1955 (having risen by just 5.4 per cent two years earlier), and although there was a steady decline for the next 3 years, they still, with the notable exception of 1958, outstripped the rate at which prices were increasing. Indeed, in 1959, the increase in earnings was more than double the 1958 figure, even though price rises had fallen from 3.1 per cent to a mere 0.5 per cent during the same 2-year period. Ministers were not solely concerned about the rate at which earnings increased each year, because this declined in some years, but the increasing disjuncture between prices rises and increases in earnings, and also the wider performance of the British economy, in which industrial output and the balance of payments were also becoming a source of growing concern.

It was Ministerial concern about these trends, particularly the figures for 1955 – when alarm over another notable increase in average earnings was buttressed by anxiety regarding the fact that the 4.4 per cent increase in prices was more than double that of 1954 – which prompted the publication, in March 1956, of a White Paper entitled *The Economic Implications of Full Employment* (the word 'Economic' was not originally in the title, but was added to the final draft).

The idea of an 'educative' White Paper – such papers are normally a direct forerunner of legislation – had originally been mooted by Rab Butler, when as Chancellor, he had also chaired the 1955 Cabinet committee on industrial relations. During its second meeting (NA CAB 134/1273, I.R. (55) 2nd meeting, 28 July 1955), Butler suggested that Treasury officials be asked to consider the feasibility of devising a formal statement which could then form the basis of a Government educational campaign to explain to the public the delicate relationship between full employment, trade union bargaining power and inflation. In particular, the intention of such an initiative would be to promote awareness of the need for moderation by those involved in collective bargaining. Other Ministers on the committee endorsed this proposal, albeit emphasising the need to avoid fuelling trade union suspicion that the Government was about to resort to an explicit policy of wage restraint.

In fact, in spite of requesting Ministerial approval for a Treasury study of this kind, Butler had already commissioned two position papers on this issue, one from the Government's Economic Adviser, Robert Hall, and the other from Clem Leslie, the Head of the Information Division at the Treasury. The former, entitled 'Full Employment and Wage Policy', explained that although the cost of imports was a factor in rising domestic prices, 'the principal reason is the regular process of wage increases which now takes place about once a year', which, since 1945, had tended to rise at a slightly higher or faster rate than that of retail prices. This upwards trajectory in pay settlements, Hall argued, was undoubtedly linked to the goal of full employment, for this not only strengthened the bargaining power of the trade unions, but the higher profits accruing from a steadily expanding, full-employment economy, with concomitantly higher consumer demand and purchasing power, 'thus reduces the resistance of employers to claims for higher wages'. Ultimately, though, this was creating a dangerous disjuncture between the relatively benign impact on industrial relations, whereby 'annual wage negotiations seem to be carried out relatively amicably' – the workers enjoying decent wage increases and the employers achieving high profits – and the increasingly damaging impact on the national economy, in terms of inflation, loss of export trade (due to the higher prices of British commodities) and the rise in imports, leading to a deteriorating balance of payments situation.

However, Hall's paper was rather longer on analysis than possible solutions, although he did suggest that since the end of the Second World War, governments had pursued a policy of 'over-full employment', and as such, he ventured to suggest that Ministers might want to consider allowing the rate of unemployment to operate at two per cent, rather than the hitherto one per cent, thereby establishing a 'policy of somewhat less than over-full employment' which might then 'help to moderate the upward movement of wages' (NA CAB PREM 11/1402, 'Full Employment and Wage Policy', 23 July 1955).

Meanwhile, Clem Leslie's paper concerning 'Economic Publicity on Full Employment and Wage Policy' claimed that as 'it would be quite unrealistic to think that any practicable economic measures would weaken the bargaining power of labour sufficiently to solve the problem', there was 'no alternative to the policy of trying to extend and clarify the understanding of economic realities in industry' by workers and managers alike. To this end, Leslie suggested that 'if better understanding of the facts will help at all in reaching agreement on a wise disposition of the product of industry among the various claims upon it, now is the time to set about new measures to achieve that understanding'. In particular, it was imperative that those involved in pay determination were persuaded that higher wages must be linked to higher industrial output and productivity, not by the cost of living, for invoking the latter as the primary criteria for annual pay increases fuelled a self-perpetuating wage-price spiral which was not only damaging to the wider domestic economy, but also weakened Britain's international economic position. The emphasis of any such campaign, Hall explained, should not be on restraining wages – this would immediately antagonise the trade unions, and arouse their suspicions about Ministerial motives – but on the need to link pay increases to industrial output and productivity.

As to the form which such a campaign might take, Leslie proposed that the main component should be 'a full-dress White Paper' delineating the economic situation, illustrated with all the relevant facts and figures. At the same time, the Chancellor should elicit the support of the editors of national and provincial newspapers, who could then publish features and editorials conveying the seriousness of the economic situation, and the consequent need for moderation. Similar approaches should also be made to the television companies, both the BBC and the independent or regional ones. Meanwhile, at a local level, leaflets or posters might be produced for fixing on work-place notice-boards – 'a cheap and potentially effective method of getting valuable ideas before a large industrial audience' – while the Ministry of Education might want to consider providing, via Technical or Further Education Colleges and adult education classes, courses on economic affairs (NA PREM 11/1402, 'Economic Publicity on Full Employment and Wage Policy', 23 July 1955).

With Ministers deeply apprehensive about Hall's proposal to tolerate slightly higher unemployment, it was Leslie's suggestion of a White Paper which was actively pursued, this yielding *The Economic Implications of Full Employment*, although Hall's analysis of the problems facing the British economy were readily incorporated. This explained that:

> In order to maintain full employment, the government must ensure that the level of demand for goods and services is high and rises steadily as productive capacity grows. This means a strong demand for labour and good opportunities to sell goods and services profitably. In these conditions, it is open to employees to insist on large wage increases and it is often possible for employers to pass these on the cost to the consumer so maintaining their profit margins. This is the dilemma which confronts the country. If the prosperous economic conditions necessary to maintain full employment are exploited by trade unions and businessmen, price stability and full employment become incompatible. The solution lies in self-restraint in making wage claims and fixing profit margins and prices, so that total money incomes rise no faster than total output.
> (HMSO, 1956: 17)

The White Paper pointed out that between 1948 and 1955, 'while consumer prices rose by nearly one-third, both wages and salaries … increased by nearly two-thirds'. Yet at the same time, Britain's share of world trade, in terms of manufactured exports, had declined by more than five per cent since 1950, which not only reflected the diminishing international competitiveness of British goods and products, but also meant a deteriorating balance of payments position, as higher earnings were increasingly expended on imports. Put bluntly, 'exports are not increasing sufficiently to meet a growing import bill and to finance other external commitments. Such a situation must be corrected', for 'as a nation whose lasting prosperity depends on a high level of overseas trade, we simply cannot afford to allow excessive demand at home to undermine our competitiveness in world markets' (HMSO, 1956: 8, 9).

What has often been overlooked, however, is that *The Economic Implications of Full Employment* identified two particular problems which were likely to arise from the need to link wage increases to increased productivity. The first such problem was that some industries could more readily achieve higher productivity or increased output than others, in which case, the ensuing wage increases would exacerbate disparities and inequalities between different sectors of the economy. Sooner or later, the less productive industries would either find it difficult to recruit or retain staff, or their employees would seek compensatory catch-up pay increases to maintain relative parity with workers in other industries. To address this particular problem, it was suggested that those employed in more productive industries should be encouraged to forgo pay increases which directly matched their increased output, in favour of lower price rises, so that those employed in less productive industries would feel less compelled to seek large wage increases themselves. Indeed, the Chancellor deemed this to constitute 'the real essence of the White Paper' (NA CAB 129/78 C.P. (55) 173, Memorandum by the Chancellor of the Exchequer, Draft White Paper on The Implications of Full Employment, 15 November 1955).

The second particular problem which was likely to arise from the attempt to link pay increases more closely to increased productivity was that, in general, higher industrial output would largely be dependent on the introduction of new technology or working methods, which, in turn, would necessitate workers and trade unions abandoning restrictive practices, prompted by their fear of job losses. It was partly to overcome this potential problem that *The Economic Implications of Full Employment* reiterated the theme of co-partnership in industry which Ministers had patiently promoted since 1951, for it was asserted that:

> The healthy functioning of the economy and the progressive growth of its output depend also on co-operation within industry in maintaining an efficient and enlightened system of industrial relations. The relationship between management and workers which this implies is a vital but intangible factor which only they can only create by common effort. It demands a full and frank exchange of opinion and information at all levels between representatives who have confidence in each other's competence and integrity. If this confidence is achieved and maintained, the gain, in terms both of physical output and human relations, can be incalculable.
> (HMSO, 1956: 11)

However, rather unconvincingly, perhaps, the Chancellor insisted that the White Paper 'avoids – deliberately – any explicit appeal for restraint in the matter of wages', and concentrated instead on 'on the conditions which must be continuously fulfilled if we are to achieve our long-term objective of maintaining relative stability of prices as one essential factor in the maximum expansion of a balanced economy' (NA CAB 129/79, CP (55) 173, Memorandum by the Chancellor of the Exchequer, 'Draft White Paper on The Implications of Full Employment', 15 November 1955). Similarly, Anthony Eden recalled that the objective of *The Economic Implications of Full Employment* was to 'provide the background for a new approach to stabilize prices and prevent a perpetual upward spiral in wage claims and the cost of living'. As such, he echoed his Chancellor by insisting that: 'The purpose of the White Paper was not to appeal for restraint in making wage claims and fixing margins of profit, but to show the need for it' (Eden, 1960: 321, 325), although such insistence seems to have been an exercise in semantic sophistry, given that the White Paper clearly asserted that full employment and price stability were ultimately dependent on 'self-restraint in making wage claims … so that total money income rises no faster than total output' (HMSO, 1956: 11).

Nonetheless, the White Paper was not viewed by Ministers as a reversion to incomes policy *per se*, because free collective bargaining between employers and trade unions was to remain the primary means of conducting annual pay negotiations, but it was clearly hoped that those involved in pay negotiations would henceforth give due consideration to the wider economic context, particularly with regard to the likely impact of their own pay increases. The Cabinet was hoping that the trade unions could be persuaded that 'economic stability could not be achieved in conditions of full employment without some degree of restraint in industrial relations and wage claims' (NA CAB 128/30, C.M. (55) 39th conclusions, 3 November 1955). Eden himself certainly appeared confident that the trade unions would respond positively to Ministerial exhortations to moderate their pay claims if they could be convinced that the economic situation warranted it, for on 27 December 1955, he wrote to the Chancellor, Harold Macmillan, informing him that:

> the trade unions do understand that if our costs go on rising we shall inevitably price ourselves out of world markets and they will be the first to suffer. Therefore they will always lend a sympathetic ear to any doctrine aimed at avoiding this danger. If … we could call for restraint in dividends and expenditure generally, and produce an attractive savings programme, we should have a fair chance of enlisting their help in trying to keep wages steady over the next few years. We have simply got to do this somehow.
> (Quoted in Eden, 1960: 322–3)

In many respects, therefore, *The Economic Implications of Full Employment* was envisaged as a long-term educational vehicle, whereby it would be studied initially by 'informed opinion', possibly prompting 'correspondence in *The Times* and the *Manchester Guardian*', whereupon 'its influence could be expected to percolate downwards' to the wider public' (NA PREM 11/1402, Hooper to Eden, 21 November 1955), thereby ensuring that 'the basic argument of the White Paper gradually soaks through into the wider public consciousness by these less formal methods'. If this wider, indirect dissemination was attained, then 'the White paper will achieve its purpose, and it will not matter greatly if the text itself is read by relatively few people' (NA PREM 11/1402, Bridges to Pitblado, 14 September 1955). This long-term approach acquired even more resonance when Macmillan ruled out, on the grounds of wider acceptability and practicability, an immediate 'voluntary standstill' of prices and incomes (NA PREM 11/1402, Macmillan to Eden, 27 March 1956).

The Economic Implications of Full Employment reflected a continued Ministerial faith that the combined impact of public opinion, and Ministerial explanation of the economic facts of life, remained the most effective and practicable means of securing desirable changes in trade union behaviour and wage bargaining, rather than legislative restriction or statutory prescription. To this end, a 'popular version' of the White Paper, this entitled *Must Full Employment Mean Ever-Rising Prices?*, was to have been published simultaneously, but rather ironically, the publication of the 'popular version' was delayed for a few weeks by a strike at the printers.

Yet within two months of the publication of *The Economic Implications of Full Employment*, the Chancellor was expressing impatience that there were no discernible signs of a reduction in the upward pressure on wages, which was deemed to be fuelling relentless price increases, and seriously damaging international confidence in the British economy. As such, it was now felt that two further initiatives were needed in order to tackle this critical situation. Firstly, immediate talks were to be held between the Prime Minister, the Chancellor and the Minister of Labour, with the TUC and employers' representatives, to explain, in the plainest terms, the urgent need for them to restrain pay claims and price increases respectively. Secondly, the Government was to 'give a firm lead and stick to it', whereby it intended to keep price increases to a maximum of 2.5 per cent in those sectors of the economy over which it had direct responsibility, most notably the nationalised industries, with the clear expectation that wages in these sectors would similarly be constrained. It was hoped that such a stance would set an example to the rest of British industry, so that private sector employers would 'make a special effort to prevent increases in prices', and that 'organised labour will show the utmost moderation in its demands' (NA CAB 129/81, C.P. (56) 118, Memorandum by the Chancellor of the Exchequer, 'Wages and Prices', 9 May 1956). Some senior civil servants, though, were deeply sceptical about the efficacy of this approach (NA PREM 11/1402, Bligh to Eden, 2 May 1956), not least because the Chancellor gave little indication about what the Cabinet would do if faced by an 'excessive' pay claim by its own employees – would the Cabinet really 'sit out' a major, highly disruptive, strike by workers in a key nationalised industry or public sector?

In spite of this shift in its stance, the Government studiously avoided using the term 'incomes policy', for the Cabinet was not seeking to place curbs on free collective bargaining, but merely urging those involved in such pay negotiations to be much more mindful of the need for moderation. Ministers still hoped that exhortation and explanation concerning the dangers of a wage-price spiral, coupled with the weight of public opinion, would yield lower pay and price increases, albeit with Ministers additionally seeking to set an example in the public sector and nationalised industries. There was some acknowledgement, however, that if this call for restraint was not heeded, then it might become necessary, at a later stage, for Ministers 'to find some discreet way of assuring reliable employers that they would have the support of the Government' if they resisted trade union demands for unwarranted pay increases (NA PREM 11/1402, Note of meeting between the Prime Minister, Chancellor of the Exchequer, Minister of Labour and Lord Privy Seal, 2 May 1956), a pledge which was reiterated 18 months later, by which time Ministers had refused to provide extra cash to finance pay claims, backed by industrial action, in the NHS and on the railways (NA PREM 11/3841, Note of a meeting between the Chancellor, the Minister of Labour and the leaders of the three main employers' organisations, 13 November 1957). Nonetheless, while it was acknowledged that Ministers should reassure employers, in both the private sector and the nationalised industries, that the Government would 'not let them down' if they sought to resist pay claims, great care was also needed to avoid giving the trade unions 'any impression that the government and employers were getting together in preparation for a battle with organised labour' (NA PREM 11/1402, Macmillan to Eden, 28 May 1956).

The Cohen Council

However, by this time, it was not economic circumstances alone which fuelled Ministerial concern over trade unions and their wage claims. What compounded the Cabinet's consternation was the 1956 appointment of Frank Cousins as General Secretary of the TGWU. Widely viewed as a leading left-wing figure in the trade union movement, Cousins' elevation to the leadership of the TGWU threatened a less harmonious relationship between the Conservative Government and the trade unions, something which apparently dismayed many senior TUC officials just as much as Cabinet Ministers.

In his first speech to the TUC annual conference since becoming TGWU leader, Cousins railed against wage restraint and any hint of incomes policy, insisting instead 'there is no such thing in this country as a place where you can say "wage levels stop here" and that we ought to be content'. Accusing the government of having thrown down the gauntlet over the issue of wage restraint, Cousins declared that the trade unions ought 'not refuse to pick it up if they were compelled to' (TUC Congress Report 1956: 400). Cousins was speaking in support of a motion – unanimously passed – which insisted upon:

> the right of Labour to bargain on equal terms with Capital, and to use its bargaining strength to protect workers from the dislocations caused by an unplanned economy. It rejects proposals to recover control by wage restraint, and by using the nationalized industries as a drag-anchor.
> (TUC Conference Report 1956: 528)

Many commentators have since suggested that Cousins' elevation to the leadership of the TGWU heralded the end of the constructive and relatively cordial relationship which had prevailed between the Conservative Governments and the trade unions since 1951. However, one commentator has argued that:

> Even whilst Monckton was Minister of Labour, the trade union picture began to change. A new generation of union leaders clearly felt that more needed to be done by the leadership to reflect increasing shop-floor pressures which that were already making themselves felt, particularly in the car industry and in the docks. Frank Cousins' appointment in 1956 as General Secretary of the Transport & General Workers Union typified this trend.
> (Seldon, 1981:205; see also Barnes & Reid, 1980: 27–8; Kavanagh & Morris, 1989: 57; Taylor, 1993: 102)

For example, by the time that Cousins had been elected leader of the TGWU, Jim Campbell had become leader of the National Union of Railwaymen, and Alan Birch leader of the Union of Shop, Distributive and Allied Workers, the combined impact of which was to imbue the TUC's General Council with a somewhat different political complexion. Whilst not becoming immediately or overtly militant or confrontational, the TUC's General Council nonetheless evinced greater caution over 'collaboration' with the Conservative Governments, particularly in the sphere of wage restraint (Dorfman, 1973: 84–5).

Meanwhile, in spite of increasing concern among Ministers and in 'the City' over apparently inflationary wage increases, the Cabinet's dual commitment to voluntarism and free collective bargaining ensured that the option of introducing compulsory arbitration to resolve disputes over pay claims was also firmly rejected. Clearly, invoking compulsory arbitration would be incompatible with the voluntarist approach to industrial relations which senior Conservatives were intent on upholding, for such arbitration would entail the government effectively compelling the 'two sides of industry' to place themselves under the jurisdiction of a state-sponsored body, which would then judge the respective merits of pay claims by the trade unions, and pay offers by employers, in cases where disagreements led to strike action. This would *inter alia* clash with the principle and practice of free collective bargaining, for as Monckton pointed out, compulsory arbitration is 'not compatible with generally accepted ideas of free negotiation and free contract', and besides, 'is contrary to [the Conservative's] political pledges given on this subject'. Consequently, Ministers could do little more in this particular sphere of industrial relations than encourage 'industries voluntarily to include in their negotiating machinery provision for finality in a dispute by way of arbitration', and 'to encourage recourse to arbitration as a means of settling disputes which cannot be resolved by negotiation … This is accepted government policy' (NA CAB 134/1273, I.R. (55) 4, 'Memorandum by the Minister of Labour: Extension of the Principle of Arbitration', 22 July 1955. See also CPA, CRD 4/8/358, 'Compulsory Arbitration', 30 October 1958).

Moreover, compulsory arbitration would almost certainly embroil the government, directly or indirectly, in pay determination, for compulsory arbitration would invariably entail evaluating pay claims and awards in the context of criteria specified by government, or its appointees. It was also recognised that 'to introduce compulsory arbitration … would be in effect to outlaw the strike weapon, and to encourage unofficial, or lightning, strikes' (NA CAB 134/1273, I.R. (55) 1st Meeting, 22 June 1955).

One further potential problem with regard to such arbitration was that those involved in pay negotiations might be less inclined to seek a voluntary agreement or resolution to a dispute, due to a calculation that they might gain a more advantageous settlement if they allowed a dispute to go to compulsory arbitration. If this proved to be the case, then the introduction of a system of compulsory arbitration was likely to foster more intransigence among trade union negotiators, and make voluntary collective agreements rather more difficult to achieve. This, in turn, of course, would seriously jeopardise the wider efforts at securing more constructive and harmonious industrial relations, and of reducing conflict in the workplace.

The Government's lack of success in persuading the trade unions to practise greater wage restraint during the mid-1950s, even after the publication of *The Economic Implications of Full Employment*, coupled with the refusal to resort either to compulsory arbitration or deflation, prompted the Chancellor to pursue an institutional initiative, in the form of a body which would be charged with examining particular pay awards and price increases in the context of the Government's call for greater restraint and moderation by trade unions and employers. Yet although the Cabinet was supportive of such an initiative in principle, the potential composition of such a body was a source of mild disagreement among Ministers – partly reflecting views held by the 'two sides' of industry themselves – particularly because this, in turn, would have implications for the manner in which it fulfilled its remit. In short, there was debate over whether this proposed forum should comprise a small membership of just three senior figures who were independent of government, trade unions and employers, and whose impartiality would itself imbue their work with greater moral authority and legitimacy, or whether 'legitimacy' would best be ensured by inaugurating a somewhat larger body, which would include one or two trade union and employers' representatives. The latter, though, prompted concern that a larger, more 'representative' body would be prone to adopt a somewhat sectional approach; trade union representatives were highly unlikely to adjudge that a pay increase attained by fellow workers was excessive or unwarranted, just as employers' representatives would hardly be likely to denounce a price increase enacted by a fellow industrialist. Indeed, the trade union representative was likely to exonerate 'excessive' pay rises on the grounds that such increases were necessary due to rising prices, while employers would probably retort that rising prices were a natural response by companies coping with higher wage bills.

Thus it was that Cabinet discussions finally veered towards the smaller, independent prices and incomes review body, which also happened to be the option preferred, on balance, by Macmillan himself. Macleod also seemed to prefer this option, envisaging that 'such a body of some independent authority considering the general economic position of the country as affected by wages, profits and prices' would yield 'a useful effect on public opinion' (NA PREM 11/2878, Macleod to Macmillan, 27 April 1957). However, there was some concern that, due to its formal independence, such a body might feel at liberty to criticise the Government itself, possibly to the extent of suggesting an alternative economic approach to that being pursued by the Cabinet. It was therefore deemed vital that this imminent review body was given a clear and sharply-focused remit, whereupon it would 'not be authorised to make pronouncements or recommendations on broader issues of economic policy' (NA CAB 128/31 Part 2, C.C. (57) 43 conclusions, 29 May 1957).

What transpired from these Cabinet discussions was the Council on Prices, Productivity and Incomes, whose brief was:

> having regard to the desirability of full employment, and increasing standards of living, based on expanding production and reasonable stability of prices, to keep under review changes in prices, productivity, and the level of incomes (including wages, salaries and profits), and to report thereon from time to time.

Chaired by a judge, Lord Cohen (hence its more common appellation, the Cohen Council), and two economists, Sir Harold Howitt and Sir Dennis Robertson, the Council had no statutory powers, but, instead, was intended to constitute 'an authoritative and impartial body to consider the wider problem of wages policy in all branches of industry'. In this respect, the Cohen Council closely corresponded to a proposal put forward at about the same time by the Conservative Industrial Research Committee, which called for an independent body to consider the relationship between wages and inflation. The rationale for an independent body was that public opinion in general, and trade unions in particular, were more likely to accept any findings or recommendations 'if they were suggested by an obviously unbiased source' (CPA, ACP/57/53, 'Wages and Inflation 1957', 6 May 1957). A few Cabinet Ministers, including the Chancellor himself, had originally wanted the Council to stipulate a 'guiding light' for pay increases, but the Cabinet had rejected this proposal for fear that such a figure would automatically be viewed by the trade unions as an automatic or minimum target for pay claims.

However, the Cohen Council had no discernible impact on wage levels and pay increases, to the extent that one commentator claims that it proved 'harmless, producing a number of hand-wringing and ineffectual reports that exhorted trade unions and workers to restrain their wage demands' (Taylor, 1993: 104–5). Consequently, the Cohen Council failed to assuage Ministerial concern over the impact of wage increases on Britain's economy, but most of the Cabinet still refused to countenance either deflation, an incomes policy (least of all a statutory one) or trade union legislation, and as such, doggedly persevered with its dual strategy of voluntarism *vis-à-vis* industrial elations and exhortation with regard to the need for moderation in pay settlements. These two approaches were inextricably linked, as evinced by Iain Macleod's insistence, at the Conservative Party's 1956 conference, that 'the British system of free voluntary negotiation in industry with the minimum of government interference is best ... I believe firmly in the trade union system. These views are fundamental to my political beliefs and I have not altered in any way. Nor will I.'

Continuing to resist deflation, but adopting a slightly tougher stance

Macmillan, meanwhile, true to his 'one nation' inclinations, was also keen to dampen down demands for legislative action against the trade unions emanating from sections of the Conservative Party. Whilst acknowledging, by the autumn of 1957, 'a wide feeling among our own supporters that the thing to do is have a row with the trade unions', Macmillan insisted that there was no point in having such a row, partly because it would fatally poison the relationship between the Conservative Government and the trade unions, but also because it simply would not tackle the underlying economic problems with which Ministers were grappling.

Macmillan also ventured to suggest that in spite of their professed belief in socialism, trade union leaders were little different to any other merchant in a capitalist society; the commodity which they control is labour, he explained, so that if the demand for labour is greater than the supply, then like anyone in control of a commodity in such a situation, they can hardly do other than push up the price. Indeed, following this analysis, Macmillan ventured to suggest that trade union leaders had actually been very moderate and restrained in exploiting their economic opportunities, certainly more so than many other people would have been in similar circumstances. Yet this perspective also led Macmillan to conclude that whilst many trade union leaders would probably like to be able to help the Government, they would be unable to do so until the government itself stopped 'the flow of the inflationary tide. If we can even get slack water, or better still, a slight ebb, then their task would be much easier' (NA CAB 129/88, C (57)194, 1 September 1957).

Macmillan was apparently enunciating a cost-push theory of inflation, implying that trade union leaders were compelled by their members to seek wage increases which kept pace with increases in the cost of living; wage increases were, he seemed to imply, a response to inflation, rather than the cause of it. As such, an agreement with the trade unions to secure wage restraint would only become feasible once inflation had already been reduced, a perspective which contrasted starkly with the orthodox view at the time which presented wage restraint as the prerequisite of curbing inflation.

This orthodoxy was certainly enshrined in the case which Macmillan's successor at the Treasury, Peter Thorneycroft, enunciated to the Cabinet in early

September 1957, when he presented proposals for a deflationary package to curb inflation. The Chancellor argued that from January 1956 to August 1957, prices had risen by about 7 per cent, while weekly wage rates had increased by 11 per cent, with further high wage claims, and demands for shorter working hours 'which are thinly disguised wage claims', imminent. Acknowledging that 'economists may never agree whether we are suffering from a cost-push or demand inflation', he suggested that 'the essence may well be that we are suffering from both', but either way, these increases reflected 'the belief in the country that the Government will always make enough money available to support full, and indeed over-full employment'. As already noted, the concept of 'over-full employment' had previously been deployed by Robert Hall, and was now being invoked by Thorneycroft in support of his claim that, with unemployment at fractionally over one per cent of the labour force, 'we are running the economy above the pressure which it can stand'. Furthermore, it was now clear, the Chancellor argued, that a decade of 'appeals to employers and unions for restraint … has been shown to be ineffectual under existing conditions of demand'. The only solution, Thorneycroft concluded, was 'to limit the level of money available in the economy', primarily by cutting public expenditure (taking money out of the economy through higher taxes would not only be even more unpopular, it would inevitably be followed by compensatory pay increases, thereby compounding the problem it was intended to tackle), even though this would entail higher unemployment. Indeed, Thorneycroft was quite explicit that the current rate of just over one per cent was untenable, and therefore, Ministers 'must be prepared to see the rate rise to around three per cent', for otherwise. 'we have no hope of curbing inflation'. He concluded by insisting that whatever hardships might be caused by higher unemployment, they were 'preferable to the evils of continued inflation', not least because the latter had a far more deleterious effect on confidence in sterling among the international financial community (NA CAB 129/88, C. (57) 195, Memorandum by the Chancellor of the Exchequer, 'The Economic Situation', 7 September 1957).

Not surprisingly, such an explicit deflationary policy of increasing unemployment in order to reduce inflation and pay increases caused considerable consternation around the Cabinet table, with the Minister of Labour in particular expressing his concern about the political implications of such an increase. Furthermore, Macleod was doubtful whether the deliberate creation of unemployment would in itself weaken the bargaining power of the trade unions (NA CAB 128/31 Part One, C.M. (57) 31st conclusions, 10 September 1957). Macmillan too remained strongly averse to adopting a deflationary policy which would produce a significant increase in unemployment, so wedded was he to the principle of full employment and the need to avoid a return to the socio-economic conditions of the inter-war years. Yet he too was becoming ever more concerned at the increases in inflation and pay awards, to the extent that at a meeting of the Cabinet early in November, Macmillan presented a draft statement of the government's policy on wages, which declared that:

> while we have no intention of interfering with the established processes of collective bargaining ... we shall refuse to create more money to finance wage awards which are not matched by increased output. This is the cardinal proposition; and on this proposition we should rest.
> (NA CAB 129/90 C (57) 261, 8 November 1957)

This toughening of the government's stance was most evident during the summer of 1958, when it was faced by a seven-week strike over pay by London bus drivers. The Government refused to yield, preferring instead to make an example of the bus drivers which would serve as a warning to other groups of workers and trade unions, particularly those in the public sector (for a full account, see Shepherd, 1994: 134–42). In endorsing the Minister of Labour's tough stance against the London bus drivers, the Minister of Transport, Harold Watkinson, revealed that in the case of public sector pay claims, his approach was now to ensure that pay increases which were not covered by higher productivity or improved efficiency should ordinarily be funded through cuts in services and/or man-power, so as to avoid unwarranted increases in fares or other charges to passengers (NA CAB 129/91, C (58) 20, Memorandum by the Minister of Transport, 'London Bus Dispute, 23 January 1958). Macleod himself alluded to such an approach when he suggested that if the London bus drivers were to secure the increases demanded, then there ought to be 'some talk about economies'. After all, he wryly observed, 'the last three weeks have proved that we do not need as many buses in London as we have' (NA PREM 11/2512, Macleod to Macmillan, 22 May 1958).

In adopting this tougher stance, the Government was also responding to criticism by private sector employers during the previous two years that whilst Ministers urged management to stand firm against 'excessive' pay claims, those same Ministers did not evince similar firmness towards their own employees in the public sector and nationalised industries. However, what also prompted this willingness to confront the London bus drivers, was a Ministerial realisation that in this particular instance, Frank Cousins and the TGWU lacked wider TUC support: 'Cousins knows, of course, that this is a bad strike and that he can't win it' (NA PREM 11/2512, Macleod to Butler, 11 June 1958). Indeed, his biographer claimed that 20 years after the bus drivers' dispute, there remained 'a bitterness in Cousins' attitude towards some of his TUC colleagues for their behaviour at that period. He felt they let him down' (Goodman, 1979: 185). What this point also reiterates is that Cousins' elevation to the leadership of the TGWU did not immediately result in a more confrontational stance between the Conservative Government and the TUC leadership, even if the composition of the latter's General Council was changing with the passing of the erstwhile right-wing junta.

Meanwhile, in spite of this new-found willingness to stand firm in the face of strike action by public sector workers, Macmillan and most of his Cabinet colleagues were not willing to countenance a deflationary policy as a means of curbing either inflation or trade union power. Indeed, February 1958 had witnessed the resignation of the Chancellor, Peter Thorneycroft (replaced by Derek Heathcoat

Amory), and his two Treasury Ministers, Nigel Birch and Enoch Powell, due to the Cabinet's refusal to accept Thorneycroft's proposals for a deflationary budget. The Minister of Labour especially had been alarmed at the proposals which the Treasury wished to include in the forthcoming Budget, not only because Macleod shared Macmillan's abhorrence of unemployment, but also because Thorneycroft wanted to include some cuts in welfare expenditure, such as abolition of child allowance in respect of a second child. Not only were such measures anathema to Macleod's own One Nation philosophy, he also feared that such cuts would merely prompt trade union pressure for compensatory wage increases (NA CAB 128/31 Part Two, C.C. (57) 3rd conclusions, 5 January 1957).

Later the same year, at the Conservative Party's annual conference, Macleod reiterated that: 'We do not believe in a national wages policy, nor do we believe in a wage freeze.' He emphasised that whilst Ministers had a duty to point out the consequences of excessive pay awards, the Government could not compel the trade unions and their members to act more responsibly, nor should it endeavour to do so. Instead, Macleod declared that 'only in a partnership independent of politics between the great partners – government, trade unions and employers – was there any real lasting hope for good, sound industrial relations'. This approach had effectively been endorsed by the Cabinet committee on wages policy, for this too had been unable to identify any viable alternative to the Government's existing approach to securing voluntary restraint, whereby great reliance continued to be placed on education and exhortation. Certainly the option of introducing a wage freeze was dismissed, on the grounds that it 'might provoke the unions to a trial of strength', while the concept of a 'guiding light' for pay increases was again dismissed on the grounds that any such specified figure was likely to 'become the minimum from which the normal bargaining processes would begin'.

With deflation and trade union legislation also continuing to be ruled out as viable policy options, the Cabinet was left with little effective choice but to continue with the policy of urging moderation and restraint concerning wage increases, with Ministers using the public sector as a means of setting an example to employers and employees in the private sector, while also hoping that the economic facts provided by the Cohen Council would serve to persuade the trade unions of the need for more responsible pay bargaining and wage settlements. Such a policy was, however, acknowledged to be 'rather negative and lacking in leadership', with the Chancellor unable to conceal his disappointment at the timidity of this approach (NA CAB 134/2573, 'Wages Policy', February 1959; NA PREM 11/2878, Amory to Macmillan, 23 February 1959. See also NA CAB 128/32 Pt 1, C.C. (58) 24th conclusions, 18 March 1958).

By the end of the decade, though, this approach was itself increasingly being called into question, as various economic indicators revealed the inadequacy of relying almost entirely on voluntary wage restraint through Ministerial exhortation. As Table 4.1 illustrated, by 1959, the increase in earnings had more than doubled from the previous year, rising from an average increase of 2.3 per cent in 1958 to 5.1 per cent in 1959, yet during the same period, price increases had fallen from 3.1 per cent to a mere 0.5 per cent. This, of course, rather undermined the view that wage increases tended merely to follow the upward trajectory in prices, which was also the argument often advanced by the trade unions themselves in defence of their pay claims. The consequent Ministerial concern over these trends, which was wholly shared among both the domestic and the international financial communities, was compounded by Britain's deteriorating balance of payments situation, as higher earnings, unmatched by corresponding increases in industrial output and productivity, yielded a concomitant increase in imports at the expense of exports. Between 1951 and 1960, exports of goods and services increased overall by 8.1 per cent, whereas imports of goods and services during the same period rose by 12.7 per cent, and between 1958 and 1959, the increase in imports virtually doubled.

In the context of such figures, there was a warning that the 'wage situation is potentially explosive', and as such, it was deemed essential that Ministers explain more forcefully than hitherto the need for pay moderation. However, this would raise the awkward question of what would constitute 'a reasonable level for wage settlements' – in effect, a 'guiding light' which Ministers had hitherto refrained from – whereupon a maximum figure of three per cent was cautiously countenanced by Treasury officials (NA T. 234/669, Stevenson to Padmore, 27 October 1959).

Such concern over seemingly inexorable pay increases also raised questions about the efficacy of the Cohen Council, to the extent that its abolition was occasionally mooted, less than two years after it had been established. Indeed, upon receiving, from the Chancellor, a summary of the Council's second report, in the summer of 1958, Harold Macmillan returned it with a hand-written annotation, pointedly asking: 'Is this Committee going on indefinitely? Does it perform any useful function?' This prompted officials discreetly to suggest that the Chancellor ought 'to talk to the Prime Minister about Cohenism' (NA PREM 11/3841, Bishop to Maude, 25 August 1958), while the Chancellor himself suggested to the Prime Minister that perhaps they ought to 'allow a short time for the digestion of the Council's Second Report before we consider the future of the Council' (NA PREM 11/3841, Heathcoat Amory to Macmillan, 29 August 1958). Just six months later, Macmillan again suggested to Amory that the Cohen Council could readily be abolished, following Lord Cohen's recent retirement, adding waspishly that the Chancellor could claim credit for having 'destroyed the C.I.C. with all its octogenarians, and the Three Wise Men, with all their platitudes. A little ceremony might then be held, at which Mr Thorneycroft, returned from his world tour, could preach the funeral oration' (NA PREM 11/3841, Macmillan to Amory, 10 February 1959).

Yet the Treasury was evidently more enamoured with the Council than the Prime Minister, for it was a further two years – and a third and fourth report – before it was finally disbanded, albeit only to be superseded by a National Incomes Commission. In the meantime, Ministers continued to exhort the trade unions to exercise restraint and responsibility in pay bargaining, thereby hoping, albeit with increasing desperation, that the Conservative Government – re-elected for a third consecutive term in 1959 – would be able to continue avoiding recourse to the three alternative policy options of deflation, incomes policy and trade union legislation.

Conclusion

Having entered Office in 1951 committed to free collective bargaining, the Conservative leadership became increasingly concerned about the extent to which full employment served to increase the trade unions' strength in negotiating higher pay. Although the vast majority of Ministers remained committed to maintaining full employment – rather than reverting to a policy of deflation and higher unemployment to reduce excess demand in the domestic economy and dampen down wage increases – their concerns about inflation, and cognizance of growing anxiety among the international financial community about the state of the British economy, meant that the Conservative leadership became increasingly anxious to educate the trade unions and their members with regard to the need for moderation in pay bargaining.

This emphasis on education as a means of securing more responsible behaviour by the trade unions neatly accorded with much of the more general voluntarist industrial relations strategy maintained throughout the 1950s, whereby Ministerial exhortation and encouragement were viewed as the most constructive and practicable means of securing desirable changes in trade union behaviour: jaw-jaw was better than class war, it was widely assumed, and this perspective similarly underpinned the stance of most Conservative Ministers with regard to eliciting wage restraint as the 1950s progressed. Such an approach was also the only viable alternative available to the Cabinet, because the refusal to countenance deflation and higher unemployment was accompanied by a similar unwillingness either to impose a formal or statutory incomes policy, or to invoke trade union legislation to curb the bargaining power of organised labour.

Nonetheless, during the latter half of the 1950s, the Conservatives' commitment to free collective bargaining was clearly being placed under increasing strain, and there was a growing urgency, occasionally bordering on desperation and exasperation, in Ministerial exhortations to the trade unions about the need for pay restraint and responsibility. Indeed, it was during this period that we can see the antecedents of the incomes policies which were subsequently to become a general tool of economic management throughout most of the 1960s and 1970s. The 1956 White Paper, *The Economic Implications of Full Employment*, the following year's establishment of the (Cohen) Council on Prices, Productivity and Incomes, and the Government's emerging willingness, as evinced in 1958, to 'stand firm' when faced with pay claims backed by strike action in parts of the public sector, can all be viewed, with the historian's benefit of hindsight, as the first steps on the road towards a more formal incomes policy, even if few realised at the time that this was the direction in which they were now heading.

Chapter 5

Voluntarism under Strain, 1960–1964

From 1960 onwards, Conservative proponents of voluntarism found themselves increasingly on the defensive in the Party. By the start of the decade, there was a growing realisation that Britain was experiencing relative economic decline, with a number of other industrial countries achieving higher rates of productivity and faster rates of growth, as was the fledgling European Economic Community (EEC), which Britain had declined to join when it was inaugurated in 1957. Moreover, Britain's share of world trade in manufactured exports, having been 33 per cent in 1900, had declined to 16.5 per cent by 1960. Cognizance of this relative economic decline, and the sluggish performance of the British economy overall, increased anxiety in the Conservative Party over the 'irresponsible' behaviour of the trade unions, and the damaging impact on industry and the economy of industrial conflict and disruption, as well as union resistance to the introduction of new working methods and technology, due to an understandable concern about potential job losses.

Nor were such concerns and criticisms confined to the Conservative Party. Several books by respected journalists and academic commentators during the opening years of the new decade painted an unflattering picture of Britain's trade unions. Among these was the industrial editor of *The Financial Times*, Michael Shanks, whose book *The Stagnant Society* accused the trade unions of 'failing to adjust themselves to the changing patterns of industry and society', thereby leaving them with 'an increasingly dated, "period" flavour' whereby the 'smell of the music hall and the pawnshop clings to them … trapped among the slogans and banners of the past' (Shanks, 1961: 44). The same year heralded the publication of *What's Wrong with the Unions?*, written by Eric Wigham, the labour editor of *The Times*. Part of his answer to the book's title was that 'the [trade union] movement as a whole has lost its drive and sense of direction', as a result of which, 'serious weaknesses and occasional abuses have developed unchecked' (Wigham, 1961: 196).

Another less than complimentary critique of contemporary British trade unionism and industrial relations was also published in 1961, by the new Organisation for European Economic Co-operation (which subsequently became the Organisation for Economic Co-operation and Development – OECD). Its report, on *The Problem of Rising Prices*, singled out the trade unions for some of the blame, for the 'haphazard fragmentation of collective bargaining and the weakness of central organisation has facilitated competitive bidding between unions' (OECD, 1961: 8).

Four other discrete developments or trends compounded this growing concern about 'the trade union problem' during the early 1960s, and thereby placed the

Conservative leadership's voluntarist industrial relations policy under increasing strain. Firstly, it was only in 1961 that the Ministry of Labour began formally categorising strikes when compiling industrial relations statistics, whereupon it was confirmed that 95 per cent of strikes were unofficial. This, of course, naturally increased the pressure on Ministers to legislate against such strikes, and thereby strengthen the authority of official or 'responsible' trade union leaders over their rank-and-file members and often more militant shop stewards on the factory floor.

Secondly, there was a growing recognition that the increasing size, scale and increasing interdependence of modern British industry and companies was such that the impact of industrial action was often greater then ever before: a relatively small number of strikes – or even a relatively small number of workers on strike – could cause widespread industrial disruption and damage, with the repercussions spreading far and wide. This was particularly true with regard to unofficial or 'wildcat' strikes, for by very definition, these were usually impromptu, and thus difficult to predict and prepare for. Consequently, their impact, and the damage thereby wreaked on British industry, was often much greater, which was precisely why militants in the trade unions were deemed to be so enamoured with such strikes (CPA, ACP (63) 103, John Hare, 'Industrial Relations – Unofficial Strikes', 28 January 1963).

As Table 5.1 illustrates, apart from 1963, the first half of the 1960s was characterised by a higher number of strikes each year than in 1959 – 2,686 in 1961, compared to 2,093 in 1959, for example – and a corresponding increase in the number of workers involved. Thus, whereas in 1959, strikes had involved 646,000 workers, over 800,000 were involved in industrial stoppages in both 1960 and 1964.

Table 5.1   Strikes commencing in each year, 1959–64

Year	Strikes commencing in year	Workers involved (000s)	Working days lost (000s)
1959	2,093	646	5,270
1960	2,832	819	3,024
1961	2,686	779	3,046
1962	2,449	4,423	5,798
1963	2,068	593	1,755
1964	2,524	883	2,277

Source: Duncan, McCarthy and Redman, 1983: 174, Table 6.1.

Of course, the final column in Table 5.1 indicates that apart from 1962, the number of working days lost in each year was actually considerably less than in 1959, but this is largely attributed to the relatively short duration of most strikes. This, in turn, largely derived from the incidence of 'wildcat' and unofficial strikes which were often ended quickly, but whose very unpredictability and relative frequency, as just noted, rendered them especially problematic.

However, as we will note in this chapter, growing concern about the incidence of such strikes did not make it any easier to devise an acceptable or practicable solution. Indeed, although concern over strikes – particularly of these unofficial and 'wildcat' variants – increased during the early 1960s, to the extent that even the most conciliatory senior Conservatives became increasingly exasperated, no legislation was enacted to curb them or punish those responsible. Instead, Ministers who contemplated this problem generally remained unconvinced that legislation would prove effective in yielding a solution. As ever, questions were raised about what sanctions could feasibly be invoked if anti-strike legislation was defied? Mass imprisonment of thousands, yet alone millions, of trade unionists was not a practicable sanction, however much it might emotionally gratify the more right-wing elements on the Conservative backbenches and among constituency activists, whose visceral hatred of trade unions was seemingly vindicated by the latter's growing 'irresponsibility' during the early 1960s, when they became, according to Robert Taylor, 'scapegoats of national decline' (Taylor, 1993: 1–15).

Nonetheless, most Ministers remained wedded to the view that any threat, or even hint, of punitive legislation against the trade unions would alienate moderate trade unionists, whose co-operation was more necessary than ever. Consequently, much of the period covered by this chapter entailed senior Ministers seeking to incorporate trade union leaders into national-level economic partnership and policy-making forums, in the increasingly desperate hope that this would help them to appreciate the problems facing the British economy, and thus of the need for a corresponding change in trade union behaviour.

Another important consequence of the increasing size and scale of British industry was a corresponding increase in the size of trade unions themselves; as Table 5.2 shows, their overall number declined slightly, but the number of workers who belonged to a trade union continually increased, resulting in gradually fewer, but larger, trade unions. The extent to which the membership of particular trade unions was increasing during this period is highlighted in Table 5.3. For example, USDAW, ETU and NUPE all saw their membership more than double between 1945 and 1963.

Table 5.2   Number of trade unions and total trade union membership 1959–63

Year	Number of trade unions	Total union membership (000s)
1959	668	9,623
1960	664	9,835
1961	646	9,916
1962	626	10,014
1963	607	10,067

Source: Taylor, 1993: 381.

Table 5.3   Membership of 10 largest trade unions, 1945 and 1963

1945		1963	
Trade union	**Membership**	**Trade union**	**Membership**
TGWU	815,675	TGWU	1,373,560
AEU	635,884	AEU	980,639
NUM	533,265	NUGMW	781,940
NUGMW	475,463	NUM	501,643
NUR	360,346	USDAW	354,701
ASW	176,000	NUR	282,801
NUDAW	168,328	ETU	271,912
ETU	127,819	NUPE	230,000
UPW	98,720	ASW	191,587
NUAW	95,200	UPW	171.200

Source: TUC Reports 1946 and 1964; Campbell, Fishman and McIlroy, 1999: 104.

Meanwhile, of the three largest trade unions in 1963, the TGWU had increased in size by 68 per cent since 1945, while the NUGMW had enjoyed a 64 per cent increase in membership, and the AEU had grown by 54 per cent. The only key trade union to suffer a decline between 1945 and 1963 was the NUM, whose membership fell by 6 per cent, reflecting the fact that the contraction of Britain's coal industry started long before the full-scale assault unleashed by the Thatcher Governments in the mid-1980s.

One other consequence of the increasing size of British industry and *pari passu* the increased membership of key trade unions was the corresponding organisational gulf which emerged or widened between trade union members and workers on the factory floor, and the full-time national-level leadership in London. For many such rank-and-file trade union members, the image of their leaders regularly meeting with, or even being wined-and-dined by, senior Conservative Ministers signified, not so much the vital importance of their unions and leaders, and how far the unions had travelled during the twentieth century, from repression to reverence, but, rather, how remote and out-of-touch their union leaders had become, especially when the outcome of such 'collaboration' was, increasingly, demands for wage restraint (discussed in the next chapter), or an exhortation to embrace new technology and working practices. It was this institutional gulf, between ordinary trade union members and their increasingly remote union leaders in larger trade unions, which largely facilitated the emergence, or increased prominence, of local union officials and shop stewards, whose very proximity and visibility enabled them to convince many of their fellow workers that they were promoting or defending their material interests on a daily basis. Hence the increase in unofficial strikes, and *inter alia* the growing problem of 'wage drift', also discussed in the next chapter.

However, the third development which exacerbated the 'trade union problem' for Conservative Ministers from the late 1950s onwards was the discernible change in the character of Britain's union leadership, which posed increasing problems for the Cabinet's voluntarist approach to trade unionism and industrial relations. As noted in the previous chapter, the TUC's 'right-wing junta' was being replaced by a younger and/or more left-wing cohort of union leaders – with Frank Cousins' election to the TGWU's leadership in March 1956 symbolising this transition – who were much less inclined to 'collaborate' with Conservative Ministers. However, this did not necessarily mean that this new cohort immediately or consistently sought confrontation with the Conservatives, but it did make it difficult for Ministers to secure the same degree of collegiality with some of the TUC leadership that they had achieved previously.

Fourthly, and more specifically, in the spring of 1961, there were new allegations of ballot-rigging by Communists, in elections held by the Electrical Trade Union (ETU), and this lent a new dimension to Conservative debates about the issue of trade union ballots. In particular, to the previous intra-party discussions about whether ballots ought to be introduced prior to strike action was now added a debate about the conduct of those ballots which already existed for the election of trade union officials, and whether these ought to be subject to some form of official regulation.

It was in the context of these developments that a growing number of Conservatives became convinced that their Party's leadership had pursued a voluntarist industrial relations strategy too far for too long, and that 'a new Tory initiative in industrial relations' was needed (CPA, ACP 3/8 (62) 94, 'A Tory Look at Industrial Relations', 29 January 1962. See also CPA, ACP 3/10 (63) 105, 'Report of the Industrial Relations Committee', 8 May 1963), with one Conservative MP alluding to the 'fears of those who believe that the Tory party is afraid of the Trade-union movement' (CPA, CCO 4/7433, Van Straubenzee to Macleod, 8 April 1963).

By this time, even the arch-conciliator, Harold Macmillan, while still fully determined to secure closer partnership, both between management and trade unions, and, more generally, between the state and industry, was unable to conceal his growing despair and frustration with the trade unions (See, for example: Macmillan, 1972: 375; Macmillan, 1973: 66). On one occasion, having been presented with a paper from the Cabinet Secretary, which reported the Minister of Labour's view that certain proposed industrial relations initiatives would 'take a little time', Macmillan ruefully added his own hand-written observation: 'It might take a life-time' (NA PREM 11/3841, Brook to Macmillan, 1 August 1961).

During the early 1960s, many senior Conservatives doubtless shared the feelings of Iain Macleod, who admitted that he 'felt frankly schizophrenic' about what the Party should do *vis-à-vis* the trade unions. He was torn between recognition that some kind of legislative action was needed and anxiety about the likely repercussions, for legislation could fuel union hostility towards the Conservative Party, and consequently undermine the efforts of the previous ten years to promote conciliation and co-partnership (CPA, ACP 2/2/50, 2 May 1962). Such anxiety was evidently shared by Ray Mawby, a former shop steward and president of the Conservative Trade Unionists Advisory Committee, who felt compelled to warn: 'Legislation in the main is negative and deters rather than initiates action', so that 'a spate of legislation could easily do irreparable damage' (CPA, CRD 2/7/7 IRC 62.16, 'Industrial Relations Committee – Notes for Mr Ray Mawby', 6 December 1962).

In response to the developments noted above, and the growing frustration at all levels of the Conservative Party, the early 1960s witnessed the Conservative Government pursue several analytically discrete, but often inter-linked, responses in a last-ditch attempt at sustaining the voluntarist industrial relations strategy, most notably: to reject the increasing demands for trade union ballots, either for the election of leaders or prior to strike action, by reiterating the problems of practicability which compulsory ballots would engender; to re-iterate the 'human relations' perspective; establish a tripartite body, the National Economic Development Council, to involve trade union leaders more closely and routinely in senior discussions about economic issues; consider the establishment of a Royal Commission on trade union law.

Continuing to reject compulsory ballots

To the perennial Conservative backbench and annual conference call for the introduction of statutory strike ballots were now added vociferous demands for secret ballots for trade union leadership elections. Although there had previously been calls for trade union leaders to be elected in this manner, the issue acquired particular resonance in 1961, in response to new allegations about ballot-rigging by Communists in the Electrical Trades Union (ETU). When concern about Communist involvement in ETU elections had arisen back in 1957, Ministers had, in accordance with the voluntarist strategy, decided against government intervention. Instead, it was anticipated that the TUC would take appropriate action to prevent any unconstitutional activity by Communists in the ETU, an expectation conveyed to senior members of the TUC's General Council when they had a private meeting with the then Minister of Labour, Ian Macleod, to discuss the developing problem (NA PREM 11/3570, Trend to Macmillan, 19 December 1957; Turner to Bishop, 19 December 1957). However, when the issue re-emerged in 1961, the furore was such that Ministers did discuss the desirability or feasibility of introducing legislation to regulate trade union elections: 'If we are ever to do anything about Trade Unions, there could hardly be a better opportunity than at the end of this case' (NA PREM 3570, R. B. [full name not given, but a senior official in the Law Officers Department] to Macmillan, 26 April 1961).

Certainly, John Hare was initially inclined towards legislative action, particularly after a meeting with the TUC's General Secretary, George Woodcock, revealed that TUC was unlikely to take action itself in response to the ETU ballot-rigging episode, partly because as a federal body, the TUC had limited authority over individual affiliated unions, and also because of its insistence that the ETU case was a one-off (in spite of this being the second such case in four years!), and so hardly warranted a new policy or initiative, either by the TUC itself or the Government. Hare adjudged the TUC's stance to be unacceptably complacent, though, and therefore mooted three possible options, although these were not mutually exclusive: model rules to govern the conduct of trade union elections; an independent body to conduct union elections; and new powers for trade unionists to seek redress of grievances when they believed that a union ballot had breached election rules.

However, voluntarism once again prevailed, because there emerged a general acceptance by Ministers that it would be inappropriate for them to impose model rules on the trade unions. Any attempt to do so would be widely viewed by the trade unions as direct governmental interference in their internal affairs; the adoption of model rules could only really be effected by the trade unions themselves, with Ministers confining themselves, as ever, to encouragement and exhortation.

The other two options, though, were certainly regarded as more feasible, with Hare impressed by both of them. As such, it was intimated that unless the TUC showed greater readiness to tackle the problems itself, the existing Registrar of Friendly Societies might have its powers and remit extended, enabling it to conduct ballots for those trade unions which requested it. This would avoid compulsion or prescriptive measures against the trade unions, for they themselves would decide whether or not to avail themselves of the Registrar's services when a ballot was being held to elect a new leader or endorse strike action. Of course, many trade unions might decide not to make use of the Registrar's services for this purpose, which would then leave unchecked the problem of irregularities in the conduct of union elections. This, though, is where the third option would be applicable and highly attractive, namely providing redress of grievances for trade union members who had grounds for believing that a ballot had not been conducted fairly and constitutionally. Again, it was envisaged that the Registrar of Friendly Societies would be the most appropriate institution, whereupon it would adjudicate in cases where complaints were lodged about the conduct of a trade union election, including alleged breaches of a unions own election rules. Although Hare was in favour of the Registrar of Friendly Societies playing both roles – organiser and conductor of trade union ballots and subsequent provider of redress of grievances – the Attorney-General, Sir Reginald Manningham-Buller, believed that the latter function ought to remain a matter for the courts. Certainly, there was some concern that if the Registrar performed both roles, a conflict of interest might arise if complaints were lodged about the conduct of a trade union ballot which the Registrar had itself been conducting; it would effectively be investigating a case against itself.

Yet Hare still hoped that the TUC could be persuaded to take appropriate action itself, on a voluntary basis, thereby reducing the growing Party pressure on him and the Government to take more decisive action in the wake of the ETU case. Although Hare was willing to contemplate these two reforms, he continued to maintain that the 'best solution would be for the TUC to deal with the problem themselves … if the unions can take effective action to prevent breaches of their election rules, this would be the most satisfactory solution' (NA PREM 11/3570, Hare to Macmillan, 14 July 1961), whereupon the Government could maintain its voluntarist stance with regard to trade unionism and industrial relations. Indeed if the TUC could be persuaded to take appropriate action, then Ministers would be able to cite this as evidence of the efficacy of voluntarism, and as vindication of their conciliatory approach to organised labour.

There still remained considerable anxiety about announcing any Government intention to legislate, for fear of offending the TUC, and thereby harming 'any chance of the government securing their co-operation in our current economic difficulties'. Once again, it was suggested that 'the TUC must be given full opportunity to consider their position first'. Moreover, the Cabinet Secretary was advising the Prime Minister that even if the Cabinet did decide to endorse legislative action in response to unwillingness by the TUC to take remedial action itself, not only was there insufficient time in the remainder of the current parliamentary session, 'there seems at present very little prospect of fitting legislation into the programme for next session: not a few important Bills have already been already been squeezed out' (NA PREM 11/3570, Brook to Macmillan, 12 July 1961, 19 July 1961, 4 October 1961). The Cabinet Secretary's emphasis on the practical and political difficulties of enacting trade union legislation in response to the ETU case certainly seemed to constitute an attempt to persuade the Prime Minister that his Government would be wise to adhere to the extant voluntarist stance for the foreseeable future.

It was certainly rather ironic that the economic circumstances of the early 1960s which were partly fuelling Conservative demands for trade union reform were then cited as a further reason why it would be unwise to invoke such legislation at that time. However, it was also the case that the TUC's general secretary, George Woodcock, was fully cognizant of growing concerns over aspects of trade union behaviour, of which the ballot-rigging episode provided a particularly unsavoury example, and was himself eager to secure more 'responsible' trade unionism, this to be pursued via an internal review conducted under the auspices of the TUC. In this context, Conservative Ministers recognised that any action or announcement on their part might well undermine Woodcock's own stance, and thereby probably destroy the last vestiges of voluntarism. Consequently, John Hare, was inclined merely to include a rather anodyne passage in the Queen's Speech for the 1961–62 parliamentary Session, blithely declaring that: 'My government are examining the possibility of providing easier redress for breaches of trade union election rules' (CAB 128/35 Part Two, C.C. (61) 54th conclusions, 9 October 1961), a pledge whose blandness caused some disquiet in Whitehall, where it was described as 'not very satisfactory' (NA PREM 11/3570, Brook to Macmillan', 4 October 1961).

Ultimately, Ministers were left adhering – albeit with increasingly desperation – to the voluntarist approach which they had repeatedly advocated since the late 1940s, and which therefore ruled out legislative measures to stipulate how or when trade unions should conduct ballots. With regard to curbing industrial stoppages, the Cabinet's official stance remained that 'legislation to prevent strikes would be unsuccessful, whether this is concerned with compulsory arbitration, secret ballots or a "cooling-off" period'. Compulsory arbitration, which effectively constituted a curb on strike action, was deemed incompatible with free collective bargaining and trade union independence from the state, and would not actually reduce unofficial strikes, while compulsory strike ballots would not address the apathy of many ordinary trade unionists who played no part in their unions' affairs, and which thereby enabled militants to acquire influence and power out of all proportion to their actual numbers. Meanwhile, a 'cooling-off' period, to enable an inquiry to be conducted prior to strike action, was likely to result in both sides adopting more entrenched positions, in the hope of obtaining a favourable recommendation (NA PREM 11/3570, Bishop to Macmillan, 17 May 1961).

The voluntarist perspective was also endorsed by a Conservative Party (as opposed to Ministerial) committee, established by Rab Butler in May 1962, to provide the extra-parliamentary Party with an opportunity to examine the problems pertaining to industrial relations and trade unionism. If the underlying rationale was to enable the wider Conservative Party to appreciate more fully the political and practical difficulties of devising or enacting industrial relations legislation, then Butler's astute initiative proved a success, for after 12 months of discussions and deliberation, the committee merely reiterated the practical difficulties which would arise from any attempt to outlaw unofficial strikes or impose statutory ballots prior to strike action. It was also reiterated that legislation to make pre-strike ballots mandatory would raise the awkward issue of ballots to call off a strike (CPA, CRD 2/7/17, Stephen Abbott, 'The 'Quid Pro Quo', 10 July 1962; CRD 2/7/17, Butler to Whitelaw, 29 May 1963).

Furthermore, the Party's industrial relations committee noted that even if legislation was introduced to prohibit strikes which had not been endorsed by a prior ballot, this would mean that only stoppages called by a trade union would be deemed lawful, thereby effectively denying non-trade unionists the right to engage in industrial action, or oblige them to join a trade union against their wishes in order to enjoy legal protection – a total absurdity. As to the perennial demand that trade union immunities should be reduced by amending the 1906 Trade Disputes Act, it was argued that, if trade unions were rendered liable for the unofficial action of some of their members, this would 'leave the door wide open for a small group of militant extremists to bring about the financial collapse of any trade union – perhaps those under moderate control'. Consequently, the committee concluded that legislation would be 'inappropriate and unenforceable' (CPA, ACP 3/10 (63) 105, 'Report of the Industrial Relations Committee', 8 May 1963), thereby effectively endorsing the classic voluntarist tenet that 'the state by itself cannot enforce better industrial relations'. Instead, 'the surest way to progress is through the encouragement of responsibility within industry itself' (CPA, CRD 2/7/7, 'Industrial Change – The Human Aspect', 15 July 1963).

This perspective was further reiterated when John Hare himself warned that:

> Legislation would cut across the present policy of trying to bring about a general improvement in industrial relations on a voluntary basis ... it would end the prospect of further progress [and] cause a head-on collision with the

trade union movement. It might lead them to withhold their co-operation over the whole field of relations with the government.
(CPA, ACP 3/10/63–103, 'Industrial Relations – Unofficial Strikes', 28 January 1963)

Consequently, the Conservative leadership continued to insist that: 'The problem of dealing with unofficial action … must be tackled, in the first instance, by the unions and employers directly concerned … the right way to get the improvements we want to see in our industrial relations is to continue … on these lines' (NA CAB 124/1618, Hare to Hailsham, 18 January 1961), and as such: 'The present government have no intention of putting the clock back by legislating against strikes in peacetime' (CPA, CRD 2/7/3, 'Note on Trade Unions and Unofficial Strikes', 30 May 1962).

Ironically, perhaps, it was subsequently reported that some moderate trade union leaders were actually 'concerned to the point of bitterness' over the Government's refusal to tackle unofficial strikes, and were equally dismayed that the Ministry of Labour 'is inclined often to promote settlements rather than face a showdown'. It was suggested that in both instances, 'the position of those Union leaders who hold out against unofficial strikes is undermined', while the hand of trade union militants promoting unofficial strikes is strengthened (NA PREM 11/4871, Shawcross to Douglas-Home, 9 March 1964). However, it was not until the Conservative Party was in Opposition from 1964 to 1970, that this perspective seemed to acquire credence among the Party leadership, whereupon the emphasis of Conservative industrial relations policy shifted from voluntarism to that of strengthening the authority of official trade union leaders, and instilling greater order into industrial relations by tackling unofficial strikes, through legislative measures.

In the meantime, senior Conservatives again sought to address the incidence of strikes, just as they had done at various junctures in the 1950s, by placing them in a more favourable comparative context. For example, it was pointed out that since the Conservatives had been returned to Office in 1951, Britain had lost fewer working days due to strike action than any other major industrial nation, apart from West Germany. Furthermore, it was claimed that in the 15 years since the end of the Second World War, the number of working days lost due to strike action was only about 11 per cent of the number of days similarly lost in the same period of time after the First World War, and that out of a total work force of 23 million, the incidence of strikes was equivalent to one day every nine years for the average worker – much less than the working days and industrial production lost due to industrial injuries or illness.

It was also noted that the majority of strikes were confined to four main industries, namely coal-mining, engineering, construction, and the car industry, which collectively employed about seven per cent of the working population: 'the undistorted picture, relatively speaking, is not unfavourable' (CPA, ACP (62) 94, Edward Brown, John Page and Paul Dean, 'A Tory Look at Industrial Relations',

29 January 1962; see also CPA, CRD 2/7/3, 'Note on Trade Union and Unofficial Strikes', 30 May 1962; CPA, CCO 4/9/433, Conservative Industrial Department, 'Strikes in the UK', 25 April 1963). Indeed, it was noted that 'more days of work are lost through the common cold than in industrial disputes', which clearly implied that 'very little actual trouble arises and relations between management and employees are friendly and pacific' (Amory, 1960: 5).

New concern over restrictive practices

In the meantime, another concern emerged, or, rather, became more pronounced during the early 1960s, namely that of restrictive practices. Although not in itself a new phenomenon, it did attract greater attention in the early 1960s, because it was increasingly viewed as an impediment to the modernisation of industry, which was itself deemed a vital prerequisite of reversing Britain's relative economic decline and thereby reviving the competitiveness of the British economy. If some Conservatives had previously criticised the trade unions for harbouring radicals and Communists, then this period now increasingly heard the allegation that the unions were too conservative and resistant to change. This alleged conservatism was generally attributed to a misguided attempt at defending their members' jobs from the perceived threat posed by industrial change and modernisation, often in the guise of automation and other innovations involving technology. This, after all, was a period when Britain was undergoing a technological 'revolution', sometimes drawing comparisons to the original 1780–1850 industrial revolution in its importance and impact, and this inevitably caused considerable anxiety among those workers who feared that their jobs would become obsolete. Such fear often seemed to underpin trade union attempts at obstructing industrial modernisation, either by resisting technological innovations in the workplace, or challenging the introduction of new working practices, both of which were viewed as a threat to the continued employment or skills and status of their members.

The Conservative leadership's 'human relations' perspective was able to empathise with this form of job insecurity, for it could explicate how such workers often felt that they were mere units of production who were increasingly expendable, or were, quite literally, becoming mere appendages of a machine. However, as with all political or governmental advocacy of modernisation, there was also an insistence that change was also a source of new jobs and employment opportunities, even if this necessitated re-training and the acquisition of new skills. Consequently, even the usually emollient and genial Harold Macmillan was again unable to conceal his increasing exasperation with the trade unions, for with regard to restrictive practices, he complained that 'until we can get over this, I see no hope of our recovery. We have spent enormously on investment. We have the machines, and we could have men if they were properly used' (NA PREM 11/3841, Macmillan to Maudling, 24 June 1961).

Yet as with other industrial relations problems, Ministers were unable to devise a feasible solution. Of course, the 'human relations' account of restrictive practices itself tended to discourage a legislative response, but even when some Ministers did occasionally contemplate firmer action, they soon became cognizant of the problems which would arise from any attempt at imposing statutory curbs on restrictive practices. This was certainly the case when, in spring 1961, the Cabinet discussed the possibility of establishing a Commission on Labour Practices (similar to the Monopolies Commission), but was then persuaded by Hare that the ostensible attractions of such an institution – regular inquiries into restrictive practices by an impartial body which could acquire growing expertise, and would reassure Party and public opinion that something was finally being done to address trade union recalcitrance – were ultimately outweighed by wider political and practical considerations, most notably the likely resentment by the trade unions at potential interference by an external institution, coupled with concern from employers that this might damage relations between management and unions.

Hare also noted that the Government itself might be placed in an awkward position by being expected to enforce decisions taken by such a Commission, particularly if it appeared to be enforcing decisions 'in favour of employers and against working-class interests'. Instead, therefore, Hare recommended that a more piecemeal and pragmatic approach be pursued, whereby the extant National Joint Advisory Council would be asked to identify the industries which were most affected by restrictive practices, and then ask the relevant sectional negotiating bodies to address the problems in their particular industry. Hare readily acknowledged that this meant proceeding 'slowly and laboriously', but insisted that was unavoidable if the Government was to 'carry with us the responsible elements in the trade unions', and thereby 'strengthen and stimulate' these moderates in the trade unions (NA CAB 129/105, C (61) 64, Memorandum by the Minister of Labour, 'Industrial Relations', 16 May 1961). However, some officials were unimpressed by this response – or lack of, as they perceived it – noting that thus far, 'little progress has been made when the industries concerned have been left to tackle the problem themselves', and pointedly asking whether 'the Minister [is] satisfied that ... a further approach on similar lines would yield useful results' (NA PREM 11/3841, Bligh to Macmillan, 12 June 1961).

In response to this thinly-veiled criticism of its rather sanguine approach, the Ministry of Labour also insisted that restrictive practices were often 'impossible to define in terms applicable to industry as a whole', and that is was invariably 'a question of degree', which therefore meant that ultimately, 'judgment on a particular case must depend on consideration of a complex of related circumstances, many of which would be peculiar to a particular industry'. It was therefore deemed necessary to tackle the problem of restrictive practices on an industry by industry basis, an approach which Macmillan himself. accepted was 'the only practicable course', even though he wished that 'there were some more dramatic method of dealing with the situation' (NA PREM 11/3841, Helsby to Bligh, 1 August 1961; Bligh to Helsby, 2 August 1961). Similar conclusions had been drawn, two years earlier, by the Conservatives' extra-parliamentary Advisory Committee on Policy, for having considered the growing problem of restrictive practices, it had concluded that:

> Legislation against restrictive labour practices would be futile. The question whether a given practice is necessary to do the job properly, or an unnecessary restriction impeding efficiency, is a question that obviously a Court of Law is not particularly well qualified to answer.
> (CPA, ACP (59) 74, 'Trade Union Reform', 4 June 1959)

Once again, therefore, growing pressure emanating from sections of the Conservative Party for legislative action to deal with a newly-identified or increasingly serious industrial relations problem was met with a restatement of voluntarism by those Conservatives most conversant with the issues and complexities involved, and a reiteration of the limits of what could be achieved merely by passing Acts of Parliament.

'Positive', not punitive, legislation enacted

Yet while Ministers and senior Conservative officials continued to espouse their faith in voluntarism, and thus refused to invoke the kind of legislation which right-wing critics were demanding with increasing impatience, the first half of the 1960s did finally herald the introduction of two Acts of Parliament, the first pertaining to relations between employers and employees, and the second concerning relationships between trade unions. However, neither were punitive or repressive in the manner that the Right invariably demanded, and as such, neither jeopardised ongoing Ministerial efforts at securing closer partnership with the trade unions. On the contrary, both Acts were beneficial to employees and the trade unions.

Contracts of Employment Act, 1963

As we have just noted, the factors which were assumed to be underpinning trade union or employees' resistance to industrial change and modernisation, and the Conservative Government's continuing reluctance to invoke legislation, both led to a strong reiteration of the 'human relations' perspective among those Conservatives most closely involved with industrial relations during the early 1960s – 'This theme of human relations has provided the basis for much Tory thought and policy at least since Disraeli's time' (CPA CRD 2/7/17, Industrial Change: The Human Aspect, 15 July 1963) – and a renewed emphasis on improving the security and status of workers, as originally recommended in *The Industrial Charter* more than a decade earlier. As the Conservative Research Department reiterated: 'the problem of industrial relations is not one which can be settled by Acts of Parliament or dictatorial intervention by ministers. It is a human problem: a question of working together' (CPA, CRD 2/7/3, 'Note on Trade-Unions and Unofficial Strikes', 30 May 1962), a stance clearly shared by Lord (Derek Heathcoat) Amory, who insisted that 'the solutions to these difficult problems … will not be found mainly in the field of politics or through Government action', but through 'industry itself tackling these problems' (Amory, 1960: 6). It was readily acknowledged that the increasing size and scale of contemporary British industry was exacerbating feelings of alienation and anomie amongst workers on the factory floor, and these served to make co-partnership schemes and dialogue between the 'two sides of industry' more important and urgent than ever, for Ministers were 'dealing with a problem which is mainly human: you cannot speedily reverse attitudes of mind which have, in some cases, influenced people's thinking for generations' (CPA, CRD 2/7/3, 'Note on Trade-Unions and Unofficial Strikes', 30 May 1962).

However, some Conservatives, whilst still subscribing to this perspective in principle, were nonetheless coming to the conclusion that a more pro-active approach by Ministers was perhaps becoming necessary, with one internal Party study referring to 'the urgent need – politically, economically and industrially – for a new Tory initiative in industrial relations … we cannot ignore the growing feeling that the government … relies too much on exhortation', and that 'the responsibility of the State must be extended'. Yet far from being a clarion call for legislation to curb strikes or regulate leadership elections – 'a showdown [with the trade unions] would be most unwise and would inevitably increase the power of the more extreme Trade Union leaders' – the authors explained that what they were recommending was governmental action to facilitate improved contracts of employment, and better arrangements for redundancy in those industries most affected by accelerating change and technological advances. The assumption here, fully in accordance with the 'human relations' perspective, was that a greater sense of status and security on the part of workers would do much to reduce employees' grievances, fear of industrial modernisation and lack of trust towards management, all of which often underpinned restrictive practices and, ultimately, strike action. Ultimately, advocates of this approach believed that the Government needed to do more by way of giving practical – and sometimes statutory – effect to aspects of *The Industrial Charter* (CPA, ACP (62) 94, Edward Brown, John Page and Paul Dean, 'A Tory Look at Industrial Relations', 29 January 1962). This, of course, was not what other Conservative advocates of governmental action and state intervention in industrial relations usually had in mind.

In accordance with such recommendations – and in spite of continued Ministerial insistence on the efficacy of voluntarism and non-intervention by the state, and the limits of the law in promoting better industrial relations – this period did witness the introduction of two legislative measures, the first of which was the 1963 Contracts of Employment Act. This sought to imbue the Conservative's 'human relations' with a statutory element, as alluded to by Edward Brown and his colleagues, by providing workers with a legal right to a written statement, from their employers, of their precise terms and conditions of employment, covering not only hours to be worked and pay, but holiday entitlement, sick leave, and, crucially, the period of notification to be given prior to termination of employment, the latter to be determined on a scale according to an employee's duration of employment. Indeed, such a measure had been deemed 'the most important question' by the Party's industrial relations committee at its inaugural meeting in June 1962 (CPA, CRD 2/7/17, Industrial Relations Committee, minutes of meeting held on 5 June 1962). In this context, the Contracts of Employment Act was intended to provide industrial workers with a greater degree of status and security, both as an important humanitarian objective in its own right, but also in the expectation that this would yield an improvement in industrial relations more generally. It was also envisaged that the greater security to be afforded by this Act might serve to eradicate some of the restrictive practices which were impeding attempts to improve industrial efficiency and competitiveness during the early 1960s.

Doubtless some on the Conservative right discerned a certain irony in the passing of the Contracts of Employment Act, given that successive Ministers of Labour had been emphatic that legislation could not and would not improve industrial relations, yet this remained the Government's official position: 'The Minister's general policy is … not to take legislative powers to control, but to encourage, mainly through informal talks, the development of better relations between employers and workers.' This stance reflected the Ministry of Labour's continued insistence that many, if not most, conflicts in the workplace were ultimately derived from 'human attitudes', and as such, 'legislation is ineffective in changing ways of thought' (NA PREM 11/3570, Bishop to Macmillan, 17 May 1961).

Although the Contracts of Employment Act was undoubtedly progressive, not prescriptive, by enhancing workers' rights, rather than curbing them, and in spite of the Ministry of Labour's insistence that it was still wedded to voluntarism and industrial relations *laissez-faire*, one prominent academic industrial relations expert nonetheless characterised it as 'a small breach [with the prevailing tradition of voluntarism and industrial self-government] … but … an important breach none the less … the old policy of leaving the two sides of industry to work out their own solutions to every problem, which often meant no solution at all, was gradually being abandoned' (Flanders, 1975: 107). Or as another writer on industrial relations expressed it, whereas previously 'the period of notice necessary before the termination of employment had been a matter left to the two sides of industry, the 1963 Act meant that it had become an area of concern to the state' (Jackson, 1991: 305).

One other possible initiative which was occasionally mooted in the context of the 'human relations' perspective was that of providing more courses in further education colleges or universities in order to disseminate a wider or deeper understanding about managerial or personnel issues in industry. For example, on one occasion, a Ministerial colleague suggested to Hare that the Government could do more to encourage the teaching of industrial relations, either as a subject in its own right, or as a component of degrees in such academic disciplines as business studies, economics, history and law (NA CAB 124/1618, Hailsham to Hare, 20 January 1961), to which Hare politely pointed out that industrial relations and cognate subjects were already taught in several universities, probably more extensively than was commonly realised (NA CAB 124/1618, Hare to Hailsham, 8 March 1961).

Trade Union (Amalgamations) Act, 1964

The second legislative measure introduced during this period was the Trade Union (Amalgamations) Act, which was enacted during the Conservative Government's final year in office. Again, though, this was certainly not the type of prescriptive or restrictive legislation which the Party's right-wing habitually craved, but, instead, a permissive measure that greatly relaxed the rules governing trade unions' mergers. Hitherto, the statutory procedure for pursuing amalgamations between trade unions was often complex and cumbersome, and required that at least 50 per cent of members voted, with at least a 6–5 majority in favour. However, it was argued that obtaining a turn-out of 50 per cent was rather rare, hence the need to reform the statutory provisions regulating trade union amalgamations. To this end, the 1964 Act – which originated as a Conservative MP's Private Member's Bill – stipulated that a simple majority of union numbers voting would be sufficient to endorse an amalgamation with another trade union; there would be no specified size of majority, nor a minimum level of turn-out, although trade unions would be entitled to stipulate either a higher majority or a minimum level of turn-out in their rules or standing orders if they so wished.

It should be noted that before introducing this legislation, the approval of both the TUC and BEC had been obtained, although the former's approval had itself necessitated a change to the original proposal, for when the Cabinet's Home Affairs committee had first drafted this proposal, it had intended to stipulate that 25 per cent of a union's membership should actually vote in order for a simple majority to be deemed sufficient in endorsing or opposing amalgamation with another trade union. However, the TUC was adamant that even a 25 per cent turn-out was often not attained, and therefore insisted that no minimum level of turn-out or participation should be stipulated in the legislation, Thus it was that Joseph Godber, the Minister of Labour, conceded that 'we must accept the TUC's view of the matter, particularly as we do not want to appear to be hampering their current attempts to rationalise the structure of the trade union movement' (CAB 21/5779, Godber to Brooke, 13 November 1963). So adamant was Godber on the need for this concession towards the trade unions that he persuaded one or two Ministerial colleagues to forgo their initial insistence on a specified minimum majority (NA CAB 21/5779, Munn to Otton, 22 November 1963). Incidentally, the low turn-out in such ballots seemed to reinforce the stance of successive Ministers of Labour who had resisted the introduction of ballots prior to strike action and leadership elections partly on the grounds that apathy among many trade unionists, and therefore low turn-out, would allow militants, who were invariably better organised and much more active, to dominate the outcomes.

Moreover, such was Godber's concern to avoid antagonising the trade unions that he also secured a last-minute redrafting of the Trade Union (Amalgamations) Bill in order to tone down an explicit reference to the consequent 'transfer', to the newly formed union, of the political levy arrangements. Godber's concern was that the original reference concerning political funds was 'drafted too prominently', and 'would lead Members to debate political funds generally', which would almost certainly have a highly detrimental impact on Conservative relations with the trade unions. As such, Godber ensured that the relevant clause was rewritten – hastily, because the Conservative backbencher who had tabled the Bill refused Godber's request that he withdraw the Bill so that it could be redrafted – to ensure that it featured 'much less obtrusively' (NA LAB 10/2068, Godber to Dilhorne, 17 January 1964; Lassen to Butler, 20 January 1964; Godber to Brooke, 10 and 27 January 1964)

Two main considerations underpinned the enactment of this particular legislation. Firstly, it reflected Conservative concern about the number – more than 600 throughout the early 1960s – of trade unions in British industry, which not only made it difficult to maintain effective and orderly collective bargaining, but also increased the scope for damaging inter-union disputes. The second consideration informing the Conservative Government's introduction of the 1964 Trade Union (Amalgamations) Act was to assuage the trade unions, in the context of the recently adopted pledge to establish a Royal Commission on the law pertaining to trade unions (discussed below), that legislation could be positive and beneficial to them, and that they need not be instinctively suspicious about Ministerial motives in promising a formal inquiry if the Conservatives won the imminent general election.

However, the Trade Union (Amalgamations) Act also enshrined or reflected a couple of contradictions or inconsistencies in the Conservative approach to trade unionism and industrial relations. Firstly, although it was, in one sense, entirely logical to rationalise the structure and number of trade unions in an era when companies and industries themselves were inexorably becoming larger – due to increasing monopolisation and economies of scale – it also meant that with correspondingly fewer, but bigger, trade unions, the union leadership would increasingly become more remote from trade union members on the factory floor. Given that a major component of the Conservative's 'human relations' perspective was that poor industrial relations were often attributable to the gulf between workers and management, and hence a feeling among employees that those who managed them were remote and consequently unappreciative of their efforts, it seemed a little odd to be facilitating fewer, but bigger, trade unions, for this would compound the problem, as industrial workers increasingly felt that their union leaders were also becoming even more remote and unaware of day-to-day grievances on the factory floor.

This, in turn, was likely to compound the problem of unofficial strikes, as disgruntled workers became disillusioned with their 'remote' union leaders, and took matters into their own hands. Indeed, one of the key industrial problems which emerged during the 1960s, and which was deemed to underpin both the incidence of unofficial strikes and the phenomenon of 'wage drift', was the growth in both the number and militancy of shop stewards and other local union officials, whose closer proximity to employees often meant that they enjoyed greater trust or respect, sometimes facilitated by allegations that the official union leadership had 'sold out' by virtue of spending most of their time in London. Thus did more militant shop stewards fill the vacuum which nature abhors, but in so doing, they exacerbated two of the key problems which Ministers were grappling with during this period, namely unofficial strikes and 'wage drift'.

The second contradiction or inconsistency which the passage of the Trade Union (Amalgamations) Act enshrined with regard to the Conservative approach to trade unionism and industrial relations was that larger trade unions would, potentially at least, make strikes more damaging, because more workers were likely to be involved. Of course, an inter-union dispute could also be deeply damaging or disruptive even if it involved only a relatively small number of key workers, but by facilitating easier trade union amalgamations, the Douglas-Home Government might unwittingly have been increasing the potential for strike action involving greater numbers of workers; if five trade unions each with 20,000 members were amalgamated to create a new union with a total of 100,000 members, then a strike called by that new union would potentially involve five times as many workers as a strike previously called by one of the pre-merger unions, notwithstanding that the latter might have involved power station workers or fire fighters, for example, and thus still have been extremely serious.

One other potential problem which might have been compounded as a consequence of the Conservative Government's passing of the Trade Unions (Amalgamations) Act concerned the closed shop. If any of the newly-formed larger trade unions operated a closed shop, then clearly rather more employees would be affected than if one or two of the smaller, pre-merger unions had done so. Moreover, facilitating fewer trade unions, by making amalgamations easier, would leave dissatisfied trade union members with less choice or scope in joining a different union. This would be a somewhat curious outcome for a Conservative Party which placed such strong emphasis on individual liberty and choice, even if it made more sense from the perspective of assisting employers in collective bargaining, by virtue of reducing the number of unions they needed to negotiate with.

Indeed, with regard to the issue of pay determination, fostering fewer, but larger, trade unions could also be viewed as an advantage to Ministers themselves as they increasingly needed to negotiate with trade union leaders in order to secure acceptance of incomes policies. It meant though, that industrial order and managerial convenience was ultimately privileged over individual liberty or choice, although many trade unions themselves welcomed the greater ease with which they could now secure their own 'economies of scale'.

Creating the National Economic Development Council

Meanwhile, the early 1960s heralded a new Conservative approach to promoting industrial partnership, for whereas the emphasis had previously been on closer and more regular consultation between employers and employees, or management and trade unions, the new initiative – which was in addition to, not instead of, partnership in the workplace – entailed a formal institutional partnership between trade unions, employers' representatives and Ministers at the very highest level. To this end, in 1962, Macmillan and his Chancellor, Selwyn Lloyd, established the National Economic Development Council (NEDC) – originally to have been called either the National Economic Advisory Council or Co-ordination of Economic Resources – a tripartite body in which the three institutional partners would meet, on a regular basis, to consider ways in which the performance of the British economy could be improved, and thereby foster increased industrial productivity and a higher rate of economic growth.

Macmillan was fully aware that this neo-corporatist forum would be viewed with deep disdain by the economic neo-liberals on the Conservative right, an expectation which was fully realised when the relevant Cabinet discussions revealed 'a rather interesting and quite deep divergence of view between Ministers, really corresponding to whether they had old Whig, Liberal, *laissez-faire* traditions, or Tory opinions, paternalists, and not afraid of a little *dirigisme*' (Macmillan 1973: 37). However, Macmillan emphasised that the Conservative Party 'has always consisted of a number holding the laissez-faire tradition, but of an equal number in favour of some direction', and that as such, we should not 'be afraid of a switch over towards more direction'. Certainly, Macmillan sought to pre-empt right-wing objections by defiantly declaring that 'I have no fear of it because these were the policies I recommended before the war', mischievously adding that 'I shall be able to claim, like Disraeli, that I have educated my Party' (NA PREM 11/3841, Macmillan to Lloyd, 15 July 1961). Support for this new approach was proffered by Quinton Hogg, on the grounds that: 'Private enterprise as our fathers knew it, and socialism, have both failed' (PREM 11/4071, Hogg [later Lord Hailsham] to Macmillan, 8 June 1962).

Meanwhile, a few weeks later, when a lead article in *The Daily Telegraph* criticised the growing enthusiasm for economic planning (the Labour Opposition, too, was increasingly enamoured with the notion of 'indicative planning' during the early 1960s, proposing both a National Plan, and a series of associated 'regional economic plans' to regenerate economically deprived regions of the UK), Macmillan dismissed this as the 'usual carping' by the paper, and reiterated that the Government should persevere. We might even, Macmillan suggested, 'devise something on the French basis which could be Conservative or "Middle Way" and would dish the Whigs'. As to the resistance which his Chancellor was likely to face from a Treasury 'which is still extremely laissez-faire by tradition', Macmillan's advice was an emphatic 'do not let this deter you' (NA PREM 11/3841, Macmillan to Lloyd, 14 August 1961).

Lloyd certainly faced criticism from the 'city editors' of several national and provincial newspapers, for when he conducted a briefing session to explain the Government's economic thinking, several of them accused him of espousing 'socialism', and accused the Conservative Government of having 'abandoned free enterprise and the use of market forces' (NA PREM 11/4314, Lloyd to Macmillan, 25 August 1961). Macmillan swiftly reassured his Chancellor that 'I do not think we need to be too alarmed by right-wing criticisms which are really heirs of the Liberal laissez-faire policy', and strongly defended 'our pragmatic approach' (NA PREM 11/4314, Macmillan to Lloyd, 28 August 1961). Meanwhile, such was the emerging penchant for planning among some senior Conservatives during the early 1960s that the Party's 1964 manifesto declared that: 'In contemporary politics the argument is not for or against planning. All human activity involves planning. The question is: how is the planning to be done? By consent or by compulsion?' (Craig, 1970: 217).

Of course, such an assertion was highly contentious – and was doubtless intended to be – because for Conservative neo-liberals, a key argument in contemporary politics was precisely about economic planning versus free markets, whereby only the latter could effectively facilitate economic growth, industrial efficiency, political liberty and wealth creation; planning, they insisted (see, for example, Coleraine, 1970: chapter 2; Powell, 1969, chapters 3 and 4; Wood, 1965: chapter IX), would inevitably lead to increasing state control and ultimately result in what Hayek, two decades earlier, had termed *The Road to Serfdom* (Hayek, 1944). As such, the 1964 Conservative manifesto's inclusion of the term 'democratic planning' would have been derided by the Party's Right as an oxymoron.

The notion of a tripartite or neo-corporatist forum such as the NEDC can be discerned in the 1959 Conservative manifesto's pledge that a re-elected Conservative government would invite trade union leaders and employers' representatives to discuss jointly the industrial relations problems which the country was likely to encounter during the next five years (Craig, 1970: 189), although as Macmillan's above comment indicates, the antecedents can be traced back to his advocacy of *The Middle Way*. Certainly, another One Nation Conservative subsequently spoke approvingly of this institutional innovation by characterising it as 'a recognizable sketch of his grand design of the 1930s' (Gilmour, 1978: 246; see also Gilmour and Garnett, 1997: 167; Walker, 1977: 26, 28). With the Conservatives having been victorious in the 1959 election, the Minister of Labour, Edward Heath was keen to instigate these talks sooner rather than later, reasoning that with the next general election four to five years away, talks involving the trade unions could be conducted 'in a non-partisan manner'. Furthermore, he argued that if the talks could be started imminently, they would benefit from relatively propitious economic, industrial and political circumstances, rather than having to be hastily arranged as a panic-stricken response to a crisis (NA PREM 11/4313, Heath to Macmillan, 6 May 1960).

However, the Ministers most closely involved – Macmillan as Prime Minister, Heath as Minister of Labour and Selwyn Lloyd as Chancellor – soon agreed that any such talks ought to be more comprehensive in scope than merely identifying specific industrial relations problems and securing agreed solutions. Instead, it was accepted that the proposed tripartite meetings should encompass a range of industrial and economic issues, not least because industrial relations problems could not be isolated from these wider societal issues; on the contrary, they invariably reflected them, and sometimes caused or exacerbated them. It therefore made little sense to hold tripartite talks about ways of improving industrial relations without simultaneously discussing how Britain's economic and industrial performance could also be improved.

Although the NEDC was not formally responsible for determining wages or formulating an incomes policy, Conservative Ministers clearly envisaged that it would serve to alert trade union leaders to the economic facts of life, and thereby tacitly persuade them of the need for wage restraint (Macmillan, 1973: 51; Heath, 1998: 280). In this last respect, the establishment of the NEDC reflected a continued belief in the efficacy of partnership with organized labour, and the enduring faith in the power of persuasion and dialogue in securing more responsible behaviour by the trade unions. Genuine discussion, not government diktat, continued to be viewed by senior Conservatives as the most desirable or realistic means of securing more harmonious industrial relations and more responsible trade union behaviour. As such, this new approach did not represent an explicit departure from the voluntarist industrial strategy of the previous 11 years, but an attempt at buttressing it: 'the Government was devising public policy remedies to try and bolster, not undermine, the traditional industrial relations system' (Taylor, 1996: 101).

Certainly, there was an implicit assumption – or hope – that, if such moderation and responsibility could be secured through the type of social partnership offered by the NEDC, then much of the backbench and grass-roots pressure for trade union legislation would dissipate, or at least become easier to disregard. It has also been subsequently claimed that Macmillan's desire to forge a closer and more constructive partnership between management and organised labour was linked 'to the need to secure support from both sides of industry for the government's emerging European policy' (Heath, 1998: 198).

Inching towards a Royal Commission on Trade Unionism

In pursuing these various approaches, the Conservative leadership initially appeared uncertain about the efficacy of responding favourably to another perennial demand from some quarters of the Party, namely the establishment of a Royal Commission or Committee of Inquiry on either trade unionism in general or trade union law in particular. On the one hand, it was recognised that such an investigation might facilitate a calm and careful examination of problematic aspects of industrial relations and trade unionism, and possibly yield a report which vindicated the Government's voluntarist approach. On the other hand, there was anxiety among Ministers that establishing a Royal Commission or Committee of Inquiry might simultaneously raise the expectations of those on the Conservative Right who routinely demanded tough measures against the trade unions, while antagonising the Left within the unions, who might then persuade moderate trade unionists that the Conservatives were preparing to attack the organised working class.

Ministers of Labour were especially sceptical about the wisdom of a Royal Commission, reflecting, as ever, the extent to which those with the closest political involvement in industrial relations were the most cautious about potential responses and proposed remedies. So, for example, when the issue was raised by the Cabinet's Home Affairs Committee in the spring of 1963, the support expressed by some Ministers for such an inquiry was countered by the firm opposition of Joseph Godber, who had recently succeeded John Hare at the Ministry of Labour, for although he recognised that 'taking action in this field … might placate a substantial number of right-wing supporters in the country', it would do so at the risk of alienating moderate trade unionists (NA PREM 11/4871, Godber to Douglas–Home, 14 February 1964). Similar concerns had already been expressed by senior officials in the Conservative Research Department, when they insisted that 'the Government's aim of improving the climate of industrial relations cannot conceivably be achieved by antagonising one of the two groups primarily concerned', for the appointment of such a Commission 'would certainly be resented by moderate trade union leaders – whose co-operation is essential if progress is to be made'. It was also suggested that although formal inquiries could be useful 'to acquire knowledge which is not already available', this was clearly not the case with industrial relations and trade unionism, which meant that 'it is extremely unlikely that any new information would come to light' (CPA, CRD 2/7/3, 'Note on Trade Unions and Unofficial Strikes', 30 May 1962. See also CRD 2/7/17, Industrial Relations Committee, minutes of meeting held on 10 December 1962).

The clear premise underpinning such a stance was the only practicable way of improving industrial relations in Britain and fostering greater responsibility by the trade unions was to persevere with the 'human relations' approach, and continue tackling the socio-psychological problems which were thought to constitute the underlying cause of poor industrial relations and restrictive practices. Neither a Royal Commission nor trade union legislation would successfully tackle such problems.

Concern about antagonising the trade unions in general, and moderate trade unionists in particular, also meant that those Conservatives who did favour a Royal Commission or Committee of Inquiry were unsure about the timing of such an investigation, or even the timing of an announcement about such an inquiry. Some Conservatives believed that if proposals for a Royal Commission were announced in the run-up to the 1964 general election, then victory for the Party at the polls could be construed as a mandate from the electorate for such an inquiry. Others in the Party (right up to Cabinet level), however, feared that any such announcement so close to the election would effectively be used as anti-Conservative propaganda by left-wing elements in the trade unions and the Labour Party, to the extent that moderate trade unionists might be dissuaded from voting Conservative. Yet if there was no allusion to a Royal Commission prior to an imminent general election, but an announcement after a Conservative victory, the trade unions would doubtless argue that its absence from the Party's manifesto meant that the Conservatives had no mandate for such an inquiry; at the very least, the unions were likely to accuse the Conservatives of duplicity or disingenuousness, and thereby claim that they could nor trust them sufficiently to participate meaningfully in such an inquiry.

So vexatious was this whole issue for Conservative Ministers that a secret official (i.e., Civil Service, not Ministerial) committee was established, in the early summer of 1963, to examine this 'highly inflammable subject' in order 'to obtain better information about the points on which reform might be considered, and about the implications of particular proposals for reform' (NA CAB 21/5779, Butler to Douglas-Home, 11 April 1963). It was envisaged that such an inquiry would pay particular attention to the phenomenon of unofficial strikes, and the relationship between trade unions and individual employees, especially the closed shop. Indeed, so secret was this committee – due to the highly-sensitive nature of its subject matter, which would have infuriated the trade unions if its existence and deliberations became known – that the majority of Cabinet Ministers themselves were not made aware of its existence, apart from the Prime Minister, and, of course, those Ministers whose Departments were directly involved.

Comprising four senior civil servants from the Ministry of Labour, and one each from the Lord Chancellor's Office, the Law Officers' Department, the Lord Advocate's Department, the Treasury Solicitor's Office and the Home Office, plus the Registrar of Friendly Societies, the committee ostensibly seemed to enshrine the tension between voluntarism, as represented by the Ministry of Labour, and advocacy of legislative remedies to Britain's industrial relations problems. However, it was actually some of the officials from the 'legal' Departments who seemed to be most hesitant about recommending legislation to regulate industrial relations or govern the internal affairs of the trade unions. For example, one of the ensuing recommendations (see below) was to make collective agreements legally enforceable, yet it was noted that such a proposal failed to acknowledge the likelihood that some employers would be reluctant to risk worsening industrial relations in their company by instigating legal proceedings against their employees or the relevant trade union. Furthermore, it was thought highly likely that some collective agreements would be worded in such a manner 'so as to escape the jurisdiction of the [proposed] Labour Court' (NA CAB 21/5779, Dudman to Cassels, 10 January 1964).

Consequently, whereas it had originally been expected that this secret official committee would issue a report to relevant Departmental Ministers by the end of the summer, such were the ensuing disagreements over specific proposals that publication of the final report had to be deferred, and even the draft interim report which was produced, in October 1963, was subject to reservations by officials from both the Lord Chancellor's office, and the Law Officers' Department. This Interim draft report offered three main recommendations, namely that:

a. The Ministry of Labour should consider legislation which would enable its Minister to establish standing 'fact-finding bodies' to investigate the underlying causes when industrial disputes occurred.
b. Collective agreements should be legally binding, enforceable through special labour courts whose membership would comprise judges and senior employers and trade union representatives.
c. Employees should have a right of appeal, possibly to the labour court, against 'unjustifiable dismissals'.

However, Sir James Dunnett, who was both chairman of the official committee and Permanent Secretary at the Ministry of Labour, recognised that these measures were unlikely to be welcomed by the trade unions, and therefore suggested that the committee examine some more positive measures which 'might produce some jam for the unions', in which case, 'it might be better not to put before Ministers any proposals until the availability of all possible jam has been considered'. Dunnett was emphatic that 'Ministers should look at the problem as a whole, and not simply at the aspects covered by the interim report.' The need for such a holistic examination would almost inevitably necessitate the establishment of a Royal Commission or similarly august body, which meant that the issue would again raise the issue of timing; should a formal public inquiry be announced before the election, but not actually be established until or unless the Conservatives were re-elected, or should it be both announced and inaugurated before the imminent election. Yet even if a Royal Commission was established immediately, it would not be able to complete its deliberations and publish its report before the election (NA, CAB 21 21/5779, Palmer to Trend, 10 October 1963), which would therefore render it difficult for the Conservatives to enunciate clear manifesto commitments regarding industrial relations and trade unionism; to do so would pre-empt, and quite possibly conflict with, the eventual recommendations of the Royal Commission itself.

It therefore seemed almost certain that Ministers would opt for the former of the two options concerning timing, namely that a pledge to establish a Royal Commission on Trade Unionism, or Trade Union Law, would be part of the Conservatives programme for the 1964 general election, but with its actual creation deferred until after that election, assuming, of course, that the Conservatives were victorious. Yet if there was to be no such Royal Commission prior to the general election, then this also seemed to preclude industrial relations or trade union legislation in the final parliamentary session, for the main purpose of the proposed Royal Commission was precisely to examine the problems or issues involved, and thereupon suggest what reforms were necessary and feasible.

In lieu of such an inquiry, however, the Conservative Party was left with something of a policy vacuum with regard to industrial relations and/or trade union reform, particularly as the Final Report of the official committee ruled out, either on grounds of voluntarist principle, or practicability and likely ineffectiveness, legislation to outlaw either unofficial strikes or the trade union closed shop, while also rejecting the introduction of compulsory arbitration or a statutory 'cooling-off' period prior to a strike. Also dismissed was the option of amending the 1906 Trade Disputes Act, in order to render trade unions or their members liable to civil action for inducement to breach contracts in pursuance of an industrial dispute. Ultimately, the Final Report was a veritable New Testament of voluntarism, a 47-page document which exuded equanimity or equivocation throughout. Even on the question of legally-enforceable collective agreements, the committee 'makes no recommendation as to whether on balance legislation to this effect would be desirable' (NA LAB 43/416, Report of the Official Committee on Trade Unions and the Law', January 1964).

The *Rookes* v. *Barnard* judgment

However, when, in early February 1964, the Prime Minister, Alec Douglas-Home, asked his Home Secretary, to 'consider urgently the possibility of setting up a Royal Commission [on trade unionism]', preferably before the general election, but if this were not possible, then 'to announce our intention of doing this if elected again' (NA PREM 11/4871, Douglas-Home to Brooke, 7 February 1964), he did so in the context of an entirely unforeseen development, namely the *Rookes* v. *Barnard* judgment in the House of Lords, in February 1964.

This long and complex case originated back to 1955, when a draughtsman employed by the British Overseas Airways Corporation (BOAC – subsequently subsumed by British Airways) resigned from his trade union, the Association of Engineering and Shipbuilding Draughtsmen (AESD), which operated a closed shop. Senior AESD officials thereupon informed BOAC that there would be a strike by the union's members if the employee in question, Douglas Rookes, was not dismissed from his employment by the company within three days. This threat was in spite of the existence of a no-strike clause enshrined in the contracts of BOAC's employees. When BOAC acceded to the union's demand by terminating Rookes' employment, the dismissed employee then instigated legal proceedings for damages – on the grounds of conspiracy – against three of the AESD's senior officials.

Rookes initially won his case, and was awarded damages, but this favourable verdict was then reversed in a subsequent appeal. The case was then pursued in the House of Lords, as the then highest and final court of appeal in the United Kingdom, which overturned the Appeal Court's decision, thereby deciding in Rookes' favour again.

This decision effectively meant that a trade union could be deemed legally liable for damages if it pursued strike action which was deemed to entail a breach of (employment) contract. There were undoubtedly legal ambiguities and complexities arising from this judicial decision, pertaining to what constituted a breach of contract, who should be deemed liable in law for inducing such breaches, and what was to constitute 'intimidation'. Consequently, Ministers themselves were uncertain about just how detrimental the *Rookes* v. *Barnard* judgment would be to Britain's trade unions (see, for example, NA 21/5779, Dilhorne to Godber, 19 February 1964). As such, before deciding how to respond politically, the Cabinet sought the advice of its own Law Officers to ascertain the precise implications of the *Rookes* v. *Barnard* decision. They advised that in this context, breach of contract meant industrial action pursued to compel an employer to act in a certain way with regard to a closed shop, or to cease trading with another company other than voluntarily for commercial reasons; for example, because the other company refused to enforce a closed shop or recognise a trade unions for bargaining purposes.

In other words, breach of contract was here defined as industrial action invoked over matters other than the immediate terms and conditions of employment of individual employees, most notably wages and hours worked. This implied that a strike by employees in pursuit of a pay claim would not be deemed to be in breach of contract provided that any stipulated period of notice had been given of the intention to strike – clearly, this would exclude wildcat strikes or walk-outs – and/or employees were breaking a no-strike agreement or were embarking on industrial action prior to exhausting agreed procedures for resolving disputes.

This reaffirmed the view that in the *Rookes* v. *Barnard* case, the breach of contract was adjudged to have occurred because BOAC operated a no-strike policy, which was written in employees' employment contracts, and also because it had established grievance procedures which the relevant trade union had not fully pursued prior to threatening industrial action against the company. However, the case was also adjudged to have involved conspiracy or inducement to breach contract, because it involved, or was directed against, a third party, and was thus, again, beyond the usual definition of a legitimate trade dispute, with one of the three defendants in the case not even employed by BOAC (NA CAB 21/5779, 'Opinion of the Law Officers for the Crown in the matter of the decision of the House of Lords in the case of Rookes v Barnard', 11 March 1964; LAB 43/416, Huxham to Godber, 26 March 1964).

Consequently, the protection hitherto afforded to the trade unions by the 1906 Trade Disputes Act was now in considerable doubt, a scenario which, some Conservatives recognised, might render the trade unions more amenable to some kind of official inquiry or review (NA PREM 11/4871, Douglas-Home to Brooke, 7 February 1964; Godber to Douglas-Home, 10 February 1964; Shawcross to Douglas-Home, 7 February 1964; CAB 128/38 Pt 2, Cabinet conclusions, 13 February and 17 March 1964). Certainly, as the Minister of Labour emphasised, the *Rookes* v. *Barnard* decision seemed 'to throw into flux some of the basic assumptions on trade union law in this country', and as such, provided a significantly changed context, for whereas the Government had previously resisted right-wing demands for trade union reform, partly due to 'the risk of antagonising a large proportion of the three million or more middle-of-the-road trade unionists who must have supported us at the last [1959] election ... the House of Lords judgment has undoubtedly changed this position'. Godber also pointed out that the increased pressure in the Conservative Party for action following the *Rookes* v. *Barnard* decision – he referred to an Early Day Motion (EDM) on this issue which had almost immediately attracted the signatures of 30 Conservative MPs, along with various other parliamentary motions and a Ten Minute Rule Bill – was further compounded by the Cabinet's pursuit of resale price maintenance[1], which served to strengthen backbench demands for corresponding 'action against restrictive practices in the trade unions' (NA CAB 21/5779, Godber to Douglas-Home, 14 February 1964; with regard to the relevance of resale price maintenance, see also NA CAB 21/5779, McIndoe to Douglas-Home, 4 March 1964).

Certainly, the Party's chief whip, Martin Redmayne, adjudged this to be an opportune moment to send the Prime Minister a copy of a published Gallup poll which purported to show widespread public support for governmental action *vis-à-vis* the trade unions, and reminding him that 'I have said on several occasions that a step in this direction … would be very popular with Conservatives both in the House and in the country' (NA PREM 11/4871, Redmayne to Douglas-Home, 4 February 1964). However, officials in the Ministry of Labour were quick to point out that the questions were somewhat 'loaded', and therefore unreliable as an accurate reflection of public opinion (NA LAB 10/2138, Barnes to Godber, 6 February; Dunnett to Godber 6 February 1964).

Meanwhile, Rab Butler noted that the trade unions were becoming 'rather agitated about the decision' in the *Rookes* v. *Barnard* case, to the extent that they were 'for the first time … recognising the dangers to their own position of the anomalies and ambiguities in the present legal position'. As such, the Conservative Government was presented with 'an opportunity which we have not had for ten years', and a context which might make the trade unions themselves more amenable to a formal inquiry into the law regarding trade unionism. Certainly, 'the only effective way to do this in practice would be to set up a Royal Commission with broad terms of reference to review the whole body of law relating to the trade unions and to recommend how it could be brought up to date' (NA PREM 11/4871, Butler to Douglas-Home, 17 February 1964).

This calculation that the trade unions might now be more amenable to such an inquiry was substantiated by Joseph Godber himself, who informed the Prime Minister that 'my private contacts with George Woodcock [the TUC's general secretary] and others show that they [the trade unions] are seriously alarmed, and Woodcock himself has mentioned to me privately the possibility of a Royal Commission on trade union law arising out of this judgment' (NA PREM 11/4871,

---

1 The 1964 Resale Price Maintenance Act was 'a political hot potato' which 'exposed the historic tension at the heart of the Tory Party … between protectionism and free trade', for the Act – after much argument and controversy (at all levels) inside the Conservative Party – abolished a system of price-fixing which kept the cost of manufactured goods higher (for the consumer) than they would otherwise be, but also protected smaller shopkeepers from being undercut by the rapidly expanding number of supermarkets (Campbell, 1993: 150–57).

Godber to Douglas-Home, 14 February 1964). Consequently, at a meeting between the Prime Minister, the Minister of Labour and the Government's Chief Whip at the beginning of March 1964 – by which time, the number of signatories to the afore-mentioned EDM had risen to 113, constituting 30 per cent of Conservative MPs – it was finally decided, subject to the approval of the Cabinet at its next meeting, just two days later, to announce that a Royal Commission on trade union law would be established if the Conservatives were re-elected, and that a pledge to this effect would be included in the Party's manifesto. This approach, Douglas-Home believed, was both safer, and 'more respectable' (NA PREM 11/4871, 'Note for the Record: Trade Unions', 3 March 1964), and would also, it was hoped, pacify at least some of the growing impatience on the Conservative backbenches, which was being expressed not only through the signing of the EDM – whose signatories had further increased to 140 by mid-March – but through meetings of the Party's [backbench] 1922 Committee (NA LAB 43/416, Lewis to Godber, 17 March 1964).

Yet immediately after his meeting with the Prime Minister and Chief Whip, Godber had second thoughts about announcing the proposed Royal Commission, for although he had been assured by George Woodcock that some trade union leaders might be amenable to an inquiry in the wake of the *Rookes* v. *Barnard* decision, the Minister of Labour remained deeply concerned that an announcement at this stage 'would give a very big handle to left-wing union leaders to stir up hostility to us among their members' by depicting the proposed Royal Commission both as 'a trick to enable right-wing Tories to attack the whole structure of the trade unions', and also as a sop 'to specific Tory MPs who were disgruntled by the RPM [Resale Price Maintenance] Bill.' Godber was therefore inclined to defer a formal announcement regarding the Royal Commission until the launch of the general election campaign (NA LAB 43/416, Godber to Douglas-Home, 4 March 1964), thereby giving the trade unions insufficient time to mobilise and campaign against it.

The following day's Cabinet meeting was itself unable to agree on the timing of an announcement, with some Ministers concerned that the timing would look somewhat odd; the sudden departure, at the end of a parliamentary session, from the hitherto voluntarist policy might be construed by the trade unions as highly partisan and politically provocative. Others in the Cabinet even wondered whether a Royal Commission was the best vehicle for identifying problems relating to the trade unions, for many of the problems were already well-known, while others, it was suggested, such as restrictive practices, might best be examined by the NEDC, on the grounds that restrictive practices were an impediment to higher industrial output and faster economic growth, and thus more appropriate to the NEDC's remit. In view of these divergent viewpoints, no decision taken at this meeting (NA CAB 128/38 Pt 2, C.M. (64) 17th conclusions, 5 March 1964). Not until nearly a fortnight later did the Cabinet finally reach a decision on this particular issue, namely that an inquiry into aspects of the law relating to trade unionism would be announced, but not actually established until after election. Also, the TUC and employers' organisations would be consulted over membership and the precise terms of reference (NA CAB 128/38 Pt 2, C.M. (64) 19th conclusions, 17 March 1964), in an attempt at securing trade union consent and co-operation in advance.

Yet even in the wake of the *Rookes* v. *Barnard* judgment, the Conservatives' Parliamentary Labour Committee remained adamant that:

> the law and its apparatus of injunctions, damages, fines, penal sanctions, etc. has little to contribute to the solution of the problems of industrial relations. Laws attempting to determine when strikes are illegal, under what conditions strikes may be held (i.e., after a secret ballot), what labour practices are legal, and what illegal, have been found from experience to be almost totally unenforceable and to do more harm than good.
>
> (CPA, PLC (64) 3, 'Trade unions, Employers' Associations and the Law', 19 March 1964)

Ironically, it was the TUC which then demanded immediate legislative action by the Government, albeit separate from, and possibly instead of, any subsequent Royal Commission into Trade Unionism or Trade Union law. This demand was made when a TUC deputation met the Minister of Labour, Joseph Godber, to discuss trade union concerns arising from the *Rookes* v. *Barnard* judgment, but what the union leaders wanted was 'immediate amending legislation' to restore the status quo *ante* prior to the *Rookes* v. *Barnard* judgment, and which, they claimed, inhibited trade union officials from undertaking normal collective bargaining. Having listened to the TUC's vitriolic denunciation of the 'intolerable' position in which the trade unions had been placed following *Rookes* v. *Barnard*, and the demand for immediate legislative action to restore the status quo *ante*, Godber could not resist pointing out to the TUC leaders that they had not considered trade union legislation important, desirable or urgent during the previous 13 years, yet were now insisting that the Cabinet should rush through legislation just months before a general election was due, and in lieu of the recommendations of a not yet established Royal Commission.

With the TUC demanding urgent legislative action 'in the most forthright terms', and Godber insistent that this was not a matter which the Government could or should not be rushed into, 'a major row' ensued, with each 'side' accusing the other of being unreasonable. However, the TUC deputation left empty-handed, as Godber remained adamant there would be no change in trade union law in lieu of the proposed Royal Commission, a stance which also frustrated the Conservative right (NA PREM 11/4871, Godber to Douglas-Home, 11 June 1964; 'Trade Unions and the Law – Memorandum by the Minister of Labour, undated, but circa 13–15 June 1964).

It is perhaps worth noting, in passing, that when he was interviewed on the *This Week* television programme[2], Godber was so keen to avoid both influencing

---

2   This was broadcast by Associated Rediffusion on 3 September 1964.

or prejudging the likely recommendations of the proposed Royal Commission and antagonising the trade unions in the run-up to the general election, that his answers were a masterpiece of non-committal equivocation and bland generalities, including this singularly opaque answer to the question of what specific aspects of trade unionism ought to be examined?:

> Well, there are many aspects, of course, but the very fact that I am proposing to set up an enquiry means that I have an open mind on this, and I want to have a broad-based enquiry and that I want those concerned to look into this matter and to advise us and ... in the light of that advice, then we will be in a much clearer position to know what, if anything, should be done.

The Conservative Party therefore contested the 1964 election pledging that 'the law affecting trade unions and employers' associations ... will be the subject of an early inquiry', although there remained a commitment to securing a closer partnership with the trade unions via the NEDC (Craig, 1970: 219). However, the election defeat ensured that the Conservative Party had to conduct its own review of trade union law in opposition, and that it was the (narrowly) victorious Labour government which actually established a Royal Commission, chaired by Lord Donovan, on Trade Unions and Employers' Associations, albeit with the former constituting the primary focus. By this time, both political parties had been obliged to acknowledge the limits of voluntarism as an industrial relations strategy. Meanwhile, Enoch Powell looked back disparagingly at the Conservative leadership's 13-year adherence to voluntarism, ruefully observing that: 'The Party came into Office ... without any specific commitment on trade-union law and practice, and it faithfully carried that non-commitment out for thirteen years' (Powell, 1968: 5).

Conclusion

The 1960s witnessed the Conservative Party's voluntarist approach to industrial relations and trade unionism being placed under growing pressure, and although it was not formally abandoned during the final four years in Office, there was an increasing defensiveness and desperation in Ministerial pronouncements on the undesirability and impracticability of seeking legislative solutions in such a delicate and complex area. Many of the issues or problems which had manifested themselves during the 1950s continued to vex Ministers into the 1960s, but they were exacerbated, and therefore acquired greater resonance, by virtue of wider economic trends and circumstances. For example, although Ministers continued to espouse the human relations perspective, and invoke the principles of the Workers' Charter, in terms of tackling employees' alienation and low self-esteem in the workplace, the growing size of British industry and the companies therein, often served to widen the gulf between employers and employees. The same trend towards industrial concentration and economies of scale also meant that many trade union leaders appeared remote and 'out of touch' with their members on the factory floor – a phenomenon exacerbated by the recourse to incomes policies, discussed in the next chapter – which enabled local union officials and shop stewards to play an increasingly prominent role in day-to-day industrial relations, their activities often most noticeable in terms of their apparent involvement in unofficial or wildcat strikes. Not surprisingly, such developments further fuelled demands from sundry Conservative backbenchers and rank-and-file activists for the Party leadership to introduce legislation to tackle unofficial strikes, while concern over the manner in which some trade union leaders were appointed or elected also prompted demands for independently-conducted secret ballots for union leadership elections.

What imbued the twin policy issues of industrial relations and trade unionism with even greater importance during the early 1960s was the growing concern over the relative decline – relative in both an historical and international comparative sense – and deteriorating health of the British economy, as evinced by the criteria and statistics for rates of economic growth and industrial productivity, inflation, balance of payments and a diminishing share of world trade in manufactured exports. In particular, growing attention was focused on the phenomenon of restrictive practices, and workers' resistance to new working practices or technologies intended to increase industrial output and efficiency, and, ultimately, to restore the competitiveness of the British economy. Yet Ministers also recognised that, very often, restrictive practices derived from workers' understandable fears about redundancies and displacement through automation, which reinforced the resonance of the 'human relations' approach. It was partly to address this problem that 1963 heralded the introduction of the Contracts of Employment Act, which also finally gave legislative effect to one of the recommendations originally enshrined in *The Industrial Charter*.

Towards the end of their time in office, the Conservative leadership was coming to the conclusion that the best way to address these industrial relations and trade union problems was to establish a Royal Commission, although this then promoted a debate about the timing of such an inquiry; whether it should be established immediately, with its recommendations possibly to be included in the Party's manifesto (whereupon re-election would be interpreted as a mandate from the electorate) or whether proposals for a Royal Commission should be announced, but with such an inquiry not inaugurated until after the election. Ministers eventually selected the second of these options, although they did so in the context of a landmark judicial decision in the *Rookes* v. *Barnard* case, the complexities of which cast considerable doubt over the legal immunities previously enjoyed by the trade unions when engaging in certain types of industrial action. Trade union fear and fury over this decision, and the resultant ambiguities over their legal position, seemed to vindicate the Conservative Party's decision to launch a Royal Commission into trade union law, albeit deferring this until after the 1964 general election. Voluntarism's days were numbered.

Chapter 6
Towards Incomes Policies, 1960–1964

As noted at the end of chapter four, increasing Conservative concern over wage increases during the latter half of the 1950s led Ministers to take a much closer interest in pay determination, and although they continued formally to eschew incomes policies, this was nonetheless the direction in which they were steadily moving. However, it was not until the 1960s that senior Conservatives explicitly adopted incomes policies, and claimed that henceforth, they would be a permanent feature of economic management. By the early 1960s, a range of economic variables were illustrating the character and scope of the problems affecting the British economy, all of which served to focus more critical attention on industrial relations, trade unionism and free collective bargaining. For example, it was discovered that the UK's inflation rate during the 1950s had averaged 4.1 per cent, compared to 1.9 per cent in West Germany and 2.1 per cent in the USA. During the same decade, the UK's average rate of economic growth, measured in terms of GDP, increased by just 2.6 per cent, compared to 7.6 per cent in West Germany, 5.9 per cent in Italy, 4.4 per cent in France, and 3.3 per cent in the USA. Meanwhile, Britain's share of world trade in manufactured exports declined from 25.5 per cent in 1950 to 16.5 per cent in 1960, which consequently fuelled concern about a deteriorating balance of payments position, as the decline in exports was accompanied by an increase in imported manufactured goods.

In the context of such economic indicators, Macmillan declared that 'the next great struggle that awaits us, and the most important, is the Battle of Wages' (Macmillan 1972: 376), whereupon, in the autumn of 1960, a Ministerial committee was established to consider the Government's response to specific pay claims and awards, primarily in the public sector and nationalised industries[1], although general questions concerning incomes policy remained within the remit of the Cabinet's Economic Policy Committee.

It was in July 1961 that two notable developments materialised, and finally set the Government on course for a permanent incomes policy. Firstly, the Cohen Council was disbanded – having almost been discontinued the previous year – its members being of the view that they had achieved as much as they could in terms of educating trade unions, and, indeed, the wider public, about the impact of wage settlements which were not matched by higher productivity, to the extent that 'further reports … are liable to be repetitive and ineffective'. Moreover, the

---

1   The relevant files at the National Archives detail Ministerial discussions concerning dozens of pay claims for individual industries, professions or specific sectors of the economy.

Council felt that, in the context of the trade unions' antipathy to the body, its continued existence 'may be a positive hindrance to trade union co-operation'. The Chancellor, with the Cabinet's approval, agreed to the Council's request that it should be disbanded after the publication of its Fourth Report at the end of July 1961, while linking such a move to his plans for a new forum to secure closer consultation and partnership between trade union leaders, employers' representatives and Ministers, namely the NEDC (NA PREM 11/3841, Lloyd to Macmillan, 18 July 1961).

Secondly, by July 1961, Macmillan was writing to Lloyd to express his anxiety about imminent pay claims which the Government would need to respond to, most notably civil servants, the public sector (teachers, fire-fighters, police, etc.), nationalised industries and workers whose pay was covered by Wage Boards or Wage Councils. What Macmillan was concerned about was not merely the vital issue of the size of many pay increases, but the extent to which the Government was obliged to adhere to arbitration agreements. On the assumption that it would be morally questionable and politically provocative for the Government to start reneging on pay settlements attained through existing arbitration procedures, Macmillan wondered whether more could be done 'to make arbitrators more keenly aware of the economic situation than some of them sometimes appear to be' (NA PREM 11/4069, Macmillan to Lloyd, 28 July 1961). Indeed, after further reflection, Macmillan ventured to suggest that 'the whole system of arbitration, that is an arbitration where ... both sides are bound to accept the arbitration award, is inappropriate in modern conditions' with regard to those employees, most notably in the public sector or nationalised industries, whose remuneration the Government was ultimately responsible for: 'It leads us to an absurd position whereby we have less control over the economy than a private employer' (NA PREM 11/4069, Macmillan to Brook, 5 August 1961).

Not surprisingly, perhaps, the Ministry of Labour was more enamoured with the system of arbitration, for it accorded with its ethos of conflict avoidance or resolution in industrial relations, while also enabling some industrial disputes to be settled without recourse to strike action. Clearly, however, and as we noted in the previous chapter, the voluntarist philosophy of the Ministry of Labour was itself being placed under increasing strain both by the deteriorating economic conditions of the early 1960s, and by continued lack of trade union responsibility or moderation *vis-à-vis* their behaviour and pay claims. As such, the Ministry's rather sanguine view of the virtues of arbitration was now increasingly at odds with those Ministers concerned with the economic costs of funding such pay awards.

The 1961 'pay pause'

In lieu of addressing such issues, and in response to the seriousness of the economic situation, the Government's immediate response was hurriedly to announce a 'pay pause', which was intended to remain in force until April 1962, by which time the government hoped to have formulated a long-term policy for wages, and *inter alia* addressed the issues raised by Macmillan. In the meantime, though, the Chancellor subsequently explained to TUC representatives that the 'pay pause' had been an emergency measure to alleviate intense pressure on sterling in the international financial markets – itself prompted, to a considerable extent, by a deteriorating balance-of-payments situation, as Britain's 'exports were suffering from a loss of competitiveness' – and that failure to have acted as he had done would probably have forced the Government to resort to devaluation, which would have had a deeply damaging impact on living standards overall. To illustrate just how serious and untenable the economic situation had become, Lloyd pointed out that in the 1960–61 financial year, personal incomes had increased by £1,450 million, but industrial production had risen by only £650 million (NA PREM 11/4314, Note of meeting between the Chancellor and TUC representatives, 22 August 1961).

Although the 'pay pause', which comprised a seven-month pay freeze, only applied to the public sector, it was intended that it would serve as an example to the private sector, and provide employers with the resolve to resist 'excessive' pay claims. It was also hoped that the 'pay pause' would alert the trade unions to the seriousness of Britain's economic problems – 'there is no other way that we can show by action rather than by exhortation that there must be a break in the vicious circle of the inflationary wage round' (PREM 11/4069, Hare to Macmillan, 10 October 1961) – and Macmillan remained quietly confident, in spite of his growing exasperation with them, that trade union leaders 'knew very well in their hearts that wage claims must lead to inflation unless accompanied by an increase in productivity', even if 'they dare not say so openly' (Macmillan, 1972: 379). To this extent, 'the pay pause was an appeal to the common sense and patriotism of all concerned – employers, employed and the general public' (Macmillan, 1973: 44).

Meanwhile, shortly after his retirement as Director of the Cabinet Office's Economic Section, Robert Hall suggested that:

> With the passage of time the number of adherents of extreme positions has diminished and a large body of opinion now thinks that some form of wage policy other than leaving wages to free collective bargaining is necessary if full employment and stable prices are to be combined.
> (Hall, 1961: 1042)

This was reflected in the appointment of Sir Laurence Helsby as Permanent Secretary at the Ministry of Labour, for whereas his predecessors had considered the pursuit of conciliation to be of paramount importance, Helsby's background as an economist in the Treasury elicited a somewhat different stance, to the extent that 'under his reign the Ministry decided as a conscious act of policy that it could no longer automatically step in to conciliate irrespective of the economic damage it produced in the process' (Brittan, 1969: 164). By this time, Treasury officials were themselves becoming convinced that, given the Government's determination to avoid both deflation and higher unemployment, 'we must obtain, either by cooperation or imposition, a considerable degree of wage restraint' (NA PREM 11/3841, Bligh to Macmillan, 12 July1961).

Another reason why some Conservative Ministers, including Macmillan himself, became convinced of the need for an incomes policy during the early 1960s was their concern that under free collective bargaining: 'The middle classes would be out-gunned by the big unions', whereas with an incomes policy, the Conservative government could offer its middle-class supporters a much greater degree of 'order and control'. Accordingly, it was argued, the middle classes 'have everything to gain and nothing to lose from a planned and imaginative incomes policy', whereas they 'would be among the first to suffer in a free-for-all' (NA PREM 11/4071, `Notes for talk to Cabinet on Incomes Policy', 25 May 1962; NA CAB 128/36 Part One, C.C (62) 37th conclusions, 28 May 1962).

A further factor steering Ministers towards a long-term incomes policy was the realisation that even when particular firms or industries could afford generous wage increases on the basis of higher industrial output or profits, without a corresponding need to increase their prices, these pay settlements then constituted the 'going rate' for workers in less successful companies, along with non-profit-making nationalised industries and the wider public sector. This particular problem was compounded by inter-union competition, for it was 'natural that when a trade union in one industry has achieved a rise for its members, the members of other unions should expect their leaders to do the same', and those leaders would feel that they had failed if they did not secure comparable pay increase for their members. (CPA, CRD 2/7/15, PFC (62) 1, 'Incomes and Prices', 26 January 1962).

The whole problem was further compounded by the tendency of higher-paid industrial workers to observe lower-paid workers trying to catch up with them through their pay claims, whereupon the former sought a higher pay claim in order to maintain or restore their differentials in relation to the latter. Ultimately, the whole annual pay cycle was being increasingly characterised by a process of 'leap-frogging', with workers and trade unions seeking to outbid each other in order to retain or regain the advantage in the annual battle over wages (CPA, CRD 2/7/16, 'Wages and Productivity', 29 December 1961). However, in refusing to countenance deflation and higher unemployment as a means of dampening pay increases and instil greater responsibility into trade union wage negotiators, Macmillan and many of his Ministerial colleagues became convinced of the need for a more long-term and politically co-ordinated approach to pay determination.

In the meantime, though, having somewhat hastily invoked the 'pay pause' in lieu of devising a more permanent incomes policy, Ministers very soon became aware of the practical problems and complexities of seeking to impose a wage freeze in the public sector. Certainly, 'when the Chancellor first proposed this temporary alleviation of our economic difficulties ... neither he nor his colleagues had a clear picture of all that was implied', for:

As the months passed, we began to realise the complexities of a policy spread over such a wide field. In many industries, there were agreements for automatic pay increases in accordance with any rise in the cost of living; in others, agreements had already been made for a rise within the near future; in others, negotiations were proceeding. In addition, arbitration agreements ruled over quite a wide field. Were these to be suspended or set aside? … were we to accept the inevitable leakages, hoping that the temporary dam … might at least stem the flood?

(Macmillan, 1973: 44–5)

Elsewhere, a Conservative MP, Thomas Moore, had a letter published in *The Times* (6 February 1962) claiming that: 'We will all admit that the Pay Pause has been badly mishandled', and as such, it served to alert Ministers and senior officials to the urgent need for greater co-ordination and planning of economic activity (NA PREM 11/4069, Bligh to Macmillan, 2 August 1961).

One particular problem which confronted Ministers following the hurried imposition of the 'pay pause' was that already vexing Harold Macmillan, as just noted, namely arbitration awards concerning public sector pay, for there was no guarantee that arbitrators would take sufficient account of the Government's putative incomes policy when adjudicating on disputed pay claims. Yet they would probably resent anything which could be construed as Ministerial interference in their work, particularly as this would undermine their independence and impartiality. However, it was deemed essential that Ministers addressed this issue as a matter urgency, to show private sector employers that the Government was serious in its determination to curb unwarranted pay increases, the intention being that a tough stance by the Government against its own employees in the nationalised industries and the public sector would similarly embolden private sector employers. This tough stance was also intended to convince 'the City' and the international financial community about the Government's determination to curb inflationary pay increases, which were themselves pushing Britain's balance of payments (on visible earnings) into deeper deficit, largely as a consequence of consumer spending on imports.

In this context, Ministers were presented with three options concerning arbitration, each of which was highly problematic and unpalatable (NA CAB 128/35 Part Two, C.C. (61) 47th and 48th conclusions, 3 and 4 August 1961). The most extreme option would have been to suspend arbitration procedures temporarily, probably for the duration of the 'pay pause', but it was feared that this was likely to 'provoke great unrest', while also being widely viewed, by the trade unions, as a political assault on free collective bargaining itself. Moreover, this would seriously undermine the painstaking efforts of the 1950s to forge a closer, more harmonious relationship with the trade unions, a relationship which would be even more important if the Government was to establish a long-term voluntary incomes policy following the 'pay pause'.

Secondly, the Government might conceivably have allowed arbitration procedures to continue, but then refuse to accept the ensuing award. This too would almost certainly have caused widespread anger and distrust among those workers and trade unions affected, possibly to the extent of prompting a number of damaging strikes in the nationalised industries, while again reducing the likelihood that the trade unions would accept a longer-term incomes policy after the expiry of the 'pay pause'. It would certainly have left Ministers open to the charge of duplicity in permitting pay disputes to be submitted to arbitration when they had no intention of honouring any subsequent award or settlement. This too would also have been interpreted by many trade unions as political interference both with free collective bargaining, and with the formal neutrality of the arbitration service. Indeed, the latter would probably be placed in an untenable position if Ministers began explicitly disavowing its recommendations to the point of refusing to implement them.

The third option theoretically available to Ministers would have been to defer any public sector pay increase awarded through arbitration, or possibly introduce it in stages. Unlike the other two options, this would entail a degree of flexibility, and would at least enable arbitration awards to be paid at a subsequent date, thereby highlighting that the Government was operating a 'pay *pause*', not a wage *freeze*. The main danger of this approach, though, was that arbitrators might 'compensate' workers for a likely deferral of their pay award by granting a higher settlement than they would otherwise have done. This would threaten an inflationary pay explosion at the end of the 'pay pause', and thereby obviate any advantages which might have accrued to the British economy in the meantime. Notwithstanding this particular risk, it was this option – with the encouragement of the Prime Minister, the Chancellor and the Minister of Labour – which the Cabinet finally endorsed, albeit only after two lengthy meetings on consecutive days, and with some Ministers preferring the option of suspending arbitration altogether for a few months.

Meanwhile, some senior Conservative officials were concerned that several months after invoking the 'pay pause', and just four months before its scheduled expiry, it was 'not clear how much progress has been made' in devising a long-term incomes policy, which raised the distinct danger that 'when the pay pause dam bursts, there is likely to be a rush of claims', in which case 'the wage spiral may continue with increased ferocity'. There was even a suggestion that the 'pay pause' should be continued 'for a number of years', during which time, unwarranted pay increases in any industry would be negated by the imposition of a special tax, possibly levied through a surcharge on employees' National Insurance contributions (CPA CRD 2/7/16, 'After the Pause', 6 December 1961).

Although this particular proposal attracted little support elsewhere in the Conservative Party – it would have been politically controversial and administratively complex, as well as almost certain to alienate the trade unions whom Ministers were, by now, desperately seeking to incorporate into economic policy-making – Macmillan was increasingly convinced that 'there must be some permanent form of incomes policy applying both to the private and the public sector', for without such a policy, at least one of the government's four objectives – full employment, stable prices, a favourable balance of payments and the expansion of the economy – would have to be abandoned, which he deemed 'unacceptable'. It was in this context that Macmillan began ruminating on the need for 'an impartial source of wage assessment operating over the whole field' (Macmillan, 1973: 70. See also NA PREM 11/4314, Note of meeting between Chancellor and the Economic Committee of the TUC, 6 December 1962). Others in the Conservative Party were similarly becoming convinced of the need for a long-term or permanent incomes policy, with one senior official admitting that whereas, prior to 1960, he had been 'against any form of interference in incomes', he had, within the last couple of years, been 'shaken' from this position, to the extent of now being convinced of the need for 'trying to check directly the rise in wages and salaries' (CPA CRD 2/7/16, Douglas to Sewill, 3 January 1962). Indeed, Brendon Sewill had already concluded that 'the present trouble arises because the trade unions ... are in the position of monopolists' which it was politically impossible to break, thereby rendering an incomes policy essential if either higher inflation or unemployment were to be avoided (CPA, CRD 2/7/16, Brendon Sewill, 'After the Pause II', 29 December 1961).

A 'guiding light'

By the early 1960s, Macmillan and his Ministers were under increasing pressure from the Treasury to pursue a deflationary policy, whilst some Conservative backbenchers were becoming ever more convinced of the need for legislation to curb trade union power, the unions increasingly being blamed for much of Britain's relative economic decline. Indeed, the problems engendered by the 'pay pause' were seen as a vindication by the proponents of both policies, with trade union power deemed to be a major underlying cause of inflation, and the very reason why incomes policies would ultimately prove unsuccessful. For those subscribing to this particular perspective, only higher unemployment or statutory curbs on trade unionism – or a combination of both – would yield lower pay increases and *inter alia* reduce inflation. Neither of these options was acceptable to Macmillan, who 'did not believe that wage inflation ... could be cured by a general deflationary policy [as] followed, so slavishly, by successive Chancellors of the Exchequer between the wars' (Macmillan, 1973: 49). Similarly, a senior official in the Conservative Research Department acknowledged that if the Government allowed unemployment to rise above the official maximum rate of three per cent, 'there would be a major political row. We should have to notify the United Nations and all the rest of it' (CPA, CRD 2/7/16, Douglas to Sewill, 3 January 1962). One further option was a statutory incomes policy, but as the Chancellor explained to his Cabinet colleagues in early December, there was 'general agreement that it would be impracticable to establish legal control over wages, profits, dividends and prices' (NA CAB 128/35 C.C (61) 68th conclusions, 7 December 1961).

Instead, Macmillan was determined to develop a closer, more constructive relationship with the trade unions and employers, in the hope that deflation could be avoided and full employment maintained, through the adoption of a voluntary long-term incomes policy, and as such, he insisted that the breathing space provided by the 'pay pause' had to be used to develop 'some other satisfactory and permanent system' (Macmillan, 1973: 49), What transpired was the creation of the National Economic Development Council (NEDC), although Ministers were anxious to assure the TUC that the NEDC would not be involved in the formulation or administration of incomes policies, an assurance which was essential to persuading the trade unions to participate. However, it was hardly likely that the NEDC would play absolutely no part in pay determination, because any incomes policy would be based on calculations about what level of wage increases the British economy could afford, and such calculations would invariably be extrapolated from the on-going economic analyses and forecasts emanating from the NEDC. Indeed, whilst preparing for the creation of the NEDC, the Chancellor made clear: 'My intention that all types of measures that encouraged economic growth would come within the purview of the NEDC ... this certainly cannot be dissociated from a sensible policy for incomes' (NA PREM 11/4069, letter to TUC's Economic Committee, 10 January 1962; see also NA PREM 11/4071, Watkinson to Macmillan, 6 June 1962).

Macmillan envisaged that the involvement of the trade unions in the NEDC 'would at least lead them to greater understanding of the real problems with which the nation is confronted' (Macmillan 1973: 51), and thereby help to persuade them of the need for greater wage restraint than had been practised previously. Certainly, Macmillan was now emphatic that: 'An incomes policy is necessary as a permanent feature of our economic life ... an indispensable element in the foundations on which to build a policy of sound economic growth' (HC Debates, 5th series, Vol. 663: col. 1757), a perspective wholly shared by Reginald Maudling, who replaced Selwyn Lloyd as Chancellor in July 1962.

One other initiative which Ministers briefly considered at the beginning of 1962 was harmonising annual pay increases, so that wage awards would all be settled at the same time each year. This, it was suggested, would eradicate the problem of pay 'leap-frogging', whereby some trade unions sought pay increases which were higher than those accepted by other unions earlier in the year. No decision was taken on such a measure, however, with Ministers merely leaving it as an option for the future – one which was never subsequently pursued (NA CAB 128/36 C.C. (62), 36th conclusions, 8 January 1962), although the following year, Treasury officials conducted their own desultory and inconclusive discussions about the 'synchronisation' of pay awards (NA T 311/86, A. Mueller, 'Synchronisation of key wage bargains', 21 June 1963).

The end of the 'pay pause' was immediately followed by a 'guiding light', whereby increases in earnings were expected to be confined to a range of 2–2.5 per cent per annum, for it was deemed 'essential that increases in personal incomes of all kinds should be brought into a more realistic relationship with increases in national production' (Treasury, 1962: 3). However, Ministers conceded that larger increases could be permitted in certain circumstances, namely 'as part of an agreement under which those concerned made a direct contribution, by accepting more exacting work, or more onerous conditions, or by a renunciation of restrictive practices, to an increase in productivity and a reduction in costs'. Conversely, though, it was suggested that: 'In many cases, there may indeed be no justification at present for any increases at all', whilst in others, some of the criteria previously cited to justify pay rises, such as a higher cost of living or comparability, 'ought not to be given the same weight as hitherto' (Treasury, 1962: 4).

The principle of a 'guiding light' for influencing pay awards – something which Lord (David Heathcoat) Amory had originally mooted back in October 1960 (Amory, 1960: 9–10) – was viewed by some Ministers as 'one of a number of middle courses between our present system of free collective bargaining and a centralised wage-fixing system such as that of Sweden or the Netherlands' (NA CAB 124/1618, Hare to Hailsham, 18 January 1961), and as such, was entirely consistent with Macmillan's advocacy, since the inter-war period, of a 'middle way' with regard to economic and industrial affairs. It also reflected Ministerial acknowledgement of the impracticability of subjecting wages to legal controls, in which case, any incomes policy would need to secure the support of public opinion, as well as the two sides of industry.

Prior to its formal Cabinet approval and public announcement, the 'guiding light' had naturally been subject to considerable discussion in the Cabinet's Economic Policy Committee, whereupon some divergence of views over the future of incomes policy had manifested themselves. For example, Lord Mills believed that any figure stipulated by the Cabinet would invariably be exceeded by employers wanting to recruit more workers in the context of labour shortages, in which case, as Iain Macleod observed, settlements which exceeded the 'guiding light' would be depicted as defeats for the Government. Besides, Lord Mills also noted that the TUC did not have any authority over affiliated trade unions to ensure their compliance. More controversially, Frederick Errol, the President of the Board of Trade, suggested that instead of tackling economic problems through incomes policies, the Government ought to deflate the economy and thereby permit a small rise in unemployment. This proposal, however, was swiftly rejected by most other Ministers on the Economic Policy Committee, who argued that such a 'solution' would be morally and politically unacceptable.

Consequently, the prevailing view was that a 'guiding light' would at least signal the seriousness of Britain's economic problems – whereas abandoning attempts at curbing pay increases would be widely viewed as 'failure to govern' – and help 'bring public opinion to bear on both sides of industry to observe constraint' (NA PREM 11/4069, Cary to Macmillan, 6 December 1961). Ultimately, in rejecting the options of allowing unfettered and unrestrained free collective bargaining, imposing statutory pay curbs, permitting a deflationary increase in unemployment, or introducing trade union legislation (as noted in the previous chapter), Ministers were left with only one feasible option, namely some form of long-term voluntary incomes policy.

In lieu of such a policy, the Macmillan Government insisted that in the context of the 'guiding light', it was 'for employers and employees to work out the application of the considerations ... to individual cases, in the light of the conditions and agreements existing in particular industries and areas'. The government merely asked that 'all negotiations affecting wages and salaries in 1962 should reflect these considerations'. The success of the guiding light, it was acknowledged, 'depends heavily on the willingness of workers not to press claims which go beyond the limits which this policy indicates' (Treasury, 1962: 5). This, in turn, reflected the view prevalent within the Cabinet at this time that 'in a free society the government should not aim to coerce but to persuade', which therefore meant that any incomes policy 'can only be made to work if it is supported by public opinion' (NA PREM 11/4069, Bligh to Macmillan, 23 November 1961).

Yet in spite of this emphasis on non-coercion in stipulating the 'guiding light', the Cabinet did give some consideration to the issue of what sanctions could be invoked if pay increases in excess of the 'guiding light' were awarded when these did not meet the relevant criteria. One option favoured by some Ministers was to invoke sanctions – such as a payroll tax – against companies who granted unwarranted wage increases in excess of the 'guiding light'. Another option mooted by some within the Cabinet was the removal of the trade unions' legal immunities, thereby rendering them liable to civil action, in the case of unlawful industrial action. From elsewhere in the Conservative Party came the demand that agreements reached through collective bargaining should be rendered legally binding for one or two years at a time (Monday Club, 1963: 29–30).

Ultimately, however, the Cabinet again decided against compulsion, preferring instead to rely upon the common sense and patriotism of the two side of industry, buttressed by the force of public opinion. It was claimed that:

> This is an adult nation and the people must accept the responsibility of being grown-up. They must be prepared to impose self-discipline. It is the government's responsibility to inform and persuade. It is no part of our way of life to try and impose an economic policy under threat of sanctions.
> (NA PREM 11/4069, Bligh to Macmillan, 23 November 1961)

The refusal to invoke sanctions against either employers or trade unions for breaching the 'guiding light' was subsequently endorsed by an official [civil servants] committee, for having considered potential responses to 'excessive' pay awards, it was nonetheless concluded that sanctions would either prove unenforceable in practice, or 'would inevitably lead towards a fully controlled economy' (NA PREM 11/4071, Frank Lee, 'A Policy for Wages, Salaries and Other Incomes – Annex C; Incomes Policy: Possible Sanctions', 9 November 1961)

Ministers also hoped that trade unions and their members would evince greater moderation and restraint if they were provided with appropriate information which placed their pay claims in a wider economic context. To this end, the 'guiding light' was accompanied by a government pledge to

> ... collect together and to publish in convenient form factual information on wage rates, earnings, hours of work and other conditions of employment, manpower, prices, production, profits and relevant subjects so that due weight can be given by all concerned ... at all stages of negotiations and at arbitration.
> (Treasury, 1962: 6).

This was an allusion to the Government's plans for replacing the Cohen Council with a standing Commission on Pay, which would be able to examine particular pay claims or awards with reference to their likely economic implications or compatibility with the 'guiding light'. In due course, it was envisaged that such a body would acquire increasing expertise, while also identifying broader trends and issues which could then provide the basis of authoritative yet independent advice to those involved in pay determination and economic management. What actually transpired was the National Incomes Commission (NIC) – announced in July 1962 but not actually becoming operational until November that year – which was given a very modest remit, whereby it could only 'review certain pay matters where the cost was wholly or partly met from the Exchequer, if the government asked it to do so, and to examine retrospectively any particular pay settlement which the government referred to it' (Blackaby, 1978: 364).

The trade unions, though, boycotted the NIC, denouncing the premise that 'some group of independent people, some outsiders [could] take on their shoulders the burden of defining what was the national interest for one section of the community – the wage earners' (TUC, 1962; 369–70). With employers also paying scant regard to it, the NIC almost inevitably proved an ineffective body, only considering a mere five cases referred to it by Ministers in its less than illustrious three-year history. Indeed, in his *Wage Politics in Britain 1945–1967*, Dorfman does not even mention the NIC in the chapter which deals with the pay pause and the guiding light (Dorfman, 1973), while Blackaby notes that the NIC 'had a short and rather undistinguished life', and 'certainly did not succeed in focusing the wrath of public opinion on excessive wage awards' (Blackaby 1978: 304; see also, Jones, 1987: 61).

Meanwhile, as part of the Government's pursuit of a long-term voluntary incomes policy, the Chancellor and Minister of Labour held a series of meetings with TUC leaders, and employers' representatives, during the summer of 1962. One particular option mooted by the Chancellor during the course of these meetings was that the 'guiding light' be applied on a long-term basis, albeit applied more flexibly after the expiry of its current 12-month term. What the Chancellor envisaged was that the stipulated figure for affordable pay awards represented an average, not a maximum, so that if the 'guiding light' stipulated pay awards averaging 2.5 per cent per annum, but a group of workers had not received a pay increase the previous year, they might then be entitled to 5 per cent the following year, because this would still represent an annual average of 2.5 per cent over the 2 years. There was a further intimation that a long-term incomes policy might be somehow linked to the Government's objective of improving the status and security of industrial workers, the implication being that for some employees, improved contracts and conditions of employment might be offered by way of compensation for accepting a lower pay settlement (NA PREM 11/4072, Minutes of meetings between the Chancellor, the Minister of Labour, and others (attendees varying from meeting to meeting), various dates early July 1962. See also: NA PREM 11/4071, Notes for talk [by Prime Minister] to Cabinet on Incomes Policy, 25 May 1962; Macmillan, 1973: 70).

Throughout these talks, Ministers were at pains to assure the trade unions that neither the National Incomes Commission nor the 'guiding light' signalled the end of free collective bargaining, nor were they intended to be instruments of wage restraint, but, instead, as means of facilitating faster economic growth without accompanying inflation. Such assurances failed to assuage trade union scepticism that, regardless of the terminology or names attached to them, these policy initiatives and institutional innovations were all concerned, in the last instance, with obliging industrial workers to accept lower pay increases, and without any corresponding restrictions being placed on profits or share-holders' dividends.

Yet there was concern among some Ministers that the Government's ability to impose curbs on their own employees in the public sector and nationalised industries risked antagonising such workers, who might well feel that the public sector was being 'singled out for restrictive treatment', a regrettable perception which might also be shared by the public. As such, it was deemed imperative that corresponding pay restraint was secured in the private sector (PREM 11/4070, Cary to Macmillan, 21 March 1962), although Ministers were understandably unsure about how to achieve this objective without resorting to draconian measures or more direct state intervention in the economy, either of which would be bitterly resented by private sector employees and the trade unions alike. Yet it was also evident that if this problem was not successfully tackled, then there would be less scope for a longer-term incomes policy. Furthermore, higher price increases in the private sector (to offset higher pay increases) were rather more detrimental to Britain's export drive, because they rendered British manufactured goods less competitive in international markets. Nonetheless, Ministers were largely left, as ever, having to rely heavily on exhortation, and the continued but seemingly forlorn hope that pay restraint in the public sector would set an example to the private sector, although John Hare did strongly urge the chairmen of the various Wage Councils to consider much more carefully, in the context of wider economic circumstances, the amount by which they raised the pay of those workers covered by these bodies.

The limited success of the Government's attempts at securing pay restraint was such that in the late autumn of 1962, in addition to the existing Ministerial Committee on Wages and the Cabinet's Economic Policy Committee, two official committees were established on incomes policy. Moreover, during the next two years, membership of the Ministerial Committee was occasionally expanded to include Ministers from Departments, such as the Board of Trade, which had hitherto been 'distinctly uncommitted on incomes policy' (CAB 21/5347, Helsby to Trend, 28 November 1963).

Nonetheless, despite the time and energy being devoted to the issue by Ministers and senior civil servants, an effective and mutually acceptable incomes policy continued to prove elusive, partly because of a continued lack of agreement in either the Cabinet or Whitehall over the precise content or format of any such policy (notwithstanding those Ministers who would have preferred a policy of deflation and higher unemployment instead), and, even more importantly perhaps, continuing trade union commitment to free collective bargaining. After another fruitless meeting with three senior TUC leaders, including George Woodcock, an exasperated Reginald Maudling reported to Macmillan that the trade union trio 'spoke with the authoritative voice of Gladstonian Liberals', for while they acknowledged the need for moderation and responsibility in pay bargaining in general, they were not willing to accept or apply it with regard to their own particular interests: 'They accept the problem, they contest our solution but they will produce no constructive alternative' (NA PREM 11/4073, Maudling to Macmillan, 18 July 1962).

Although many Ministers shared Macmillan's conviction that a long-term incomes policy would henceforth constitute an essential tool of economic management in the constant struggle against inflation and unemployment, as well as to tackle Britain's increasing balance of payments deficits, it was rapidly becoming apparent that, quite apart from the vital issue of securing trade union acquiescence, any incomes policy would highlight or exacerbate problems pertaining to such principles as fairness and comparability, as well as differentiation and consequent tensions between the private and public sectors. There was also the unresolved issue of what sanctions, if any, Ministers could invoke in the case of breaches of any incomes policy, either by employers or trade unions.

The problem of 'wage drift'

The Conservative Government's increasing recourse to incomes policy from 1961 onwards also served to highlight another problem, namely that of 'wage drift'. This referred to the tendency for actual earnings to increase at a higher or faster rate than the figure officially agreed through national pay bargaining. Ministers discovered that in many industries – particularly engineering – regardless of what was agreed by trade union officials formally negotiating with employers' representatives or/and Ministers in London, local-level managers and trade union officials or shop stewards often negotiated additional or supplementary agreements, entailing somewhat more generous pay increases. For example, in the financial year 1961–62, actual average earnings (excluding overtime payments) were almost one per cent higher than official or hourly wage rates, while in 1963–64, the difference was 1.3 per cent. Some of this discrepancy could be attributed to productivity bonuses, which Ministers ordinarily encouraged as a means of increasing industrial output, but it was also recognised that part of this divergence was due to differences between official pay deals agreed at national level and unofficial pay deals agreed at factory or workshop level, and it was the last of these causes which increasingly vexed Ministers, the Treasury and the Ministry of Labour during the 1960s.

Furthermore, even if local level employers paid these higher earnings without raising their prices, the overall effect was still considered to be inflationary, because other groups of workers would invariably seek to obtain compensatory wage increases, with lower-paid workers seeking 'catch-up' pay rises, while better-paid workers sought higher pay increases in order to maintain or restore differentials. Moreover, 'wage drift' was extremely difficult to measure or factor into economic plans, such as those devised by the NEDC during this period. This led the Government, in its written submission to a 1964 NIC inquiry into recent pay awards in the engineering and shipbuilding industries, to ask:

> how as a nation we can ensure that the results of a dual system of wage negotiation operating simultaneously at the national and local level are consistent with incomes policy, which requires incomes of all kinds to be kept in line with the trend in productivity if further inflation is to be avoided.
> (Quoted in Treasury, 1964)

This problem was depicted more starkly four years later, in the (Donovan) Report of the Royal Commission on Trade Union and Employers' Associations, when it explained that:

> Britain now has two systems of industrial relations. The one is the formal system embodied in the official institutions. The other is the informal system created by the actual behaviour of trade unions and employers' associations, of managers, of shop stewards and workers… The informal system undermines the regulative effect of industry-wide agreements. The gap between industry-wide agreed rates and actual earnings continues to grow.
> (Royal Commission, 1968: 12)

Not surprisingly, the Treasury was particularly concerned about the development of 'wage drift' from the early 1960s onwards, with some officials calling for employers' organisations to be made more fully aware of the problem, and their own contribution to it as a consequence of acceding to 'excessive' trade union pay claims (NA T 331/86, Note of meeting of officials from the Treasury and the Ministry of Labour, 3 July 1963).

Struggling to maintain an incomes policy

Due to the problems of securing wage restraint in accordance with the 'pay pause' and the 'guiding light', Ministers were inevitably going to find it difficult to secure agreement for a further incomes policy for 1963 and 1964. Although they sought to persuade both the TUC and employers' representatives of the need for a continuation of pay and price restraint to follow the scheduled (spring 1963) expiry of the 'guiding light', the records of various meetings and negotiations convey the impression that senior Conservatives themselves were rapidly becoming pessimistic about their chances of success. This does not mean that they were willing to resort to deflation instead, or to invoke legislation to tackle trade union 'irresponsibility' – not yet, anyway – but there was a discernible shift of emphasis towards fostering faster economic growth through the NEDC, in the desperate hope that higher industrial output and productivity would simultaneously make non-inflationary pay increases more affordable, while also boosting British manufactured exports, and thereby reduce or eradicate the country's balance of payments' deficit.

Consequently, with the NEDC promulgating an annual rate of four per cent for economic growth, and the existing 'guiding light' pay norm of 2.5 per cent proving untenable, it was generally accepted that wage increases during 1963 and 1964 should be no more than 3.5 per cent, although the continued emphasis on a voluntary incomes policy meant that Ministers would again be unable to enforce such a limit on the private sector, and this, in turn, would make it extremely difficult to contain mounting pressure – and anger – in the public sector. In spite of this more generous 'limit' for pay increases, the trade unions remained implacably opposed to an incomes policy which they considered to be primarily concerned with wage restraint – although they were, during this period, coming to an agreement with the Labour Party for a 'planned *growth* of incomes', which is precisely what exasperated Conservative Ministers could claim they were also seeking – and this reluctance to accept another incomes policy was compounded by the realisation that 1964 would herald a general election.

Indeed, both for senior Conservatives and the trade unions, from late 1963 onwards, thoughts were increasingly dominated by the imminent general election, and although they would never admit it openly, Ministers were not inclined to impose pay restraint too vigorously in the approach to an election, for this is a period when incumbent governments invariably seek to facilitate an economic 'feel-good' factor among voters, in order to increase their chances of re-election. As such, there was something half-hearted about the Government's call for pay increases to be limited to 3.5 per cent after the expiry of the 'guiding light', particularly as Ministers were also talking in terms of using the forthcoming general election as the basis for seeking a new agreement over prices and incomes, with the Conservative Party's 1964 manifesto pledging that: 'We shall take a further initiative to secure wider acceptance and effective implementation of such a policy' (Craig, 1970: 217). In the meantime, at a meeting with the TUC's Economic Committee in July 1963, the

Chancellor was talking in terms of an improving economic situation, to the extent that he was increasingly thinking about stimulating demand in order to boost both public and consumer spending, although the implication was that this would be jeopardised if wage restraint was abandoned (NA PREM 11/4314, Note of a meeting between the Chancellor of the Exchequer and the Economic Committee of the TUC, 10 July 1963).

What might also have somewhat weakened the Cabinet's commitment to an incomes policy during the Government's final year was the autumn 1963 resignation, on health grounds, of Harold Macmillan himself, for he had been the major impetus in steering Ministerial colleagues towards both indicative economic planning and the search for a long-term voluntary incomes policy. Immediately following Macmillan's departure, some of this impetus seems to have dissipated, and his successor – whom he actually endorsed to replace him – Alec Douglas-Home, had never shown the same interest in economic affairs as his predecessor. Indeed, Douglas-Home's expertise and reputation were primarily in foreign affairs, having been appointed Secretary of State for Commonwealth Relations in 1955 and Foreign Secretary in 1960, which, incidentally, might explain why the first two pages of the Conservative Party's 1964 manifesto were devoted to foreign policy and international relations. It is certainly notable that after Macmillan's resignation as Prime Minister, there was very little discussion of incomes policy in the Cabinet. There also seemed to be a rather naive hope that the 1964 abolition of resale price maintenance, by promoting competition, would lead to lower prices for consumers, and thereby help to alleviate upward pressure on wages.

Consequently, in September 1964, with the general election just weeks away, the Cabinet heard the Chief Secretary to the Treasury explain that progress towards securing trade union agreement for an incomes policy had proved 'disappointingly slow'. It was therefore agreed that if they were re-elected, the Government would invite employers' representatives and trade union leaders to a special conference on incomes policy (NA CAB 128/38 Pt 2, C.M (64) 47th conclusions, 10 September 1964).

Conclusion

Recourse to an incomes policy also raised new issues and problems for Ministers during the early 1960s, and ultimately undermined this putative new approach to economic management. Pay restraint was heavily dependent not only upon trade union willingness to accept lower wage increases, in accordance with limits recommended by senior Ministers, but also on the readiness of private sector employers to resist pay claims which exceeded those limits. Yet when such co-operation and voluntary restraint were not forthcoming, the Cabinet found it difficult to impose its will, partly because this would have entailed an unacceptable degree of interference in the economic decisions of private employers and companies who could claim to have been responding to 'market' circumstances, and partly because of an inability to impose sanctions against recalcitrant trade unions or employers themselves. After all, Ministers were searching for a *voluntary* incomes policy, which meant that it could not credibly enforce wage restraint on the private sector. Only a statutory incomes policy would have legitimised governmental penalties for breaches or defiance, but even then, Ministers would almost certainly have been unable to enforce punitive measures in such instances. It could not, for example, imprison thousands of trade unionists for securing an 'excessive' pay increase, nor could it invoke similarly draconian punishment against employers who granted such a pay increase. Short of much stronger state control over industry, there was little that Ministers could do to secure wage restraint than rely, as ever, on exhortation, and explanation of the need for such moderation.

Of course, Ministers hoped that by curbing pay increases in those sectors of the economy in which it did have some direct control, namely the nationalised industries and the public sector, this would persuade the private sector to reciprocate. After all, the Government had sometimes been criticised by private sector employers for not setting an example by imposing pay restraint on is own employees. Yet Ministers then found when they attempted to do so, these very same private sector employers did not follow suit, thereby leaving public sector workers aggrieved at this inequity.

Following on from such problems, the reversion to incomes policies served to highlight two other inter-linked problems. Firstly, attention was drawn to the inability of national trade union leaders to ensure the compliance or acquiescence of their members. Indeed, the attempted incorporation of the national union leadership into regular elite-level discussions over economic affairs, particularly concerning the issue of pay, exacerbated the gulf between union leaders and their rank-and-file members on the factory floor, to the extent that the latter increasingly looked to local officials and shop stewards to secure better pay settlements, regardless of any specified 'guiding light' or 'norm' decreed from above.

Secondly, but following directly on from this problem, there was the phenomenon of 'wage drift', whereby actual earnings rose at a faster or higher rate than envisaged or intended by Ministers and senior officials pursuing incomes policies. Indeed, this was also another manifestation of the willingness, on many occasions, of local employers or managers to grant more generous pay increases in order either to recruit and retain staff in their company at a time of labour shortages (itself a consequence of full – or 'over-full' – employment) or to forestall strike action instigated by local union officials or shop stewards.

These problems served further to undermine Ministerial efforts at securing a long-time incomes policy, and consequently increased the mounting pressure from elsewhere in the Conservative Party for a rather different, less conciliatory or constructive, approach. Many in the Cabinet had hoped that if lower pay settlements could be attained through incomes policies, thereby curbing inflation and improving Britain's balance of payments by reducing imports, then pressure from elsewhere in the Party for either legislation to curb trade union power and irresponsibility, or a deflationary policy whose higher unemployment would elicit a corresponding erosion of the trade unions' bargaining power, would dissipate, while vindicating the 'voluntarist' strategy. Instead, the difficulties encountered by Ministers in securing an effective voluntary incomes policy during the early 1960s merely served to draw further attention to problematic aspects of trade unionism, and consequently strengthened the conviction among many others in the Conservative Party that a wholly different approach was required.

Conclusion

Prior to 1945, and again after 1964, many Conservatives tended to view trade unionism with considerable anxiety, if not considerable and unconcealed hostility, not least because the trade unions' collectivist ethos, often accompanied by a professed commitment to Socialism, clearly conflicted with the Conservatism's core tenets of individualism, competition, 'the market' and, ultimately, Capitalism. This ideological incompatibility was confirmed when many trade unions formed, and subsequently aligned themselves, with the Labour Party.

There have therefore been several specific trade union practices which have variously been condemned by the Conservative Party, and which have thus reflected and reinforced British Conservatism's frequent distaste for trade unionism. In particular, the closed shop, whereby union membership was a prerequisite of obtaining or retaining a job, was frequently denounced by many Conservatives as a gross infringement of individual liberty, and a form of industrial conscription. Similarly, the political levy, invariably used by many trade unions to finance the Labour Party, was routinely condemned, particularly the 'contracting-out' aspect, which placed the onus on those who did not wish to pay the levy to declare this unwillingness, by signing a form exempting them from such payment. Also routinely condemned by Conservatives have been strikes, particularly those of an unofficial variety, and/or which were not endorsed by a prior secret ballot of the trade union members concerned. The absence of secret ballots was also cited by some Conservatives in their condemnation of the appointment or selection of trade union leaders. In both cases, the absence of secret ballots led some Conservatives to condemn the trade unions for their lack of internal democracy. Another routine Conservative criticism of trade unionism has been, somewhat paradoxically, the latter's conservatism, as manifested by restrictive practices and other forms of resistance to new modes of working or the introduction of technologies, deriving from a concern to protect members' jobs. Finally, Conservatives have routinely condemned annual pay rises sought or secured by trade unions, variously alleging that such wage increases are inflationary, or likely to cause unemployment among employees who 'price themselves out of a job' by demanding to be paid more than their employer can afford – although it should be noted that Conservatives hardly ever condemn the salary increases of company directors and chief executives in this manner; these are always warranted, apparently, by successful performance or the need for recruitment and retention in an intensely competitive market.

It is clear, therefore, that British Conservatism has historically found much about trade unionism to condemn or disapprove of, thereby providing ample scope for remedial or repressive legislation. Yet this makes it all the more remarkable that the 1951–64 Conservative Governments deliberately and patiently refrained from legislating to tackle these aspects of trade unionism, while also resisting, for as long as possible, involving themselves in pay settlements, in spite of growing concern about inflation and the problems of maintaining full employment. We have noted, in the previous chapters, how much of this 'voluntarist' stance, with regard industrial relations and trade unionism, derived from the prevalence, among senior Conservatives, of the 'human relations' perspective, whereby conflict or distrust in the workplace tended to derive, ultimately, from a perception among employees that their contribution or role was not appreciated or valued by management. These feelings or sentiments often created grievances or resentments which festered until they manifested themselves openly, usually in the form of strike action, or other forms of industrial disruption. Moreover, it was these feelings and emotions among alienated industrial workers which were apparently exploited by militants in the trade unions, who therefore exploited the grievances of such employees for their own political purposes. Such problems, though, were not deemed amenable to legislative remedies, and hence senior Ministers avoided recourse to the statute book to deal with industrial relations problems.

What also underpinned this steadfast refusal to invoke industrial relations or trade union legislation throughout the 1950s and into the early 1960s was the issue of practicability, for senior Conservatives repeatedly argued that even if they did introduce Acts of Parliament, they would be unable to enforce them effectively, usually due to the problem of invoking sanctions or penalties if they were breached. For example, Ministers rejected demands for statutory ballots prior to strike action partly on the grounds that if such legislation was defied – if a trade union embarked upon strike action without conducting a prior ballot – then there would be little that a Conservative government could do as a consequence. It would hardly be feasible or practicable to imprison thousands, or even tens of thousands, of trade unionists for participating in industrial action for which no ballot had been held. Furthermore, it was consistently argued that as most strikes were unofficial, and thus, by definition, not endorsed by the trade union leadership anyway, legislation to curb strikes would be futile. All that would probably be achieved would be to antagonise the whole trade union movement and alienate moderate trade unionists, and thereby destroy any hope of securing a more constructive relationship between the Conservative party and the unions.

Also deemed impracticable was legislation to outlaw the closed shop, for as Ministers routinely explained to those Party members who demanded such a measure, prohibition would merely drive the closed shop underground, where abuses and injustices would be even harder to detect and condemn. Besides, even if the closed shop was formally banned by a Conservative government, it was envisaged that any worker who subsequently exercised their new right not to join a trade union would be vulnerable to more subtle forms of victimisation than actually losing their job, such as being 'sent to Coventry', that is, ignored or ostracised by their workmates as 'punishment', or liable to find that their tools 'disappeared' or repeatedly 'broke', so that their position became untenable. Such appalling treatment would almost certainly be more difficult to prove and seek redress for, and as such, the evils which were supposed to be exorcised by banning the closed shop would almost certainly be replaced by others of a more covert nature.

One other reason why Ministers refrained from actually outlawing the trade union closed shop throughout the 1950s and early 1960s was the Conservative leadership's desire to see more employees become involved in trade unions. Although the loss of individual liberty which the closed shop entailed was still condemned by Conservatives, Ministers recognised not only that many employers preferred all employees to belong to a (specified) trade union for collective bargaining purposes, but that those workers who would probably exercise any statutory right not to join a trade union would be those who were 'moderates'. However, throughout the 1950s, another concern harboured by Conservative Ministers was that of militancy inside the trade unions – particularly infiltration by Communists – deriving from the fact that the left was invariably more active in union affairs, and certainly more inclined to vote in favour of strike action. From this perspective, therefore, rhetorical condemnation of the closed shop was tempered, in practice, by a Ministerial desire to maximise trade union membership, in order that 'moderates' – and the Conservative Trade Unionists – could mobilise against the left, and reduce the latter's strength. In this respect, senior Conservatives were inclined to tolerate the closed shop because maximum trade union membership potentially facilitated greater stability in industry, and fostered the increased involvement of 'moderates' in the trade unions who could then outweigh the left. Industrial order was thereby privileged over individual liberty, and pragmatism again prioritised over principle.

The dominance of 'One Nation' Conservatism among senior Conservatives

Also crucial to understanding the Conservative Party's predominantly conciliatory and constructive approach to trade unionism from 1945 until the early 1960s, was the character of its leading parliamentary figures during this period, both in terms of ideological outlook, and also in terms of their own personal backgrounds, Indeed, the two aspects seem to inform and reinforce each other.

Ideologically, the early post-war Conservative Party was notable for the intellectual dominance of the 'One Nation' strand of Conservatism, whose origins are generally attributed to Benjamin Disraeli, as signified by his paternalistic approach towards the industrial working class during the 1870s especially, and his denunciation of the extremes of wealth and poverty arising from unfettered Capitalism. On some occasions, Disraeli used characters in his novels, particularly *Sybil, or The Two Nations*, first published in 1845, to articulate his concern at the gulf between the working and upper classes. Probably the most notable of such examples is the conversation between Egremont (brother of Lord Marney) and two strangers whom he meets at the ruins of Marney Abbey:

'Well, society maybe in its infancy' said Egremont slightly smiling, 'but say what you will, our Queen reigns over the greatest nation that ever existed.'

'Which nation?' asked the young stranger, 'for she reigns over two'.

The stranger paused; Egremont was silent, but looked inquiringly.

'Yes', resumed the young stranger after a moment's interval. 'Two nations between whom there is no intercourse and no sympathy: who are as ignorant of each other's habits, thoughts and feelings, as if they were dwellers in different zones or inhabitants of different planets; who are formed by a different breeding, are fed by a different food, are ordered by different manners, and are not governed by the same laws.'

'You speak of ...', said Egremont hesitatingly.

'THE RICH AND THE POOR.'

(Disraeli, 1995: 58, capitalisation in original)

Although Conservatives believe – for a variety of reasons which we do not have time to explain here – that inequality is a natural and necessary feature of all societies (Dorey, forthcoming), One Nation Conservatives have been concerned that if inequality becomes excessive (although what constitutes excessive in this context is never made explicit or quantified) then the legitimacy of capitalism and parliamentary democracy is liable to be questioned, with the industrial working class becoming more susceptible to the blandishments and false promises of utopian political doctrines and radical parties, especially those of a Marxist hue.

In this respect, One Nation Conservatism constitutes a philosophy of enlightened self-interest, for the propertied and the privileged in society can only be confident and secure in the enjoyment of their wealth and status if there is little likelihood of revolt from the masses. As Disraeli himself once crisply expressed it: 'The castle cannot rest if the cottage is not happy.' For One Nation Conservatives, therefore, it behoves the propertied or moneyed classes to ensure that the working classes enjoy tolerable material conditions, and are accorded a certain degree of respect, if only to minimise the likelihood that those workers will turn against their masters or established political leaders.

Furthermore, during the period covered by this study, the paternalism of many prominent Conservatives was seemingly reinforced or underpinned by their personal backgrounds or experiences. For example, we noted in chapter three how Macmillan's first-hand observation of the devastating impact of unemployment in his Stockton-on-Tees constituency during the inter-war years subsequently made him determined to avoid a repeat of such demoralisation and deprivation. A working class which had suffered so much, especially in the 1930s, but which then fought so valiantly against the threat of Nazism during the first half of the 1940s, deserved rather better than it had hitherto received, a conviction which naturally and neatly accorded with Macmillan's determination to forge a more humane or compassionate Conservatism. Macmillan himself noted that 'the older ones have not forgotten. I was a Member of Parliament in those years [the 1930s] on Tee-side. As long as I live, I can never forget the impoverishment and demoralisation' and consequently, he was 'determined, as far as it lies within human power, never to allow this shadow to fall again upon our country' (quoted in Ramsden, 1977b: 448–9).

Elsewhere, Anthony Eden's experience of leading conscripts while he was a young officer during the First World War seemed to imbue him with much greater respect for the working class, and consequently made him much more sympathetic towards them in peace time. As such, he too was not willing to adopt a deflationary economic policy which would fuel unemployment, nor was he willing to countenance legislation either to curb trade union power, or to regulate their internal affairs. On the contrary, like Macmillan, who succeeded him as Conservative leader and Prime Minister in 1957, Eden viewed industrial relations in terms of fostering closer partnership between management and workers, and thereby eradicating the notion that there existed 'two sides of industry'.

Meanwhile, Rab Butler's paternalism, particularly in the sphere of industrial relations, as evinced by his intimate involvement in developing *The Industrial Charter*, seems to have derived, to a considerable extent, from the fact that he became the son-in-law of the chairman of Courtaulds, a family firm which was run on progressive lines (Howard, 1987: 155). Indeed, it should be noted at this juncture that another reason why the Conservative Party of the 1950s proved so reluctant to invoke industrial relations or trade union legislation was that during this decade, more than a third of Conservative MPs were (or had been) company directors. Now, it might be intuitively assumed that Conservatives with such occupational backgrounds would have been particularly hostile towards the trade unions, and therefore keen to pursue legislation against them. Yet, in fact, it was often precisely those Conservative parliamentarians with direct experience of management or leadership in industry who were most cognizant of the complexities of relations in the workplace, and thus of the strong likelihood that legislation would be inappropriate or impracticable. This effectively provided One Nation Conservatives with further endorsement for their conciliatory approach, for they could claim, or at least imply, that those in the Party demanding a tougher, legislative, approach towards trade unionism were often those most removed from life in industry, and who therefore had little, if any, real understanding of workplace problems and politics.

The conciliatory character of Ministers of Labour

Throughout the 1951–64 period, the Conservatives who successively occupied the post of Minister of Labour were, to a large extent, the embodiment and personification of 'One Nation Conservatism'. Personally and 'ideologically', they were concerned to foster closer and more constructive relations, both between management and workers and between the Conservative Party/Government and the trade unions. The promotion of 'one nation' principles through the British economy and society was to include, also, the advocacy of something more akin to 'one nation' in the workplace. Just as Benjamin Disraeli had bemoaned the existence of 'two nations' in mid-nineteenth century Britain, 'between whom there is no intercourse and no sympathy; who are ignorant of each other's habits, thoughts and feelings, as if they were dwellers in different zones or inhabitants of different planets' (Disraeli, 1995: 58), so did senior Conservatives during the mid-twentieth century lament the existence of 'two sides of industry', a duality which was deemed both to reflect and reinforce old-fashioned notions of 'workers versus bosses' and the Marxist notion that capital and labour had conflicting, contradictory and irreconcilable interests.

Successive Conservative Ministers of Labour during the 1950s and early 1960s were therefore determined to counter such assumptions by emphasising the commonality of interests between employers and employees, and the need for a new conception of partnership in the post-war British workplace. Moreover, whereas Disraeli had placed great emphasis on the need for enlightened and humane leadership by social and political elites in order to pacify and integrate the working classes so did his 1950s successors emphasise the role to be played by similarly enlightened and humane employers in ameliorating the anxieties and suspicions of their employees in order to bridge the perceived gap between the 'two sides of industry'.

The Conservatives' first post-war Minister of Labour was the 'hyper-emollient' (Hennessy, 1990: 453) Walter Monckton, whose brief from Winston Churchill, as we noted in chapter three, was to do the utmost to avoid industrial conflict. In one particular respect, Monckton's marked reluctance to invoke the law was surprising, given his professional background as a barrister, for it might have been expected that he would have immense faith in legal solutions to various problems. Certainly, a couple of decades later, one of the criticisms of the ill-fated 1971 Industrial Relations Act was that it was unduly legalistic, much of it having been drafted by Geoffrey Howe, himself a barrister. In Monckton's case, however, it may well be that his professional background in the legal profession fostered the opposition response, namely cognizance of the limits of the statute book in tackling certain kinds of problems, particularly those involving behaviour and inter-personal relations in the workplace, a circumspection which would have perfectly accorded with the 'human relations' approach.

As Monckton himself explained in a speech in Birmingham shortly after becoming Minister of Labour, he would be 'sorry to see party politics enter the factory gates and embitter our industrial life'. As such, Monckton declared that he was 'a firm believer in government by consultation and consent, and I shall do everything I can to carry out that principle in the conduct of my Ministry' (quoted in Hyde, 1991: 167).

There was another reason, too, why Monckton might have been so averse to invoking legislation in the twin spheres of industrial relations and trade unionism, namely that he was only notionally a Conservative, for although he had been elected as a Conservative MP for the Bristol West constituency in 1951 (Churchill having personally asked him to stand), Monckton had, a few years earlier, confessed to Churchill that he was 'not a Conservative', and one eminent political historian subsequently described him as 'a man almost without party affiliation' (Middlemas, 1979: 406). Consequently, much of Monckton's ensuing good relationship with key trade union leaders whilst he was Minister of Labour was because 'they did not regard him as a Tory minister' (Butler, 1982: 135, 136). Thus did G.G. Eastwood, a trade union leader interviewed by one of Monckton's biographers, explain how:

> ... one had the feeling that Sir Walter was not simply trying to be fair, but that he really was unbiased and was desperately anxious to get to the kernel of a problem and help towards a mutually acceptable solution. Sir Walter must have sensed that, as the first Conservative at St James's Square following six years of Labour rule, union leaders were cautious and indeed sometimes suspicious during initial contacts. My experience was that he soon gained one's complete confidence ... He really made one feel: 'Here is a man who is genuinely trying to understand the situation and do what he can to help.'
> (Quoted in Birkenhead, 1969: 287)

These effusive sentiments were echoed by Vincent Tewson, the TUC's General Secretary during Monckton's tenure at the Ministry of Labour, when he explained that Monckton:

> was not a politician and could take his own incisive and down-to-earth line. He was nor weak ... It was true that he saw both sides of a question, but as Minister he had to see both sides, and the consequence was that both sides liked and trusted him. If he had been weak, he would have offended both. He was a bending cane, but he was always on his own axis.
> (Quoted in Butler, 1982: 65)

Of course, such a commitment to conciliation was condemned by some Conservatives, for whom Monckton's congenial approach was equated with a lack of courage and conviction, and thus regular recourse to the path of least resistance. For example, according to Churchill's private secretary, John Colville: 'The trouble with Monckton, almost the only trouble, was that he could not bear to make anyone unhappy. He was thus a natural appeaser ... poor Monckton earned the reputation as the architect of slippery slopes' (Colville, 1981: 182–3).

Although Monckton's successor at the Ministry of Labour, Iain Macleod, was deemed to be a little tougher towards the trade unions – an image given credence by his unyielding stance during the 1958 London bus strike – he nonetheless largely maintained the voluntarist approach to industrial relations, and generally sought to avoid antagonising or alienating the trade unions; even when confronting the TGWU in 1958, he knew that his stance was tacitly endorsed by the TUC General Council, a point to which we will return subsequently. One of Monckton's closest Ministerial colleagues, Rab Butler, recalled how:

Iain's qualities were entirely suited to this Ministry, for he was a negotiator par excellence, able to conduct his talks with the unions on a friendly basis ... He was anxious to introduce a positive industrial, or worker's, charter [although did not do so due to trade union and managerial resistance to such governmental 'interference' in industrial relations] ... He was moreover adept at remembering people and talking to them: his talent for negotiations could not have found better ground than this particular Ministry.

(Butler, 1982: 98. 99, 102)

Similarly, one of his biographers emphasised that Macleod readily accepted the conciliatory ethos of the Ministry of Labour (discussed below), for it 'represented his personal policy' and he 'wished to preserve it' (Fisher, 1973: 125).

Macleod's successor, Edward Heath, only served as Minister of Labour for nine months (and later became associated with a major departure from the 'one nation' approach by presiding over the introduction of the ill-fated 1971 Industrial Relations Act), but his short stint at the Ministry was nonetheless characterised by continuity with his two predecessors. As Heath himself recalled, 'my main aim was to reassure the British worker that, if he put his back into making the nation more prosperous, a "One Nation" Conservative government would treat him fairly and do its best to ensure that he was properly rewarded'. Moreover, when faced with the perennial demands from the Conservative Right for either a Royal Commission on trade unions or legislation to curb strikes, Heath's response was to reiterate that most trade union leaders appreciated the need for great responsibility in industrial relations and moderation in collective bargaining, and therefore 'the TUC should be given a further chance to deal themselves with their undisciplined minority' (Heath, 1998: 195; see also Laing, 1972: 125; *The Times* 4 January 1960). Part of Heath's apparent optimism was because, even during his short tenure at the Ministry of Labour, he established cordial relations with the new TUC General Secretary, George Woodcock, and his deputy, Vic Feather, and was seemingly heartened by their professed desire to tackle acknowledged problems concerning the operation and conduct of British trade unionism (Campbell, 1993: 110–11).

Indeed, in contrast to his later reputation as someone who was personally aloof and somewhat lacking in inter-personal skills and warmth towards others (see, for example, Berkeley, 1972: 108; Norton, 1978: 235–8), Feather was impressed by Heath's readiness 'to depart from the formal procedures and see people informally', and his recognition that 'the Minister's job is to be a conciliator ... the traditional role of being neutral ... he never adopted any attitude of political partisanship'. This role, Feather believed, 'rather suited his temperament' (quoted in Hutchinson, 1970: 89). At the same time, most of the TUC leadership seemed to share the concerns of Heath and his Ministerial colleagues about the damage being wrought by irresponsible or extremist minorities in the trade unions, and the need for a restoration of authority by the official, national union leadership, as the key to ensuring the more orderly conduct of industrial relations and wage negotiations.

The generally conciliatory and constructive approach was continued when John Hare replaced Heath at the Ministry of Labour in July 1960. Although Hare's tenure (until October 1963) coincided with rapidly growing concern about aspects of trade unionism (particularly in the context of increasing awareness of the problems pertaining to the British economy, for which the unions were variously apportioned much of the blame), he broadly resisted perennial right-wing demands for legislation to curb strikes and tackle restrictive practices, usually by reiterating the argument that such phenomena could not be eradicated by Acts of Parliament, while also insisting that invoking legislation would alienate moderate trade unionists. This, in turn, would make it even more difficult for Ministers to develop a closer partnership with the TUC, through which they could educate union leaders about the need for greater responsibility and wage restraint. Like his predecessors, Hare was adamant (as he explained to delegates at the Conservatives' 1960 conference) that: 'Our main job is to do everything we can to ... smooth the relationships between employers and unions. We must hold the ring and ensure that each side has no unfair advantage over the other ... Our aim must be to strengthen the sense of responsibility of both sides of industry.'

Hare consequently refused to yield when faced with growing demands for a Royal Commission into trade unionism. In spite of such demands – or possibly because of them – he remained adamant that the only way of improving industrial relations and addressing Britain's economic problems was to adhere to the existing policies, entailing exhortation and encouragement, for ultimately, it was only through the joint efforts of responsible employers and trade union leaders that industrial conflict would be reduced, and impediments to improved productivity removed (NA CAB 124/1618, Hare to Hailsham, 18 January 1961). He reiterated this stance nine months later, at the Party's 1961 conference, where he claimed that in spite of 'faults in the way the trade unions conduct their affairs ... their leaders are, in the large majority, honourable men for whom I personally have a high respect', and as such, any genuine improvement in industrial relations or trade union behaviour could only be attained through 'persuasion and by constant appeal to common sense and common interest'.

Hare was replaced, in September 1963, by Joseph Godber, who was also strongly committed to the voluntarist approach of his predecessors at the Ministry of Labour. Although Godber's one-year tenure coincided with mounting pressure in the Conservative Party for legislative action against the trade unions, or at the very least, a Royal Commission to examine trade union law, especially in the wake of the *Rookes* v. *Barnard* court case early in 1964, Godber – 'a wise and cautious man' (Taylor, 1993: 353) – strove to resist such pressures, and consistently reiterated the view that more harmonious industrial relations or more responsible trade unionism could not be secured by statutory measures or Ministerial command, but only by patiently encouraging moderates on all sides to work more closely together to tackle problems for the benefit of all. Thus did Godber succeed in deferring the proposed Royal Commission on Trade Unionism until after the 1964 general election, lest the more immediate establishment of such an inquiry undermined responsible elements within the trade unions, and thereby provided political ammunition to the Left. In the meantime, when he was urged, early in 1964, to display more urgency in tackling restrictive practices, Godber insisted that 'the best way to make progress is through identifying and eliminating these practices by discussion and negotiation between the employers and workers concerned', for it was up to both sides [of industry] to help us overcome it', as such, Godber insisted that 'I have no plans for legislation' (HC Debates, 5th series, Vol. 688, col. 21).

The role of the Ministry of Labour

The character of these Ministers of Labour seemed both to reflect and reinforce the ethos of the Ministry of Labour itself throughout the 1950s and early 1960s, for it evidently viewed its role as being one of resolving industrial conflicts in an impartial and constructive manner, and even then, only when asked to do so by the 'two sides' of industry. Political scientists have long noted how Departments often enshrine their own philosophy or in-house ideology, which consequently shapes their perceptions of the issues and problems which fall within their remit, and therefore strongly determine how they respond them. The dominant operational paradigm of the Ministry of Labour during this period undoubtedly enshrined the 'human relations' and voluntarist perspectives which similarly permeated the senior echelons of the Conservative Party throughout most of this time, and which thus eschewed legislation as a means of resolving industrial relations problems or reforming trade union practices. Instead, it generally pursued 'peace-at-almost-any-price', an approach widely viewed as commendable and sensible at the time, but which has since been criticised (Hennessy, 1990: 453), the clear implication being that, with the benefit of hindsight, this resolute refusal to legislate *vis-à-vis* industrial relations or trade unionism, largely for fear of antagonising the unions, unwittingly permitted trade union power and irresponsibility to increase, until it wrought havoc in the 1970s, thereby significantly contributing towards the collapse of the post-war consensus and precipitating the rise of Thatcherism.

Reflecting on his 12 year (1944–56) tenure as Permanent Secretary in the Ministry of Labour, Sir Godfrey Ince clearly encapsulated the voluntarist operational paradigm by explaining how 'traditional policy is that industry should be given the fullest encouragement to settle its own affairs, and that the State should take action only when there is no effective bargaining machinery in industry, or when negotiations through an industry's machinery have broken down.' Such a system of collective bargaining, Ince emphasised, 'rests on the effective organisation of both employers and workers ... Together, they have played a large part in ensuring that industrial relations in this country were established on a sound basis', and that this voluntarist policy 'has been eminently successful' (Ince, 1960: 117, 118, 21. See also Ministry of Labour, 1957: 16).

Furthermore, the Ministry of Labour, throughout much of the 1940s and 1950s, fully subscribed to the 'human relations' philosophy, believing not only that 'good relations between management and workers are an end in themselves' but that they are also 'a direct contribution to human happiness and peace in industry', by virtue of seeking 'to make a man's work a satisfying and satisfactory part of his life', whereupon this would contribute to 'increased production and productivity'. Indeed, it was accepted that the promotion of mutual trust and respect between management and workers, so that the latter felt that their economic and industrial contribution was appreciated and valued, 'is probably one of the most important tasks in a free society', particularly as the growing size and scale of industry had resulted in management becoming increasingly remote or impersonal in relation to their employees (Ince, 1960: 26).

Perhaps not surprisingly, the conciliatory stance and human relations perspective of the Ministry of Labour strongly informed the advice proffered to its Ministers during the 1950s and early 1960s, thereby reaffirming and reinforcing the similarly cautious approach of those Ministers to industrial relations issues and trade union affairs. As the Cabinet Secretary (Norman Brook) explained to the Prime Minister in the mid-1950s, the Ministry of Labour was 'strongly imbued with a laissez-faire philosophy and ... frightened to death of doing anything which might be thought to impair the impartiality of their Minister as a "conciliator" in industrial disputes' (NA PREM 11/1238, Brook to Eden, 30 May 1956). Meanwhile, one of Iain Macleod's biographers noted that 'the trade unions did not think of the Ministry of Labour as part of the Government. They felt they could always go to St James's Square for advice, and that the Minister would hold the ring impartially between them and the employers' (Fisher, 1973: 125).

The character of the trade union leadership

Throughout much of the period covered by this book, the 'One Nation' character of many senior Conservatives, particularly successive Ministers of Labour, was matched by the moderate character of most of the leaders of Britain's largest trade unions, and particularly those serving on the General Council of the TUC. Although these senior trade unionists remained ideologically aligned to the Labour Party, they nonetheless evinced a remarkable pragmatic readiness to work with senior Conservatives, especially those of the conciliatory 'one nation' variant who served at the Ministry of Labour during the 1950s and early 1960s. These trade union leaders often shared the concern of senior Conservatives about Communist infiltration of certain unions, and the damage caused, not least to their own authority and credibility, by unofficial strikes and inter-union disputes. In this regard, many such trade union leaders were motivated by a form of enlightened self-interest just as the 'one nation' Conservatives were. Such was the moderation and stature of such union leaders that one study suggested that: 'To run through the list of leading TUC figures is not unlike running through a list of leading

Civil Servants: Sir Vincent Tewson, Sir William Lawther, Sir Thomas Williamson, Sir Lincoln Evans', and added that these four major trade union figures 'could mobilise about one-third of the votes at Congress', which, when buttressed by the support of various medium-sized unions ensured that they were 'in a position to determine Congress policy' (Lovell and Roberts, 1968: 162, 156).

Even though these stalwarts were being eclipsed by the mid-1950s, thereby placing the TUC's hitherto cordial relationship with Conservative Ministers under increasing strain – with the election of Frank Cousins as leader of Britain's then largest trade union, the TGWU, symbolising this shift – the degree or rapidity of the transformation should not be exaggerated. It was not an immediate or overnight change, but a more general and gradual one, perfectly in accordance with the incremental character of much of British politics and policymaking during the 1950s and early 1960s. Indeed, as we noted in chapter four, when the TGWU pursued a seven-week strike in support of London bus drivers in 1958, support from other trade unions was conspicuous by its absence, a point not lost on Conservative Ministers.

Even by the early 1960s, when a degree of exasperation was manifesting itself among some senior Conservatives – not least Harold Macmillan himself – over the refusal of the trade unions to act with greater responsibility and moderation, and at a time when the right-wing 'TUC junta' (Taylor, 2000: 124) of the mid-1950s had largely been superseded, many trade union leaders still enjoyed a relatively good working relationship with those Conservative Ministers with whom they were in regular contact, particularly through the NEDC. For example, Reginald Maudling, who succeeded Selwyn Lloyd as Chancellor in July 1962, recalled 'the cordial relations that were established with the Trade Union representatives on the [National Economic Development] Council, particularly George Woodcock, Harry Douglas and Sidney Greene' (Maudling, 1978: 111). If many of the TUC leaders of the early 1960s had not maintained a largely cordial relationship with their Conservative counterparts, then they would probably have boycotted the NEDC.

Instead, what was probably more important in altering the relationship between the trade unions and Conservative Ministers from the early 1960s was the changing internal organisational dynamics of British trade unionism, which itself naturally reflected changes in the structure of British industry and the trend towards economic centralisation. This was to highlight a paradox concerning trade unionism, because although an increasingly frequent and widespread criticism was that the unions had become too powerful, largely due the combined impact of full employment and legal immunities, there was one particular sense in which some of the problems pertaining to industrial relations and collective bargaining derived partly from the weakness of the trade union leadership *vis-à-vis* their ordinary members. Indeed, this problem pertained both to the relationship between the leaders of individual trade unions and their rank-and-file members, and to the relationship between the TUC and affiliated trade unions (discussed later).

With regard to relations between the leaders and ordinary members of trade unions, the ever-increasing scale or size of industries and firms meant that it was not only managers and employers who appeared increasingly remote from industrial workers on the factory floor; trade union leaders themselves seemed increasingly distant, both organisationally and geographically, due to the extent to which they spent much most of their working week in London, taking part in regular meetings with national level managers and/or politicians and senior civil servants. Indeed, with the expansion of many industries and companies, an intrinsic part of a general trend towards monopolisation in the British economy at this time, and the concomitant increase in trade union membership underpinned by full employment, trade unions exhibited many of the features originally identified, in 1911, by Robert Michels, whereby organisational expansion leads inexorably to a bureaucratisation and professionalisation of institutional leadership; the more members an organisation recruits, the less influence those members have on the organisation they have joined, because the amorphous or atomised mass membership is susceptible to, or even largely dependent upon, the minority of full-time, increasingly specialised or expert, leaders to take decisions and then direct the membership (Michels, 1968).

However, the clear manifestation of this process in Britain's trade unions during the 1950s and 1960s resulted in a further development not apparently foreseen by Michels (whose focus, admittedly, was primarily on political parties, albeit with his findings intended to have wider applicability to other organisations), namely attempts by some ordinary trade unionists and officials to wrest back a degree of control or power from their 'out-of-touch' leaders. It was this counter-phenomenon which underpinned many of the unofficial or 'wildcat' strikes which vexed both Ministers and many senior trade union leaders during these two decades, more especially in the 1960s. As trade unions underwent a process of bureaucratisation, and many union leaders seemed to undergo a parallel process of *embourgeoisement* – to the extent that some of these leaders were wined and dined by Conservative Ministers, especially Ministers of Labour, at prestigious London restaurants, or even at 10 Downing Street – so local-level officials or shop stewards increasingly secured the allegiance or respect of rank-and-file trade unionists, for their day-to-day proximity and visibility meant that workers could see for themselves what these trade union figures were doing on their behalf in terms of pay negotiations or tackling workplace grievances. This trend was compounded, of course, by the transition towards incomes policies, whereupon trade union leaders increasingly appeared, to their ordinary members, to be collaborating with national-level employers' representatives and Ministers to hold down their wages.

The changing character of wage determination

As we noted in chapters four and six, Conservative attitudes towards wage determination experienced a gradual, but cumulatively profound, change, during the 1950s and early 1960s. Throughout the first half of the 1950s, the emphasis was on the sanctity of free collective bargaining, a principle which the trade unions themselves deemed to be inviolate, whereby wages – along with other terms and conditions of employment – were routinely determined through annual negotiations conducted between trade unions and employers, free from political direction or government intervention, although obviously, such a principle was somewhat difficult to apply in the vastly expanded public sector and nationalised industries. To the extent that the state did intervene, this was primarily through the auspices of the Ministry of Labour's arbitration service, although even this intervention – in accordance with 'voluntarism' – was only invoked if both 'sides' involved in a dispute requested it.

From the mid-1950s, however, Ministers took a closer interest in wage determination, although they certainly did not seek to interfere directly with collective bargaining arrangements. Instead, governmental attempts at securing lower pay rises during the latter half of the decade took the form of 'educational' campaigns which sought to present trade unions and their members with the economic facts of life, and thereby persuade them of the need for greater moderation and responsibility. The 1956 White Paper *The Economic Implications of Full Employment* heralded the first explicit attempt at a high-profile Ministerial campaign to highlight the need for voluntary self-restraint by organised labour in its annual pursuit of pay increases. Then, when this failed to elicit the desired response from the trade unions, and economic circumstances continued to deteriorate, Ministers established (in 1957) the Council on Prices, Productivity and Incomes, a body whose annual reports were intended to provide further evidence of the need for lower pay increases. Of course, these two initiatives reflected Ministerial determination to avoid alternative means of lowering pay settlements, namely either a deflationary policy whereby trade union bargaining strength would be weakened by higher unemployment, or legislation to curb trade union power.

It was not until the early 1960s, though, that Conservative Ministers increasingly became convinced that the continuation of free collective bargaining was untenable in the context of the continued commitment to full employment, for the latter was enhancing the bargaining power of trade unions, not least because many employers, anxious to fill vacancies, were only too willing to accede to demands for higher pay to attract or retain staff. Conservatives became concerned that these pay increases were not only inflationary, but were also, indirectly, pushing Britain's balance of payments into deficit, as higher earnings were increasingly expended on imported manufactured goods, while relatively low rates of economic growth and industrial productivity affected British exports, and led to a diminution of Britain's share of world trade.

It was in this economic context that, from 1961, many senior Conservatives, particularly Harold Macmillan, became convinced that an incomes policy was now necessary, and would henceforth constitute a vital tool of economic management. This shift initially manifested itself in the temporary 'pay pause' applied to the public sector and nationalised industries, the intention being that this would serve to alert the trade unions and private sector employers alike to the urgency of the economic situation, and the need for a corresponding degree of restraint. In lieu of the search for a long-term, voluntary incomes policy, to be agreed through tripartite discussions, the 'pay pause' was followed by a 'guiding light' which stipulated that pay increases should be no more than 2.5 per cent – later increased to 3.5 per cent – unless certain specified criteria were fulfilled.

Yet incomes policies themselves yielded intractable problems for Ministers, not least the attempt at linking pay rises to increased productivity, because some industries were more amenable to increased output than others, which would, as a consequence, lead to increased disparities and inequalities between sectors, particularly between the private and public sectors (how could nurses, teachers or police officers increase their productivity, for example?). Sooner or later, the festering grievances in the less productive sectors would lead to them seeking to catch up, so that any period of restraint would almost certainly be followed by a pay explosion – unless Ministers were willing to stand firm and 'face down' such workers, often the Government's own employees, which would merely exacerbate feelings of unfairness and inequity, while also enhancing the shift in rank-and-file loyalties to more militant local level union officials and shop stewards. Of course, the 1956 White Paper on *The Economic Implication of Full Employment* had recognised this, and argued that in those more productive industries, workers should not assume that their higher output would always or automatically translate into higher wages, for there was a need to consider the wider economic context.

Another notable problem which confronted Ministerial efforts to secure wage restraint through the imposition of incomes policies was that of what sanctions could realistically be enforced against those who defied any stipulated figure or target. Not only was the sheer impracticability of imprisoning thousands of trade unions once again acknowledged, there was also the question of culpability in cases when 'excessive' pay rises were awarded. Who should be held responsible? Trade union leaders who pursued such an increase, or the employers who conceded such claims? Private sector employers would probably claim they were operating in the context of 'market criteria' or other commercial considerations, in which case, it would hardly be fair for Ministers to penalise them. Meanwhile, in cases where pay increases were awarded ostensibly on the grounds of increased productivity, there was the issue of how was this to be measured and verified? (For further discussion these, and other, 'implementation' problems *viz* incomes policies, see Dorey, 2001: 236–7; Towers, 1978: chapter four).

The 'weakness' of the trade union leaders and the TUC

However, in raising some of these issues, the drift towards incomes policies also inadvertently exacerbated some of the industrial relations and trade union problems which had been increasingly vexing Conservative Ministers – quite apart from the trade unions' long-standing commitment to free collective bargaining anyway. Moreover, the pursuit of incomes policy also reinforced the paradox alluded to previously, concerning the 'weakness' of the trade union leadership *vis-à-vis* the mass membership, for as the linkages were increased or strengthened between trade union leaders and Conservative Ministers, most visibly or symbolically through the NEDC, it also served to ensure that, from the perspective of many ordinary industrial workers, those union leaders increasingly became associated with efforts to impose wage restraint on ordinary working people. This, in turn, compounded the trend whereby local-level trade union officials and shop stewards could play a more active and visible role, not infrequently successfully negotiating higher wage increases at factory or plant than those recommended by the official union leadership in London. Local level managers were often willing to concede such pay claims, either to avert industrial action and thus loss of production, or to recruit and retain workers when the alternative might be unfilled vacancies, which would also detrimentally affect production and output. Of course, this divergence between national or official pay deals concerned to secure wage restraint, and the *de facto* higher wage increases secured locally, then gave rise to problem of 'wage drift'.

Having spent many years wooing trade union leaders, while also increasingly urging greater 'responsibility' and 'moderation' in pay bargaining, any success which Conservative Ministers might eventually have enjoyed in these respects was undermined by the fact that, as a consequence, those union leaders seemingly lost the trust and loyalty of those whom they officially represented. It was in response to this phenomenon that, in the latter half of the 1960s, political attention regarding industrial relations turned towards the need to strengthen the authority of national level or official trade union leaders over their members, as evinced initially, by the 1966–70 Labour Government's legislative proposals based on the (1969) *In Place of Strife* White Paper, and then the 1970–74 Conservative Government's ill-fated 1971 Industrial Relations Act. Prior to these two legislative initiatives, the 1968 Donovan Report – based on a 1965–68 Royal Commission inquiry into trade unionism and employers' associations – had noted the extent to which two parallel industrial relations systems had become established in Britain: the first was the official system based on agreements secured through national level collective bargaining conducted between senior trade union leaders and their counterparts on the employers' side, while the second was an unofficial system based on agreements secured at local or factory level between shop stewards of local union officials and work-place managers. The latter, needless to say, seriously undermined the former, hence the subsequent political imperative of restoring the authority of national trade union leaders over their members, and thereby promoting the restoration of orderly collective bargaining and the durability of agreements entered into.

Meanwhile, with regard to the relationship between the TUC and affiliated trade unions, a similar problem manifested itself concerning authority, for the TUC was, and still is, a federal body which therefore has little power over the trade unions affiliated to it. This, needless to say, continually undermined efforts at securing wage restraint, for as one commentator has noted, the TUC itself is 'splintered ... made up of an enormous number of individual unions organised on an occupational basis', the combined effect of which was seriously to reduce 'the chances of any centrally imposed incomes policy working' (Jones, 1987: 140–41). In similar vein, Lovell and Roberts once declared that: 'The untidy structure ... of the trade unions in Britain has long been recognised as a major handicap to the development and the carrying out of an effective central policy' (Lovell and Roberts, 1968: 178). Certainly, while he was Minister of Labour during the early 1960s, John Hare occasionally felt obliged to explain to some of his Ministerial colleagues that 'the unions in the Trades Union Congress are autonomous, and would not be prepared to limit their own bargaining powers and freedom of action. Indeed, the T.U.C. has no powers of bargaining about wages' (NA CAB 124/1618, Hare to Hailsham, 18 January 1961). Walter Citrine had made a similar point at the start of the Second World War, when faced with Treasury demands that the TUC should ensure wage restraint by the trade unions, to which he pointed out that: 'the General Council [of the TUC] had no authority to control the activities of the unions in regard to wage applications, and it would be resented were they to attempt to do so' (TUC, 1940: 169).

Consequently, the problems of authority and ensuring compliance which pertained to the leadership of individual trade unions *vis-à-vis* their members was replicated in the relationship between the TUC and affiliated trade unions. In both cases, a key consequence was the ensuing gulf which became apparent between trade union leaders and the TUC entering into agreements at national level, and the reluctance or outright refusal of their constituent members to adhere to them. Nor, incidentally, was this particular problem confined to the trade unions and the TUC. A similarly loose relationship existed between the main employers' organisations, namely the Federation of British Industries, the British Employers' Confederation and the National Union of Manufacturers, which meant that they too found it difficult to 'deliver' the compliance of their members when asked to curb price rises, or stand firm against wage demands.[1]

These problems grievously undermined the 1959–64 Conservative Government's attempts (and those of subsequent governments, until the 1979–90 Thatcher Governments explicitly eschewed such efforts entirely) at fostering a more neo-corporatist and *dirigiste* approach to managing and modernising the British economy. Thus has one political economist suggested that the 1960s are 'best characterised as failed corporatism', this failure deriving, in large part, from the state's inability to ensure the compliance of the industrial partners after economic decisions had been taken, even when those industrial partners had themselves been privy to these decisions: 'corporatist policies ... failed because due to the unwillingness of the major private economic interests to accept the price

---

1   These three organisations merged in 1964, to form the Confederation of British Industry (CBI), largely to lend greater coherence and unity to employers' representation, and thereby provide a more effective counter-weight to the TUC. Ironically, however, the creation of a larger federal body compounded the problems of ensuring that the affiliated members abided by decisions entered into the by the CBI leadership (see, Grant, 1977; Jones, 1987: 141).

of state-induced modernisation'. This unwillingness to accept corporatist modes of economic management, indicative planning and incomes policies, largely derived form 'the anti-state, liberal values of the mass of the populace and the ability of the trade union, industrial and financial interests to ignore government policies' during the 1960s and 1970s, even though the unions demanded that the state maintained full employment and legislated to ensure certain statutory employment and union rights. (Cox, 1989: 207, 220–21; see also Crouch, 1979; Dorey, 1993; Dorey, 2002: 72–5; Marquand, 1988: 148 and *passim*); Shonfield, 1965: 93). The trade unions were not, however, willing to countenance governmental intervention to regulate their internal affairs or activities, nor were they willing to accept a long-term or permanent incomes policy whose primary objective was to secure wage restraint.

Conclusion

From 1945 to 1964, a unique set of circumstances, ideas and individuals combined to ensure that the Conservative Party and the trade unions enjoyed their most harmonious relationship ever. Prior to 1945, many Conservatives were hostile or suspicious towards the trade unions, viewing them as ideologically incompatible with the philosophy of Conservatism, while also fearing that they posed a threat to industrial stability and, ultimately, economic prosperity. A few senior Conservatives were willing to adopt a more charitable or tolerant stance towards the trade unions, but they often encountered strong unease or disagreement elsewhere in the Party, particularly during the nineteenth century, when the ideology of *laissez-faire* was at its strongest, and the emergence of an organised industrial working class was a source of deep concern to many industrialists and property owners, especially in the context of the development of Marxism during the 1840s and 1850s. Although more progressive and prescient Conservatives like Benjamin Disraeli wanted to incorporate industrial workers and the trade unions as a means of neutralising potential radicalism or revolution, others in the Conservative Party feared that this would merely embolden organised labour, and thereby increase the risk of insurrection.

Although this fear was never realised – and, we can see with hindsight, was never likely to have been – many Conservatives still harboured apprehension about trade unionism, and readily blamed them when economic downturns occasionally occurred, and unemployment increased. Furthermore, there was disapproval of newer, specific aspects of trade unionism which attracted Conservative condemnation, most notably the organisational and financial links which many trade unions established with the newly-formed Labour Party during the early twentieth century. By this time, most Conservatives had accustomed themselves to the permanent existence and growth of trade unionism, but now sought to draw a distinction between industrial objectives, which were deemed to be legitimate, and political objectives, which were roundly condemned. This apparent distinction was strongly reiterated both with regard to the operation of the trade union political levy following the 1909 Osborne judgment (and ensuing 1913 Trade Union Act) and the 1926 General Strike. The latter prompted the 1927 Trade Disputes Act, which imposed a number of statutory restrictions on trade union activity, and was thus warmly welcomed by many Party members. This, of course, also did much to reinforce the popular conception, not least among the trade unions themselves, that British Conservatism and trade unionism were incompatible and irreconcilable.

Some younger, more progressive, Conservative MPs were determine to dispel this belief, and consequently promoted the concept of partnership, both within industry, and between the state, the economy, capital and organised labour, although it was not until during the exceptional circumstances wrought by the Second World War that such partnership was given practical effect. This served to illustrate the efficacy of such partnership, with the trade unions widely acknowledged to have played a crucial, constructive role in aiding the war effort, during which time Ernest Bevin, leader of the TGWU, served as Minister of Labour.

Although the Conservatives lost the 1945 general election, the Party did not jettison the idea of industrial partnership or its recently-acquired respect for the trade unions. On the contrary, the years in opposition immediately after the war were utilised to give more substance and credence to such ideas, thereby firmly committing the Party to greater governmental regulation of economic affairs, the maintenance of 'high and stable' levels of employment, improved status and security for industrial workers, a *rapprochement* with the trade unions, including the avoidance of legislation to regulate their activities or internal affairs, and support for free collective bargaining. These principles and policy commitments were duly adhered to after the Conservatives had been returned to Office in 1951, and provided the framework for much of the Governments' approach to industrial relations and trade unionism until 1964. During this time, Ministers – particularly Ministers of Labour – did their utmost to resist pressure from other parts of the Conservative Party for legislation to curb the trade unions, or to permit higher unemployment to weaken their bargaining power. As such, what Conservative critics of the Party leadership's 'voluntarist' approach denounced as weakness and pusillanimity, Ministers defended as wisdom and practicability.

Of course, relations between Conservative Ministers and their trade union counterparts were not always smooth, and from the late 1950s onwards, tensions did increase over particular issues, particularly that of 'excessive' pay increases, but the predominant approach of senior Conservatives remained that of conflict avoidance, dialogue and exhortation concerning the need for greater moderation and responsibility. Indeed, in the context of mounting concern about the relative decline of the British economy during the early 1960s, the response of senior Conservatives was to strengthen industrial and economic partnership, and the incorporation of trade union leaders, through the establishment of the NEDC. This, in turn, it was hoped, would 'educate' union leaders about the need for pay restraint, and thereby render them more amenable to the adoption of – voluntary – incomes policies.

However, this approach unwittingly served to widen the gulf between the trade union leadership and their rank-and-file members, whereupon the latter increasingly turned to local level union officials and shop stewards to represent their day-to-day interests, and secure better pay. Not only did this highlight the problems of unofficial strikes and 'wage drift', it also drew attention to the limited authority which national-level trade union leaders had over their members, and which the TUC exercised over its affiliates. For a growing number of Conservatives, the efficacy of both 'voluntarism' and incomes policies was now open to serious doubts, and by 1964, pressure in the Party for a serious reconsideration of the leadership's approach to industrial relations and trade unionism – boosted by the *Rookes* v. *Barnard* judgment early that year – had become so strong that the Cabinet was promising to establish a Royal Commission on Trade Union Law after the general election, having spent several years trenchantly rejecting calls for just such an inquiry. The Conservative Party's 'voluntarist' experiment was about to be abandoned, and hostilities between British Conservatism and trade unionism were about to be resumed.

Bibliography

Many of the sources cited in this book come from the National Archives (formerly the Public Records Office) at Kew, London, and the Conservative Party Archives, which are held at the Bodleian Library, Oxford University, but are not additionally listed in the bibliography, in order to avoid undue complexity and length.

Materials from the National Archives (NA) consist of the following:
    Minutes and conclusions of Cabinet meetings, prefix CAB 128.
    Minutes and conclusions of Cabinet committees, prefix CAB 134.
    Discussion papers or policy proposals by individual Ministers, prefix CAB 129.
    Papers by senior civil servants or Cabinet Office officials, prefix CAB 21.
    Correspondence between Ministers and/or civil servants, prefix PREM 11.
    Papers and correspondence from the Ministry of Labour, prefix LAB.
    Papers and correspondence from the Treasury, prefix T.

Materials from the Conservative Party Archives (CPA) consist of the following:
    Papers from Conservative Central Office, prefix CCO.
    Papers from the Conservative Research Department, prefix CRD.
    Papers from the Conservative Party's Advisory Committee on Policy, prefix ACP.

Addison, Paul (1977) *The Road to 1945: British Politics and the Second World War*, London: Quartet Books.

Allen, V.L. (1960) *Trade Unions and the Government*, London: Allen and Unwin.

Alport, Cuthbert (1946) *About Conservative Principles*, Publisher unknown.

Amery, Leo (1946) *The Conservative Future*, Conservative Political Centre.

Amory, Derek Heathcoat (1960) *A Positive Partnership*, London: Industrial Co-Partnership Association.

Baldwin, Stanley (1926) *On England, and other Addresses*, London: Philip Allan.

Barnes, Denis and Reid, Eileen (1980) *Governments and Trade Unions: The British Experience, 1964–1979*, London: Heinemann.

—— (1982) 'A New Relationship: Trade Unions in the Second World War' in Ben Pimlott and Chris Cook (eds) *Trade Unions in British Politics*, Harlow: Longman.

Beer, Samuel (1969) *Modern British Politics: A Study of Parties and Pressure Groups*, London: Faber and Faber.

Berkeley, Humphrey (1972) *Crossing the Floor*, London: George Allen and Unwin.

Biffen, John (1968) 'Intellectuals and Conservatism: A Symposium', *The Swinton Journal*, summer.

Birkenhead, Lord (1969) *Walter Monckton*, London: Weidenfeld & Nicolson.

Blackaby, F.T. (1978) 'Incomes Policy' in F.T. Blackaby (ed) *British Economic Policy 1960–1974*, Cambridge: Cambridge University Press.

Blake, Robert (1969) *Disraeli*, London: University Paperbacks/Methuen.

—— (1985) *The Conservative Party from Peel to Thatcher*, London: Methuen.

Boyd-Carpenter, John (1950) *The Conservative Case*, London: Wingate.

Brittan, Samuel (1969) *Steering the Economy*, London: Secker and Warburg.

Brooke Stephen (1992) *Labour's War: the Labour Party during the Second World War*, Oxford: Clarendon Press.

Bryant, Arthur (1929) *The Spirit of Conservatism*, London: Methuen.

Bullock, Alan (1967) *The Life and Times of Ernest Bevin: Volume Two; Minister of Labour, 1940–1945*, London: Heinemann.

Butler, Lord (Rab) (1971) *The Art of the Possible*, London: Hamish Hamilton.

—— (1982) *The Art of Memory*, London: Hodder and Stoughton.

Campbell, Alan., Fishman, Nina and McIlroy, John (1999) 'The Post-War Compromise: Mapping Industrial Politics, 1945–64' in Alan Campbell, Nina Fishman and John McIlroy (eds) *The Post-War Compromise: British Trade Unions and Industrial Politics, 1945–64*, Aldershot: Ashgate.

Campbell, John (1993) *Edward Heath: A Biography*, London: Jonathan Cape.

Cazalet-Keir, Thelma (1967) *From the Wings*, London: The Bodley Head.

Churchill, Winston (1906) *Randolph Churchill, Volume Two*, London: Macmillan.

Citrine, Walter (1967) *Two Careers*, London: Hutchinson and Co.

—— (1942) *British Trade Unions*, London: William Collins.

Clarke, David (1947) *The Conservative Faith in the Modern Age*, Conservative Political Centre.

Coleman, Bruce (1988) *Conservatism and the Conservative Party in Nineteenth Century Britain*, London: Edward Arnold.

Coleraine, Lord (1970) *For Conservatives Only*, London: Tom Stacey.

Colville, John (1981) *The Churchillians*, London: Weidenfeld & Nicolson.

Conservative Central Office (1951) *Britain Strong and Free*.

Conservative Industrial Department (1963) *Trade Unions and the Government*.

Conservative Research Department (1956) *Notes on Current Politics, 2: Economic and Industrial Affairs*, January.

Conservative and Unionist Central Office (1947) *The Industrial Charter: A Statement of Conservative Industrial Policy*, Conservative and Unionist Central Office.

Conservative and Unionist Central Office (1949) *The Right Road for Britain*, Conservative and Unionist Central Office.

Cox, Andrew (1989) 'The Failure of Corporatist State Forms and Policies in Post-War Britain' in Andrew Cox and Noel O'Sullivan (eds) *The Corporate State:*

Corporatism and the State Tradition in Western Europe, Cheltenham: Edward Elgar.

Craig, F.W.S. (1970) *British General Election Manifestos, 1918–66*, London: Political Reference Publications.

Criddle, Byron (1994) 'Members of Parliament' in Anthony Seldon and Stuart Ball (eds) *Conservative Century: The Conservative Party since 1900*, Oxford: Oxford University Press.

Crouch, Colin (1979) 'The State, Capital and Liberal Democracy' in Colin Crouch (ed) *State and Economy in Contemporary Capitalism*, London: Croom Helm.

Dilks, David (1977) 'Part Three: Baldwin and Chamberlain' in Norman Gash, Donald Southgate, David Dilks and John Ramsden, *The Conservatives: A History from their Origins to 1965*, London: George Allen and Unwin.

Disraeli, Benjamin (1995) *Sybil, or The Two Nations*, London: Wordsworth Classics, originally published in 1845.

Dorey, Peter (1993) 'Corporatism in the UK', *Politics Review*, Vol. 3, No. 2, pp. 24–7.

—— (2001) *Wage Politics in Britain: The Rise and Fall of Incomes Policies since 1945*, Brighton: Sussex Academic Press.

—— (2002) 'Britain in the 1990s: The Absence of Policy Concertation' in Stefan Berger and Hugh Compston (eds) *Policy Concertation and Social Partnership in Western Europe*, Oxford: Berghahn.

—— (forthcoming) *British Conservatism: The Philosophy and Politics of Inequality*, London: I.B. Tauris.

Dorfman, Gerald (1973) *Wage Politics in Britain 1945–1967*, London: Charles Knight.

Duncan, J., McCarthy W.E.J. and Redman G.P. (1983) *Strikes in Post-War Britain*, London: George Allen and Unwin.

Eden, Anthony (1947) *Freedom and Order*, London: Faber.

—— (1960) *Full Circle: Memoirs*, London: Cassell.

Egremont, Max (1980) *Balfour: A Life of Arthur James Balfour*, London: William Collins.

Fisher, Nigel (1973) *Iain Macleod*, London: Andre Deutsch.

Flanders, Allan (1975) *Management and Unions: Theory and Reform of Industrial Relations*, London: Faber.

Fraser, Michael (1948) *The Worker in Industry*, London: Conservative and Unionist Central Office.

Gamble, Andrew (1974) *The Conservative Nation*, London: Routledge and Kegan Paul.

Dorothy, George (1936) 'Revisions in Economic History: IV. The Combination Acts', *Economic History Review*, Vol. 6, No. 2.

OECD (1961) *The Problem of Rising Prices*, Paris: OECD.

Gilmour, Ian (1978) *Inside Right: A Study of Conservatism*, London: Quartet Books.

—— and Garnett, Mark (1997) *Whatever Happened to the Tories? The Conservative Party since 1945*, London: Fourth Estate.

Girvin, Brian (1994) *The Right in the Twentieth Century: Conservatism and Democracy*, London: Pinter.

Goodman, Geoffrey (1979) *The Awkward Warrior. Frank Cousins: His Life and Times*, London: Davis-Poynter.

Grant, Wyn (1977) *The CBI*, London: Hodder and Stoughton.

Greenleaf, W.H. (1983) *The British Political Tradition, Volume Two: The Ideological Heritage*, London: Methuen.

Hall, Robert (1961) 'Britain's economic problems', *The Economist*, 16 September.

Harris, Nigel (1972) *Competition and the Corporate Society*, London: Methuen.

Hayek, Friedrich (1944) *The Road to Serfdom*, London: Routledge and Kegan Paul

Heath, Edward (1998) *The Course of My Life: My Autobiography*, London: Hodder and Stoughton.

Hedges, Robert Yorke and Winterbottom, Allan (1930) *The Legal History of Trade Unionism*, London: Longmans, Green.

Hennessy, Peter (1990) *Whitehall*, London: Pimlico Publishers.

Hill, Charles (1964) *Both Sides of the Hill*, London, Heinemann.

Hinchingbrooke, Lord (1944) *Full Speed Ahead: Essays in Tory Reform*, London: Simpkin.

—— (1946) 'The course of Conservative politics', *Quarterly Review*, January.

HMSO (1956) *The Economic Implications of Full Employment*, Cmnd 9725.

Hoffman, John (1964) *The Conservatives in Opposition, 1945–51*, London: Macgibbon and Kee.

Hogg, Quintin (1944) *One Year's Work*, Conservative Political Centre.

—— (1945) 'Too many Micawbers in the Tory party', *Daily Mail* 11 September.

—— (1947) *The Case for Conservatism*, Harmondsworth: Penguin Books.

Howard, Anthony (1987) *RAB: The Life of R.A. Butler*, London: Jonathan Cape.

Hutchinson, George (1970*) Edward Heath: A Personal and Political Biography*, London: Longmans.

Hyde, H. Montgomery (1991) *Walter Monckton*, London: Sinclair-Stevenson.

Ince, Sir Godfrey (1960) *The Ministry of Labour and National Service*, London: George Allen and Unwin.

Inns of Court Conservative Association (1958) *A Giant's Strength*, London.

Jackson, Michael P. (1991) *An Introduction to Industrial Relations*, fourth edition, London: Thomson.

Jessop, Bob (1974) *Traditionalism, Conservatism and British Political Culture*, London: Allen and Unwin.

Jones, Russell (1987) *Wages and Employment Policy 1936–1985*, London: Allen and Unwin.

Kavanagh, Dennis and Morris, Peter (1989) *Consensus Politics: From Attlee to Thatcher*, Oxford: Blackwell.

Laing, Margaret (1972) *Edward Heath: Prime Minister*, London: Sidgwick and Jackson.

Leather, Ted, Macmillan, Harold, Bevins, Reginald, Harris, Reader, McAdden, Steve and Tilney, John (undated, but circa 1951) *A New Approach to the Problem of Economic Survival for Our Generation*, Publisher unknown.

Lindsay, T.F. and Harrington, M. (1979) *The Conservative Party 1918–1979*, London: Macmillan.

Lovell, John and Roberts, B.C. (1968) *A Short History of the TUC*, London: Macmillan.

Macdonald, D.F. (1976) *The State and the Trade Unions*, second edition, London: Macmillan.

Mackenzie, Robert and Silver, Allan (1968) *Angels in Marble: Working Class Conservatives in Urban England*, London: Heinemann.

Macleod, Iain and Maude, Angus (eds) (1950) *One Nation: A Tory Approach to Social Problems*, Conservative Political Centre.

Macmillan, Harold (1937) *The Middle Way*, London: Macmillan.

—— (1946) 'Strength through – what?', *Oxford Mail*, 26 January.

—— (1969) *Tides of Fortune 1945–1955*, London: Macmillan.

—— (1972) *Pointing the Way*, 1959–1961, London: Macmillan.

—— (1973) *At the End of the Day, 1961–1963*, London: Macmillan.

——, Boothby, Robert, de V. Loder, John and Stanley, Oliver (1927) *Industry and the State*, London: Macmillan.

Marquand, David (1988) *The Unprincipled Society*, London: Jonathan Cape.

—— (1999) *The Progressive Dilemma: From Lloyd George to Kinnock*, London: Weidenfeld & Nicolson.

Maudling, Reginald (1978) *Memoirs*, London: Sidgwick and Jackson.

Michels, Robert (1968) *Political Parties: A Sociological Study of the Oligarchical Tendencies of Modern Democracy*, New York: The Free Press, originally published in 1911.

Middlemas, Keith (1979) *Politics in Industrial Society: The Experience of the British System since 1911*, London: Andre Deutsch.

—— and Barnes, John (1969) *Baldwin: A Biography*, London: Weidenfeld & Nicolson.

Ministry of Labour (1957) *Industrial Relations Handbook*, revised edition, London: HMSO.

Molson, Hugh (1945) 'The Tory Reform Committee', *New English Review*, Vol. XI.

Monday Club, The (1963) *Strike Out of Strike Bound*, London: Conservative Political Centre.

Monypenny, William and Buckle, George (1929) *The Life of Benjamin Disraeli, Earl of Beaconsfield: Volume One*, London: John Murray.

Moran, Lord (ed) (1965) *Diaries*, London: Weidenfeld & Nicolson.

National Union of Conservative and Unionist Associations (1952) *Report of the Committee on Trade Unionist Policy and Organisation*, London.

National Unionist Association (1924) *Unionist Worker handbook: Co-partnership*, London.

Nordlinger, Eric (1967) *The Working Class Tories: Authority, Deference and Stable Democracy*, London: Macgibbon and Kee.

Norton, Philip (1978) *Conservative Dissidents: Dissent within the Parliamentary Conservative Party 1970–74*, London: Temple Smith.

—— and Aughey, Arthur (1981) *Conservatives and Conservatism*, London: Temple Smith.

One Nation Group of Conservative MPs (1950) *One Nation: A Tory Approach to Social Problems*, London: Conservative Political Centre.

—— (1954) *One Nation at Work*, London.

Pelling, Henry (1976*) A History of British Trade Unionism*, Third Edition, Harmondsworth: Penguin.

Powell, Enoch (1968) *Conference on Economic Policy for the 1970s*, The Monday Club.

—— (1969) *Freedom and Reality*, London: Elliot Right Way Books.

Price, John (1940) *Labour in the War*, Harmondsworth: Penguin Books.

Ramsden, John (1977a) 'Winston Churchill and the Conservative Party' in Lord (Rab) Butler (ed) *The Conservatives: A History from their Origins to 1965*, London: George Allen and Unwin.

—— (1977b) 'From Churchill to Heath' in Lord (Rab) Butler (ed) *The Conservatives: A History from their Origins to 1965*, London: George Allen and Unwin.

—— (1980) *The Making of Conservative Party Policy*, London: Longman.

Renshaw, Patrick (1982) 'The Depression Years, 1918–1931' in Ben Pimlott and Chris Cook (eds) *Trade Unions in British Politics*, Harlow: Longman.

Rowe, Andrew (1980) '*Conservatives and Trade-unionists*' in Zig Layton-Henry (ed) *Conservative Party Politics*, London: Macmillan.

Royal Commission on Trade Unions and Employers' Associations, 1965–1968 (1968) *Report*, Cmnd 36234, London: HMSO.

Salisbury, Lord (1860) 'The Budget and the Reform Bill', *Quarterly Review*, April.

—— (1866) 'The Reform Bill', *Quarterly Review*, April.

Self, Robert (ed) (2000) *The Neville Chamberlain Diary Letters, Volume 2: The reform years, 1921–1927*, Aldershot: Ashgate.

Seldon, Anthony (1981) *Churchill's Indian Summer*, London: Hodder and Stoughton.

Shanks, Michael (1961) *The Stagnant Society*, Harmondsworth: Penguin.

Shepherd, Robert (1994) *Iain Macleod: A Biography*, London: Hutchinson.

Shonfield, Andrew 1965) *Modern Capitalism*, Oxford: Oxford University Press.

Smith, Paul (1967) *Disraelian Conservatism and Social Reform*, London: Routledge and Kegan Paul.

Stevens, Richard (1999) 'Cold War Politics: Communism and Anti-Communism in the Trade Unions' in Alan Campbell, Nina Fishman and John McIlroy (eds) *The Post-War Compromise: British Trade Unions and Industrial Politics, 1945–64*, Aldershot: Ashgate.

Stevenson, John (1982) 'Early Trade Unionism: Radicalism and Respectability, 1750–1870' in Ben Pimlott and Chris Cook (eds) *Trade Unions in British Politics*, Harlow: Longman.

Taylor, Andrew (1994) 'The Party and the Trade Unions' in Anthony Seldon and Stuart Ball (eds) *Conservative Century: The Conservative Party since 1900*, Oxford: Oxford University Press.

Taylor, Robert (1975) *Lord Salisbury*, London: Allen Lane.

—— (1996) 'Industrial Relations' in David Marquand and Anthony Seldon (eds) *The Ideas that Shaped Post-War Britain*, London: Fontana.

—— (1993) *The Trade Union Question in British Politics*, Oxford: Blackwell.

—— (2000) *The TUC: From the General Strike to New Unionism*, Basingstoke: Palgrave.

Towers, Brian (1978) *British Incomes Policy*, Leeds and Nottingham: University of Leeds and University of Nottingham (Occasional Papers in Industrial Relations).

Treasury (1962) *Incomes Policy: The Next Step*, Cmnd 1626, London: HMSO.

—— (1964) 'Wage drift: some broad considerations', *Bulletin for Industry*, July 1964.

TUC (1940) *Report of Annual Congress*, London: TUC.

—— (1962) *Annual Report 1962*, London: TUC.

Walker, Peter (1977) *The Ascent of Britain*, London: Sidgwick and Jackson.

Wigham, Eric (1961) *What's wrong with the unions?*, Harmondsworth: Penguin.

Williamson, Philip and Baldwin, Edward (eds) (2004) *Baldwin Papers: A Conservative Statesman, 1908–1947*, Cambridge: Cambridge University Press.

Wood, John (ed) 1965) *A Nation Not Afraid: The Thinking of Enoch Powell*, London: B.T. Batsford.

Woolton, Lord (1959) *Memoirs*, London: Cassell.

Young, G.M. (1952) *Stanley Baldwin*, London: Rupert Hart-Davis.

Index

Modern Economic and Social History Series

General Editor
Derek H. Aldcroft, University Fellow, Department of Economic and Social
History,
University of Leicester, UK

Derek H. Aldcroft
Studies in the Interwar European Economy
1 85928 360 8 (1997)

Michael J. Oliver
Whatever Happened to Monetarism?
Economic Policy Making and Social Learning in the United Kingdom Since 1979
1 85928 433 7 (1997)

R. Guerriero Wilson
Disillusionment or New Opportunities?
The Changing Nature of Work in Offices, Glasgow 1880–1914
1 84014 276 6 (1998)

Roger Lloyd-Jones and M.J. Lewis with the assistance of M. Eason
Raleigh and the British Bicycle Industry
An Economic and Business History, 1870–1960
1 85928 457 4 (2000)

Barry Stapleton and James H. Thomas
Gales
A Study in Brewing, Business and Family History
0 7546 0146 3 (2000)

Derek H. Aldcroft and Michael J. Oliver
Trade Unions and the Economy
1870–2000
1 85928 370 5 (2000)

Ted Wilson
Battles for the Standard
Bimetallism and the Spread of the Gold Standard in the Nineteenth Century
1 85928 436 1 (2000)

Patrick Duffy
The Skilled Compositor, 1850–1914
An Aristocrat Among Working Men
0 7546 0255 9 (2000)

Robert Conlon and John Perkins
Wheels and Deals
The Automotive Industry in Twentieth-Century Australia
0 7546 0405 5 (2001)

Geoffrey Channon
Railways in Britain and the United States, 1830–1940
Studies in Economic and Business History
1 84014 253 7 (2001)

Sam Mustafa
Merchants and Migrations
Germans and Americans in Connection, 1776–1835
0 7546 0590 6 (2001)

Bernard Cronin
Technology, Industrial Conflict and the Development of Technical Education in
19th-Century England
0 7546 0313 X (2001)

Andrew Popp
Business Structure, Business Culture and the Industrial District
The Potteries, c. 1850–1914
0 7546 0176 5 (2001)

Scott Kelly
The Myth of Mr Butskell
The Politics of British Economic Policy, 1950–55
0 7546 0604 X (2002)

Michael Ferguson
The Rise of Management Consulting in Britain
0 7546 0561 2 (2002)

Alan Fowler
Lancashire Cotton Operatives and Work, 1900–1950
A Social History of Lancashire Cotton Operatives in the Twentieth Century
0 7546 0116 1 (2003)

John F. Wilson and Andrew Popp (eds)
Industrial Clusters and Regional Business Networks in England, 1750–1970
0 7546 0761 5 (2003)

John Hassan
The Seaside, Health and the Environment in England and Wales since 1800
1 84014 265 0 (2003)
Marshall J. Bastable

Arms and the State
Sir William Armstrong and the Remaking of British Naval Power, 1854–1914
0 7546 3404 3 (2004)

Robin Pearson
Insuring the Industrial Revolution
Fire Insurance in Great Britain, 1700–1850
0 7546 3363 2 (2004)

Andrew Dawson
Lives of the Philadelphia Engineers
Capital, Class and Revolution, 1830–1890
0 7546 3396 9 (2004)

Lawrence Black and Hugh Pemberton (eds)
An Affluent Society?
Britain's Post-War 'Golden Age' Revisited
0 7546 3528 7 (2004)

Joseph Harrison and David Corkill
Spain
A Modern European Economy
0 7546 0145 5 (2004)

Ross E. Catterall and Derek H. Aldcroft (eds)
Exchange Rates and Economic Policy in the 20th Century
1 84014 264 2 (2004)

Armin Grünbacher
Reconstruction and Cold War in Germany
The Kreditanstalt für Wiederaufbau (1948–1961)
0 7546 3806 5 (2004)

Espen Moe
Governance, Growth and Global Leadership
The Role of the State in Technological Progress, 1750–2000
978 0 7546 5743 9 (2007)

Peter Scott
Triumph of the South
A Regional Economic History of Early Twentieth Century Britain
978 1 84014 613 4 (2007)

David Turnock
Aspects of Independent Romania's Economic History with Particular Reference
to Transition for EU Accession
978 0 7546 5892 4 (2007)

David Oldroyd
Estates, Enterprise and Investment at the Dawn of the Industrial Revolution
Estate Management and Accounting in the North-East of England, c.1700–1780
978 0 7546 3455 3 (2007)

Ralf Roth and Günter Dinhobl (eds)
Across the Borders
Financing the World's Railways in the Nineteenth and Twentieth Centuries
978 0 7546 6029 3 (2008)

Vincent Barnett and Joachim Zweynert (eds)
Economics in Russia
Studies in Intellectual History
978 0 7546 6149 8 (2008)

Raymond E. Dumett (ed.)
Mining Tycoons in the Age of Empire, 1870–1945
Entrepreneurship, High Finance, Politics and Territorial Expansion
978 0 7546 6303 4 (2009)